Christian Socialism:
Scott Holland to Tony Blair

Also by Alan Wilkinson and published by SCM Press

The Church of England and the First World War

Christian Socialism:
Scott Holland to Tony Blair

The 1998 Scott Holland Lectures

Alan Wilkinson

SCM PRESS

Copyright © Alan Wilkinson 1998

0 334 02749 7

First published 1998
by SCM Press
9–17 St Albans Place, London N1 0NX

SCM Press is a division of SCM-Canterbury Press Ltd

Typeset by Regent Typesetting, London
and printed in Great Britain by
Biddles Ltd, Guildford and King's Lynn

To
my twin grandchildren
Beatrice and Maximilian
born 25 November 1996
for the future they represent
and the past they will inherit

Contents

Foreword

by The Right Honourable Tony Blair, MP

I am pleased to contribute this Foreword to Alan Wilkinson's book, based on his Scott Holland lectures. In them he examined the strong tradition of Christian Socialism that began to take shape in the middle of the last century when Christian thinkers asked themselves how the gospel could best be interpreted in the terms of modern industrial society – as F.D. Maurice and his colleagues put it, 'socializing Christianity and Christianizing socialism'.

Some of the most notable names in the development of political and social thought over the last century and a half have shared this broad approach – Charles Kingsley and F.D. Maurice, Bishops Westcott and Gore, R.H. Tawney and Archbishop Temple among them.

In founding the Christian Social Union in 1889 Scott Holland and his colleagues gave to the general approach shape and direction. It is interesting that at much the same time the 1888 Lambeth Conference reported (rather cautiously) that there was no necessary contradiction between socialism, interpreted broadly, and Christianity. But it went further and called on clergy to learn 'how much of what is good and true in socialism is to be found in the precepts of Christ'. Looking back on Christian Socialism over a hundred years later Alan Wilkinson says in his concluding chapter that 'it has drawn . . . Christians from all classes into politics, social action and work for the poor and for a more just society'. And it still does.

Christian Socialism had had a long and well supported history within the Labour Party and Labour movement. As Tawney and

Temple taught, the view that Christian faith and belief is all to do with personal morality and nothing to do with the needs of society as a whole is too partial a perspective. Similarly, the belief that only through the good offices of a benign state can the good of all be achieved leaves out the sense of individual responsibility which is essential if society is to function at all. My politics have always been based on the belief that individuals best thrive in a strong and active community, where rights are matched by responsibilities and where individuals count most when they are able to play a full part. As John Macmurray said, 'we are what we are, in part, because of the other'.

Alan Wilkinson's book provides a fascinating perspective on the way in which in this country successive generations of Christians in public life have wrestled with the demands that their faith places on them and their countrymen as citizens. As a study of ideas and their application it makes an illuminating read.

Preface

When in 1994 I was invited by the Scott Holland Trustees to give the 1998 Scott Holland Lectures, I was very much aware that this was a great privilege and honour. I thought of some of my predecessors who have given the lectures since 1922 when R. H. Tawney gave the first series, later published as *Religion and the Rise of Capitalism*: William Temple, Donald MacKinnon, Alec Vidler, Michael Ramsey, Ronald Preston, Ann Loades, Stephen Clark, Lord Plant. I was also conscious of the great contribution to Anglican social thought made by Henry Scott Holland (1847–1918), founder of the Christian Social Union in 1889. Scott Holland lecturers are bidden to consider 'the religion of the incarnation in its bearing on the social and economic life of humanity'. So in 1994 I chose as my theme Christian Socialism from Scott Holland and Charles Gore to Tony Blair. Tony Blair had been Leader of the Labour Party for only five months when I chose this subject. But I knew that whether he won or lost the General Election there would be much to consider in the present as well as in the past. In the event, I gave the lectures in Portsmouth Cathedral and in the Leeds University Chaplaincy just a year after the election of the first Labour government for eighteen years. This book is an expansion of those lectures.

In this Preface I wish to draw attention to three of the main themes of the book. First, the important contribution Christianity has made to the Labour Party and British socialism. Second, I believe that Tony Blair can claim to have rediscovered aspects of the very varied Christian Socialist tradition which have been marginalized by the dominant statism of the Labour Party of the last eighty years. Third, I take issue with the progressivist understanding of history. This I believe should be questioned in the light of both theology and experience.

One theme of the book is the considerable influence of Christianity on the Labour movement. Yet this is often ignored. A photograph in *The Independent* for 30 September 1996 from the 1996 Labour Party Conference was an example of this. It depicted the Blairs, a smiling couple, walking in the rain towards a building. Two men hold umbrellas over them. The caption simply states that Tony Blair was sheltering from stormy weather. It did not say that they were going to the Conference religious service and that the two men with umbrellas (admittedly in mufti) were both priests, one Anglican (chairman of the Christian Socialist Movement) the other Roman Catholic (the co-ordinator of the CSM). The exclusion of the religious heart of the story is typical of our society which ignores religious motivation, allegiance and institutions in both popular and academic publications. So, Andrew Thorpe's recent *History of the British Labour Party* (1997) tells a wholly secular story. Shaw in his play *Candida* (1895) was better informed. Its hero is an Anglican socialist priest. Among his books is one by F. D. Maurice, who began Christian Socialism in 1848. Shaw also tells us that he was a member of two societies which were part of the Christian Socialist movement, the Guild of St Matthew (1877) and the Christian Social Union (1889).

Aspects of this book may be surprising to some readers. The depth and extent of Christian concern for society in the period is often ignored in historical studies. Many know the great contribution made by Nonconformists to the formation of the trade unions and the Labour Party, but may be unaware of the ambiguity in the relationship between Labour and Nonconformity. Others may not have realized how many Anglicans were involved in Christian Socialism and the Labour movement. This was brought home to me recently. A Labour Party supporter refused to believe that the first Christian Socialists were Anglican priests. A Roman Catholic priest told me he could not understand what a

Christian Socialist like George Bell was doing as a bishop in the Church of England. Again, it is not always realized how hostile Roman Catholic teaching has been towards socialism and the welfare state. Marx declared in the *Communist Manifesto* (1848): 'Christian socialism is but the holy water with which the priest consecrates the heart-burnings of the aristocrat.' But Pope Pius XI was also dismissive in *Quadragesimo Anno* (1931): '"Religious Socialism", "Christian Socialism" are expressions implying a contradiction in terms' (III.2.b). Despite such rebuffs, in recent years Christian Socialism has revived remarkably, inside and outside the Labour Party, after a long period when secularity triumphed in Left-wing circles. As we shall see, 'Christian Socialism' is a portmanteau term which covers a wide range from those who were (in Edwardian days) New Liberals to those in our own day who advocate a Marxist liberation theology. Christian Socialists are united more by a religious faith than one particular political programme. They are not simply socialists who go to church from time to time, but Christians who, having thought about the political implications of their faith, have concluded that the good of individuals cannot be realized in isolation, or in enmity with other groups, but only through promoting the common good of all. They do of course differ as to how this should be realized.

Second, Tony Blair's socialism clearly marks a break with the predominant statism of Labour Party history since 1918. But it can be seen as in part a rediscovery of certain themes in Christian Socialism. The advent of Blair, like any other new and un-expected development, compels a reinterpretation of previous history. This leads to a recovery of ideas and groups from the past which had been suppressed or ignored by the dominant ortho-doxy. One thinks, for example, in the church of the process of reinterpretation of the past set in train by the rise of feminist theology or the Second Vatican Council. Blair himself made clear his desire for such a reinterpretation in a speech commemorating the fiftieth anniversary of the 1945 Labour victory. He called for 'a new political consensus of the left-of-centre' whose history

would include Liberals as well as Labour. He obviously warms to
the New Liberals at the turn of the century:

> The New Liberals were people who were both liberals with a
> small 'l' and social democrats, also in lower case, living on the
> cusp of a new political age – transitional figures, spanning the
> period from one dominant ethic to another.[1]

Some Christian Socialists have been motivated by the Tory
Anglican tradition of *noblesse oblige*. Others have preached the
panacea of self-help in the context of mutual benefit. They
owed much to the evangelical tradition which started with the
individual, rather than with society, and was sceptical about the
benefits of transforming structures without transforming individuals. To this tradition, the 'full life' promised by socialism was
moral and spiritual, not hedonistic and secular. So too, several
factors (some of them external to Labour) combined to assist the
birth of New Labour and the revival of ethical and Christian
Socialism: the collapse of Communism; the way in which
Thatcherism turned attention to certain features of the Victorian
tradition such as the virtuous role of self-interest and self-help;
Mrs Thatcher's own encouragement of a theological debate about
politics in her address to the General Assembly of the Church
of Scotland in 1988; the failure of Labour for the fourth time
in a row to be elected in 1992 and the contribution that John
Smith's traditional tax proposals made to that defeat; the growth
of a global economy and communications network which make
inconceivable the type of socialism which requires a siege
economy; Blair's moral appeal which seemed to many inside and
outside the churches concerned with ethical politics, to articulate
values which had been absent for some years, both on the Left
and on the Right. Yet if Blair represented the rediscovery of some
old values, he seems to have pushed others aside which used to be
central to Christian Socialism, such as: the suspicion of acquisitiveness; the determination to keep the market and its values out
of significant areas of national life; admiration for disinterested
service; overt rather than covert redistributive taxation.

Third, this book questions the progressivist ideology with its belief that history is (or should be made to be) an escalator ever leading upwards. This has been an important emotional engine in socialist thinking and propaganda, both Christian and secular. The Anglican socialist priest, Conrad Noel for example, entitled two chapters in *Socialism in Church History* (1910) 'The Night of Christendom' and 'Before the Dawn'. This progressivism is allied to romanticism, and I have explored the baleful effects of romanticism on society in *Dissent or Conform?* (1986); *The Church of England and the First World War* (1996); in 'The Poetry of War' (*Theology*, November 1986); in 'Is Poetry a part of History' (*Modern History Review*, April 1996). Some Christian Socialists so surrendered to optimism (which is different from hope) that they came to believe that the kingdom of God could be established by political means. Theologically the kingdom of God is an eschatological reality of which we only get glimpses, hints, temporary manifestations in this life. So it would be quite foolish, for example, to write this history as though Blairism was the goal of British socialism, whereas it is simply its contemporary mutation. Rather surprisingly, it was the utopian socialist William Morris who in 1896 grasped the provisional nature of all human and political achievement:

> I pondered . . . how men fight and lose the battle, and the thing they fight for comes about in spite of their defeat, and when it comes it turns out to be not what they meant, and other men have to fight for what they meant under another name.[2]

This is the fourth of my quartet of books about the church on the frontier. My two books on the churches and the wars explored what faith might actually mean in the trenches, in the peace movements of the 1930s, in the debates about obliteration bombing. My third book, the centenary history of the Community of the Resurrection, pondered how a Religious Order lived and wrestled on several frontiers: on the primary one, that with God, but also (in its early days) with Christian Socialism, and later in

South Africa as it confronted apartheid. Throughout I have had in mind Martin Luther King's question as to whether the church was to be a thermometer registering the surrounding temperature or a thermostat attempting to affect it.

I am deeply grateful to the Prime Minister for finding time, amidst his many commitments, to contribute such a generous Foreword to this book.

I wish also to thank the Bishop of Basingstoke, chairman of the Scott Holland Trust, the Revd Dr Peter Jupp, secretary, and other Trustees for their invitation to me and for their subsequent support. I have been fortunate to receive financial help for my research from the Chichester Institute of Higher Education during my Visiting Fellowship there 1995–97 and from the George Bell Institute, Birmingham, since my appointment as a Fellow in 1996. I wish also to express my appreciation to the Provost and Chapter of Portsmouth Cathedral and to the Anglican Chaplains of Leeds University for their warm welcome and efficient organization which helped to make the four Saturdays both enjoyable and (I hope) instructive. I learned much from the questions and discussion initiated by the audiences, and I have incorporated some points that were made into the final text. The Christian Socialist Movement and particularly Chris Bryant, David Cairns, Alison Webster and Catherine Shelley have been generous in helping in various ways, not least by giving the lectures publicity, even though I am not a member. The Community of the Resurrection, Mirfield, once again gave me hospitality and allowed me to use its library and archives with its fine collection of material on the subject and its newspaper cuttings about Charles Gore, its founder. It also kindly helped with the expenses of repeating the lectures in Leeds.

The staff at Portsmouth City Library have dealt with my constant flow of requests with efficiency and equanimity. It has been a pleasure also to use the libraries at Lambeth Palace and at Pusey House (by permission of the Principal and Chapter).

The Rt Hon. Frank Field, MP, formerly Minister for Welfare Reform, has taken a keen interest in this project throughout its gestation, generously found time to chair two of the lectures at Portsmouth Cathedral, provided me with copies of his speeches and lectures and gave me permission to quote from those which are as yet unpublished. (The book was written before he resigned from the government in July 1998.)

Dr Peter Catterall, the Revd Dr C. S. Ford, Laurie Fricker, the Revd Dr John Heidt, the Revd Dr Philip Newell, Dr Gillian Nicholls (on behalf of the late Revd Dr David Nicholls) have kindly given me permission to make use of their theses. I have been unable to trace Mrs A. A. Eckbert whose thesis on the Christian Social Union I found so valuable. I am obliged to Lord Plant for giving me permission to quote from his unpublished 1995 Gore Lecture.

Among others to whom I am indebted are: Canon John Atherton; Dr Thomas Buchanan; the Revd Dr Peter Davie; Graham Davies; Professor Alan Deacon; Daniel Hartley; Emma Heron; Canon Eric James; the Revd Dr Richard Jones; the Revd Kenneth Leech; David Livett; the Revd A. V. Longworth; Dr Patrick Logan; Dr Alistair Mason; Councillor Frank McManus; the Revd Peter Millar and the staff of Iona Abbey; Professor R. H. Preston; Professor Donald Read; Bishop Alastair Redfern; the Revd Dr John Vincent; the Revd John Wall; Professor Haddon Willmer; Dr Watcyn Wynn.

Finally, I want to say how much I owe to my wife Fenella. She gave indispensable help by checking the typescript and by organizing the Lectures at Portsmouth Cathedral. But above all she has sustained me during those times when, like other writers, I have been beset by glooms. She has remained always equable when the tasks of completing first the lectures and then the book have been so preoccupying.

Portsmouth Cathedral   Alan Wilkinson
Petertide 1998

Abbreviations

COS	Charity Organisation Society
CR	Community of the Resurrection
COPEC	Conference on Christian Politics, Economics and Citizenship
CSL	Christian Socialist League
CSM	Christian Socialist Movement
CSU	Christian Social Union
DLB	Dictionary of Labour Biography
GSM	Guild of St Matthew
ICF	Industrial Christian Fellowship
ILP	Independent Labour Party
SDF	Social Democratic Federation
SDC	Society of the Divine Compassion
SSM	Society of the Sacred Mission
WEA	Workers' Educational Association

Nineteenth-Century Background

Histories of Christian Socialism used to depict Christian attitudes to society in the early nineteenth century as cruel and barren until F. D. Maurice emerged in 1848 to lighten the darkness. But such a picture draws too sharp a distinction between Maurice and other strands of Christian social thought of the period. In any case, Maurice was in many ways a very traditional figure. Nor was there a simple polarization between the advocates and opponents of *laissez-faire*. The same church leader might advocate state action as a solution to one social ill, but promote philanthropy and self-help as a remedy for another. In short, there was more inter-action between different traditions of social thought than has been granted by propagandists of the Left. So evangelical beliefs in self-help and self-improvement found their way (partly through Samuel Smiles) into the trade union and cooperative movements and into the ethos of the Friendly Societies. The Tory Anglican tradition of *noblesse oblige* motivated a number of middle and upper-class people to become Christian Socialists. The main story of this book begins with the resurgence of Christian Socialism under Henry Scott Holland and Charles Gore in the 1880s. But it is essential to map the various tributaries which flowed into this late-Victorian Christian Socialism from other parts of the nineteenth century. Christian Socialism arose partly as a response to the threat of revolution, partly as a response to poverty and inequality, so we need to be aware of Victorian atti-tudes to both these issues.

In our own time, debates about social policy since the advent of Thatcherism have made parallel debates in the last century more

comprehensible. We had thought we had arrived at final solutions
to certain key social problems. We began to realize how interim or
even wrong they were. So the thinking of earlier generations has
become much more relevant than seemed possible twenty years
ago.

At the beginning of the nineteenth century, English political
and ecclesiastical leaders shared a common aim: the maintenance
and defence of a traditional social hierarchy.[1] The French
Revolution of 1789 made the leaders of church and state in
England fearful of social change. Only when fears of a similar
revolution here receded in the 1820s did reform become possible.
But fears of an uprising recurred from time to time during the
century. When the majority of the bishops voted against the
Reform Bill in 1831, they became targets of abuse. Fearing the
mob and public opinion, the clergy began to huddle close to the
Tories who presented themselves as the protectors of the church,
so forming an alliance which persisted until the beginning of this
century and in some areas of national life until Mrs Thatcher.[2]
Throughout the century the middle and upper classes worried
about the alienation of the working classes from the churches and
whether this meant they were also alienated from the state.
Panaceas for this alienation ranged from repression and church
building at the beginning of the century to Christian Socialism
and social and electoral reform later on.

Christian Political Economy

In the early nineteenth century, evangelicalism was the main
religious tradition. Its social thought was dominated by eschatology. But there was a division between post-millennarians who
believed in a gradual amelioration of social conditions as history
continued towards the millennium, and pre-millennarians who
regarded social reform as a dangerous diversion from the imminent return of Christ, though some believed reform would soften
divine judgment. Some Evangelicals were uneasy about the use of
political agitation even to further the abolitionist cause.[3]

Far from being indifferent to social questions, as was once alleged, Anglican clergy, including Thomas Malthus, Bishop Edward Copleston and Archbishops Whately and Sumner, made important contributions to political debates and economic thought. It was widely believed that social inequality was divinely ordained and that the principle of subordination was fundamental to society. On the other hand, the powerful had the duty to rule justly and with paternal compassion. On their part, the poor had the duty of conscientious service and deference. By these means all classes were bound together. Inequality served God's purposes because life was to be an education in virtue and inequality provided moral challenges and choices. But this world's injustices would be righted in the next.[4]

The 1662 Prayer Book Catechism speaks of 'that state of life unto which it shall please God to call me'. It was often misquoted to teach obedience to the status quo, as in this sermon of 1842 on behalf of sufferers in Manchester from the trade depression:

> If inequality of rank and condition be an ordinance of providence, no man is to be blamed for simply belonging to one class or another, but each is to be judged by the way in which he, as an individual, discharges his duty in that state of life into which it *has* [my italics] pleased God to call him. Woe then be to him . . . who attempts to set master against man and man against master – who fails to see that both are as necessary in the economy of civil life as hill and valley in the economy of nature.[5]

Hence those trying to create trade unions (for example) were regarded as rebels against God's order.

However, Chartists as well as Evangelicals could appeal to the Bible. In August 1839 a group in Blackburn asked the Revd John Whittaker, the vicar (who had rebuilt the parish church and eleven new ones) to preach on James 5.1–16 which begins 'Go to now, ye rich men, weep and howl for your miseries are coming upon you', and condemns those who have witheld payment of wages. He did so, but claimed that the passage did not apply to

England where the rich were beneficent to the poor and needy. Such morality was essentially personal. 'For unto whomsoever much is given, of him shall much be required' (Luke 12.48). One squire in mid-century conducted daily prayers for the household, prepared his footmen for confirmation, visited and prayed with the poor, paid wages to men unable to work to keep them out of the workhouse, gave coal at Christmas and exhorted his servants to receive the sacrament.[6]

Political Economy, the dominant social theory of the first half of the nineteenth century, was popular among progressive Tories as well as Whigs, but disliked by paternalistic squires and country priests. Political Economy could be presented as a new philosophy for a new age, but also as a tough Christian social policy for testing times and recalcitrant sinners. Failure to learn lessons and to improve morally and spiritually had consequences here and hereafter. However, some felt that this new harshness was contrary to the Gospel.[7] J. B. Sumner, the evangelical Archbishop of Canterbury from 1848 to 1862, believed that the creator desired that

> the human race should be uniformly brought into a state in which they are forced to exert and improve their powers: the lowest rank, to obtain support; the one next in order, to escape from the difficulties immediately beneath it; and all the classes upward, either to keep their level, while they are pressed on each side by rival industry, or to raise themselves above the standard of their birth . . . [8]

How did Sumner and other church people regard the poor? Sumner believed that life was meant to be a place of trial. Inequality was an inevitable consequence of the unequal capacity of human beings. Poverty was a natural and honourable condition. But indigence was the result of intemperance, lack of foresight and dependence on welfare. Sumner wrote: '"Turn not your face from any poor man"; but inquire into the circumstances of his distress, and point out to him the mode in which the prudent regulations of society have directed that it should be relieved.' Education would enable the poor to understand the way out of poverty. Poverty would be alleviated by a market economy and by the habit of saving.[9] However Edward Copleston (Bishop of Llandaff 1827–49) questioned this simple approach. Perhaps the poor were helpless victims of circumstances beyond their control? Why was the gap between rich and poor growing? He appealed to farmers and gentry to reduce profits and increase wages.[10]

Another response to the threat of revolution was a building programme of churches and schools. The laws of supply and demand did not apply to religion and education. Between 1818 and 1824, parliament voted £1,500,000 for new Anglican churches in urban areas. In Leeds, between 1837 and 1859, the vicar, W. F. Hook, raised enough money to build 21 churches, 27 schools and 23 vicarages. He gave up £400 of his own annual stipend to abolish pew rents, though as late as 1842 Bishop Wilberforce defended the division of church seating according to class. By 1861 the Church of England was educating 76.2% of children in elementary day schools. The educational work of the church was not disinterested. The continuance of the establishment depended upon it having some form of contact with the majority of the people. In the early nineteenth century upper and middle class people feared that educating the working classes would make them reject their subordinate status. So church elementary education was presented as a means for making children into better workers and more obedient servants.[11] In 1868 the Dean of York said:

So long as the working man maintained order and decorum, and kept the peace and observed the laws of the land, and was a respectable member of the community, so long he felt satisfied the working man would meet with the sympathy and approval of those who in the order of Providence were placed in a higher and another position in life.[12]

Church people and politicians discussed how the poor might be helped without pauperizing them. Evangelicals in particular warned against removing the consequences of sin through a mistaken soft-heartedness. They pointed out that Christ only fed people in the wilderness because they had no other source of food. Private philanthropy had moral value whereas state aid had none. During the Irish famine of 1846–49, Richard Whately (Archbishop of Dublin 1831–63) gave away nearly £8000 to the needy, but bitterly resisted outdoor relief by the state as likely to prolong the misery. He believed that the famine would soon be over once the poor realized that the only solution was hard work and increased production.[13] Whatever Political Economy might teach, many clergy continued their tradition of philanthropy to anyone in need in the parish, whether churchgoers or not. One vicar combined his clerical duties with giving medicine to the sick and extracting teeth. He took food, clothes, fuel, beer and medicine to a group of unemployed labourers, gypsies and vagabonds – all paid for out of his own pocket. But bridges between church and community were being removed. Parishes were losing their civil functions as a result of the 1834 Poor Law and the creation in 1836 of civil registration of births, marriages and deaths. Influenced by Political Economy, some clergy restricted charity to the churchgoing poor.[14]

Nevertheless, clergy went on initiating large numbers of ventures which benefited working people: allotments (though sometimes fiercely opposed by farmers); clothing, medical, coal and blanket clubs; reading rooms and village institutes; cooperative stores, savings schemes and Friendly Societies; a number of clergy campaigned for housing and sanitary reform from mid-century. By such means, the aspiring poor who were drawn to the churches tended to be re-classed within a generation, especially if they became Nonconformists. A small Primitive Methodist group began worship in a nailer's shop in the Black Country in 1821. By 1901 the now well-to-do congregation had built its new church in Tudor Gothic with stained glass windows.[15]

The new Poor Law of 1834 was the culmination of decades of

debate about poverty and represented the triumph of Political Economy. Critics, including Sumner, argued that relief had become indiscriminate and encouraged dependency, and quoted St Paul: 'If any would not work neither should he eat.' The poor ought to do more to help themselves through mutual benefit associations and savings banks.[16] Compassion was best expressed through individuals working through voluntary societies, not by state action. Copleston argued: 'it destroys the very essence not only of benevolence, but of all virtue, to make it compulsory'.[17]

C. J. Blomfield (Bishop of London 1828–56) was chairman of the Poor Law Enquiry Commission appointed in 1832, and Sumner was a member. It accepted the Benthamite principle of making relief as unattractive as possible. It was hoped that the abolition of outdoor relief and the threat of the workhouse would abolish poverty and unemployment. The result has been described as a 'blend of evangelical retribution and utilitarian optimism'. Blomfield felt called to reform the morals of the working classes. So, for example, he supported clergy who refused to 'church' single mothers.[18] However in 'a very large number of places, squires and parsons came together to protect the existing parish administration of poor relief against the centralizing tendencies of the London thinkers'. Workhouses were particularly disliked by clergy.[19]

By the 1840s Blomfield realized that the new Poor Law was not being, and could not be implemented at a time of economic depression and social unrest. In 1839 four-fifths of relief was still given in the form of outdoor assistance. Thomas Chalmers (1780–1847), the outstanding Scottish Presbyterian minister, praised the new law for deterring the undeserving poor, but unexpectedly attacked it for deterring the deserving poor. Workhouses would undermine family, parish and other sources of charity. Like other church leaders he found it very difficult to understand the change from rural societies which could be controlled by squirearchy and church, to the anonymity and pluralism of the cities. A leading advocate of Political Economy, he believed that private charity was always preferable to state intervention. The apostles had refrained from charitable works in order to concentrate on the Word. Christ had relieved want and hunger only twice. So he advocated a 'godly commonwealth' based on establishment and rural ideals, for irreligion was the chief cause of poverty. Paradoxically it was he who led the secession from the Kirk in 1843, so decisively easing the way for an increase of secular authority as there was no longer one national church. In 1845 the church's participation in poor relief was ended. Chalmers' voluntarist and ruralist approach, which until mid-century dominated Scottish Presbyterianism, could not cope with the sheer scale of urban poverty.[20]

What was the contribution of evangelicalism to social thought? The widespread distrust among Evangelicals of state action, their preference for voluntary philanthropy and their belief that conversion was the only true antidote to poverty: such beliefs have been treated with incomprehension by those who regard the modern welfare state as the goal of social policy. But evangelical social attitudes were far from uniform. Some promoted factory reform, others thought anti-popery a more important cause. Life was a God-given pattern of rewards and punishments. Souls could be lost if in mistaken compassion the consequences of sin were removed. Bankruptcy, for example, was a providential punishment for profligacy. Though the pursuit of profit and self-interest seemed un-Christian, both served the general good by a wonderful divine contrivance.

The Irish famine was decisive for Evangelicals. Chalmers believed that relief should be provided out of taxation because the famine was not a divine punishment. Others thought it was divine retribution for popery and fecklessness. Evangelical attitudes to the famine seemed so harsh that some people felt a moral revulsion like that against hell, the Athanasian Creed, and retributory theories of the atonement. Hilton believes that the legislation for limited liability in 1856 symbolized the end of the dominance of evangelical social thought. Significantly the change was initiated by a group of philanthropists, most of them Christian Socialists. It had become clear that some who failed in business were not guilty people deserving punishment, but innocent victims of others' misdeeds.[21]

Don Cupitt once described the tension between those Christians who think in terms of two opposing cities and those who aspire to one unified city. Christianity, he contended, had always been dualistic: a way to death, a way to life; heaven or hell; good and evil; Christ or the world. If it comes to power it sees itself as an instrument of divine judgment. One-city Christians are accused of having no cutting edge, of taking away the *raison d'être* of the church by making it co-extensive with creation.[22] Cupitt oversimplifies. But it is difficult – perhaps impossible – to run a democratic society on the basis of a two-cities Christianity with its negative attitude to the 'world', to the 'natural' and the 'non-Christian'. It was very difficult for Evangelicals to share the growing belief in the determining effects of social environment. Edwin Chadwick in his *Sanitary Report* of 1842 illustrated the different mortality rates between different classes and between different districts of the same town. But for Evangelicals to accord environment such a crucial role would seem to diminish that awesome sense of personal responsibility which was at the heart of their faith. The solution to social problems had a way of turning out to be complex and to require much empirical investigation, whereas Evangelicals wanted simple solutions based on *a priori* beliefs. Therefore it was easier to concentrate on a few emotional issues like sabbatarianism and temperance. 'The powers that be are ordained by God' said St Paul in Romans 13. Evangelical Anglicans were therefore Erastians. Radical dissent from the state in the name of Christ was not an option for them as it was for Anglo-Catholics and Nonconformists. This is one reason why so few Christian Socialists were Evangelicals.

Critics of Political Economy

The Romantic Movement, and Anglican and Roman Catholicism, which were so influenced by it, were often hostile to Political Economy and Utilitarianism. Romantic Catholics were more at home in rural than industrial society. To Utilitarians, lighting candles on the altar in broad daylight was simply wasteful. The *Quarterly Review* in 1855 attacked 'the numberless . . . holidays with which the Romish calendar encourages idleness and baffles thrift'.[23] John Keble thought Malthus hard and vulgar and felt most at home in a rural economy where everyone was interdependent economically and in the life of the church: 'the rich man wants the poor man's labour, and the poor man wants the rich man's meat, and both want the love and prayers of each other'. E. B. Pusey, by contrast, was deeply concerned about the great cities and in 1838 proposed colleges of celibate priests and sisterhoods to minister to them. In 1837, he felt a call to simpler living, and sold his carriage and horses, and his wife sold all her jewellery. They gave the money to needy London churches. In 1847 he told a well-off West End congregation on a fast day for the Irish famine:

> We *will* not limit our self-indulgence; and so in order to obtain it cheaply, we pare down the wages of our artisans. They who have seen it, know that full often the very clothes we wear are, while they are made, moistened by the tears of the poor.

But Pusey was not politically minded.[24]

The novels of Disraeli, A. W. Pugin's drawings *Contrasts* (1836) and the passionate writings of R. H. Froude, the Tractarian, blamed the Reformation and the dissolution of the monasteries for many social evils. Froude also blamed the Reformation for producing rationalism and commercialism. But earlier, the radical William Cobbett had also disparaged the Reformation when 'this land of meat and beef was changed all of a sudden to a land of dry bread and oatmeal porridge'. His nostalgia for the old cottage economy of a pre-industrial society has been a persistent feature of English socialism. When he denounced the 'Graspalls' he cited Amos. When a group of Chartists attend a Roman Catholic church in Norwich in 1839 the priest told them their sufferings were caused by the robbery of endowments at the Reformation. Even Frederick Temple (Archbishop of Canterbury 1897–1902 and father of William Temple) in 1844 sympathized with W. G. Ward's view that the Reformation was a 'robbery of the poor'. Temple thought it had been 'maintained solely by selfish interests'.[25] Carlyle in *Past and Present* (1843), so influential on socialists, contrasted the life of a mediaeval monastery with the individualism and cash mentality of the nineteenth century. An important strand of Christian Socialism has been nostalgic, mediaevalist and ruralist.

Robert Owen (1771–1858), acting like a paternal Tory squire, had created at Lanark model mills, schools and community institutions. It proclaimed the message often echoed since, that cooperation not competition should be the basis of society. Owenites established a cooperative society in 1821. Unlike some radicals he accepted industrialism, but believed it required 'legislative interference and direction'. Political Economy he described as a 'thoroughly selfish system' which must be superseded.[26]

Thus, even during the heyday of Political Economy, alternative views of society continued. Waterman suggests that as early as the mid 1820s, the unity between classical Political Economy and Christian leaders was beginning to break up. So when Political Economy began to wane, an alternative theology and ideology was available to support the shift towards a more positive view of the state, which eventually fed into Christian Socialism. For example W. F. Hook, the energetic vicar of Leeds, in an Open Letter of 1846 to the liberal-minded Connop Thirlwall (Bishop of St David's 1840–75) dramatically pronounced the voluntary (largely church) system of education a failure and proposed a national state system. Thirlwall responded that the clergy should no longer regard the state as 'a necessary evil' but as 'an eminently sacred institution' with the object not only of protecting but also promoting the progress of all citizens.[27] Kitson Clark considered that 'the middle of the nineteenth century was in England a period of survivals, anticipations and contradictions'. The old aristocratic methods of government were being replaced by centralized controls and paid officials, but the old titled classes still dominated the political system.[28]

Thus during even 'The Age of Atonement' (as Hilton calls the first half of the century) an incarnational and immanentist tradition was maintained by Blake, Coleridge, Wordsworth, Carlyle and Keble. William Blake (1757–1827) celebrated the real humanity of Jesus (then a novel idea) and God's identification with the poor and outcasts of every race and religion (also novel), for example in 'The Divine Image'. This was included as a hymn in the Anglo-Catholic *English Hymnal* (1906) by Percy Dearmer, its editor and a leading member of the Christian Social Union. By then, incarnationalism and immanentism dominated theology. Blake offered a radical version of part of the Lord's Prayer: 'Give us the Bread which is our due & Right, by taking away Money, or a Price, or Tax upon what is Common to all in thy Kingdom.' He described industrial work as 'sorrowful drudgery to obtain a scant pittance of bread'.[29]

Edward Norman regards Coleridge with Carlyle and Thomas Arnold as the three immediate intellectual sources of Christian Socialism.[30] Though S. T. Coleridge (1772–1834) and Wordsworth had been bitterly disillusioned with the French Revolution, both retained something of its initial hope. Coleridge, with his strong sense of the church as an organic body, believed we are members one of another. His rejection of the mechanistic view of life put him at odds with Political Economy:

> It is not uncommon for 100,000 *operatives* (mark this word, for words *in this sense* are things) to be put out of employment at once in the cotton districts, and, thrown upon parochial relief . . . you say to a man – 'You have no claim upon me; you have your allotted part to perform in the world, so have I. In a state of nature, indeed, had I food, I should offer you a share from sympathy, from humanity; but in this advanced and artificial state of society, I cannot offer you relief; you must starve . . .'[31]

As a nation we had grown (he complained) 'to look at all things through the *medium* of the market, and to estimate the worth of all pursuits and attainments by their marketable value'. He criticized 'Christian Mammonists' for not challenging the commercial spirit.[32] Coleridge had an indirect influence on the Tractarians, but a direct influence on F. D. Maurice and his circle. He provided the group with an organic view of the state and a new model for a church-state relationship. The church (he said) ought to be 'the compensating counterforce to the inherent and inevitable evils and defects of the State, as a State'.[33] Thomas Carlyle (1795–1881) was a pugnacious opponent of *laissez-faire*, critical of democracy, yet angry about the treatment of the workers. 'Of these successful skilful workers some two millions . . . sit in Workhouses, Poor-law Prisons; or have "out-door" relief flung over the wall to them, – the workhouse Bastille being filled to bursting . . .' Traditional bonds of society had been replaced by 'Cash Payment the sole nexus; and there are so many things which cash will not pay!' Like Coleridge, Carlyle pleaded for life against mechanism and summoned his fellows to forsake Mammon and to return to God.[34] Thomas Arnold (1795–1842) wrote:

> Society has been regarded as a mere collection of individuals looking each after his own interests, and the business of government has been limited to that of a mere police whose sole use is to prevent these individuals from robbing and knocking each other down.

The purpose of both church and state was the moral happiness of man, yet government had come to be regarded 'as a mere necessary evil, an encroachment upon individual liberty'. Yet the condition of the poor showed the consequences of a policy of 'letting alone'.[35]

However, it was the pressure of experience rather than changes in ideology which began to modify *laissez-faire*. Factory conditions, issues of public health and education focussed minds. Of course the application of *laissez-faire* had always been partial.

Those keenest to let the market decide might decry regulation of working hours, but use laws to prevent Sunday work. As early as 1802, parliament agreed on a measure to restrict children's working hours. Even though it remained largely a dead letter, it began a process of factory regulation. But the Ten Hours Bill was only passed in 1847 after fifteen years' hard campaigning by Tory Anglican paternalists, George Bull ('the Ten Hours Parson') Michael Sadler, Lord Ashley (Shaftesbury), Hook and others. Up to this point the bishops had rarely been leaders of opinion in such questions, but they strongly supported this bill. Bishops were concerned not only about the physical effects of long working hours, but also that these prevented children attending church schools. Bishop Wilberforce used what was becoming a regular argument – that the legislation was not contrary to Political Economy, but an exception: 'it was wrong to create wealth by the sacrifice of the health and morals of a portion of the people'.[36] 'By the middle of the century the episcopate could no longer be described as indifferent or hostile to the physical needs of the working classes.'[37] Exceptions to the rules of Political Economy began to multiply. 'Expert opinion, in the name of particular acts of social improvement – sanitation, industrial employment, food adulteration, and so forth – appealed increasingly to the central authority of the State as the effective agency for change.'[38]

But however hard the bishops tried to understand the needs of the workers and the poor, they lived in a totally separate world. In the early 1830s the Archbishop of Canterbury received £19,000 a year (say £718,000 today). But a curate might receive less than £100 a year (£3,780). When starving labourers south of the Thames marched in 1830 demanding 2/6d a day (say £1,400 a year) three were hanged and 420 transported. The style in which wealthy clergy lived conveyed more eloquent and memorable messages than any sermon. The fact that in the first half of the century many clergy were also magistrates made them seem an arm of the government and further alienated them from working people.[39]

Some Christians, particularly Dissenters and Evangelicals, remained economic purists. John Bright, the Quaker mill-owner and MP, throughout his life opposed factory legislation. He said after the repeal of the Corn Laws in 1846:

. . . all legislative interference with the labour market, all attempts of Government to fix the wages of industry, all inter- ference of a third party between employers and employed, are unjustifiable in principle and mischievous in their results.

When Ashley, and other landed aristocrats, argued that factory workers needed protection, Bright accused them of bias and ignorance. The workers had more reason to thank the Anglican aristocrat from the south than the Dissenting manufacturer from the north. Yet historians of the Left have been reluctant to recognize the contribution of Anglican Tory paternalism to both the Labour Party and Christian Socialism. Ashley illustrates the way in which the same person could mix traditional and new approaches to social issues. Certain problems, he believed, such as the treatment of children in factories, could only be tackled by legislation and he called for the state to be 'a faithful and pious parent'. But in 1883 he attacked suggestions that the state should ease the housing problem by providing houses at nominal rents, because it would 'utterly destroy their moral energies'.[40]

F. D. Maurice and his circle

The 1840s were bleak years for many British workers. But unlike most of Europe, Britain avoided a revolution in 1848 because of a measure of reform, the influence of religion and a tradition of def- erence. Nevertheless, Chartism agitated for radical reform and between 1836 and 1846, fourteen Socialist Congresses were held which Robert Owen often chaired.

In 1848, F. D. Maurice (1805–72) heard that a Chartist demonstration was to be held on Kennington Common on 10 April.[41] A month before, he had been alarmed by a first-hand account by his friend J. M. Ludlow of the Paris revolution.

Maurice determined that action must be taken to prevent something similar happening here. Maurice was an Anglican priest and Professor of Theology at King's College. He had gathered round him a group of young men eager to do social and religious work among the poor in local parishes. The authorities, alarmed by the proposed Chartist demonstration, set up barricades. Maurice, because he was a conventional patriot, volunteered to be a special constable, but because he was ordained, he was rejected. Charles Kingsley (1819–75), a country priest, went to the demonstration with J. M. Ludlow, a young barrister. Kingsley was as well informed about rural as urban poverty and publicized both in his novels *Alton Locke* (1850) and *Yeast* (1851). He had become Maurice's disciple after reading Maurice's *Kingdom of Christ* in 1843. Kingsley was an English nationalist and imperialist, a Tory paternalist with little sympathy for the unions, but passionate about technological progress, sanitary reform and the poverty and estrangement of the workers from the church. In the preface to *Alton Locke*, 'Cheap Clothes and Nasty', he demonstrated that society was bound together not by fraternity but by disease (as in Dickens' *Bleak House*) transmitted from underpaid, ill-clad tailors and seamstresses to their aristocratic and clerical customers. 'Lord —'s coat has been seen covering a group of children blotched with small-pox.' But in an 1854 Preface he assured working men that the propertied classes were now facing their responsibilities. J. M. Ludlow (1821–1911) had been brought up in Paris and much of his understanding of socialism derived from France. Maurice and Ludlow had met in 1846. They believed that socialism must be Christianized, otherwise there would be catastrophe.

In the event, the Chartist demonstration was curtailed by a downpour, and the smaller than expected crowd dispersed peacefully. Kingsley spent that night making placards addressed to the 'Workmen of England':

Many of you are wronged; and many besides yourselves know it. Almost all men who have heads and hearts know it – above all, the working clergy know it. They go into your houses, they see the shameful filth and darkness in which you are forced to live crowded together . . . you have more friends than you think for . . .

He told them that they had friends who loved them and regarded them as brothers, who were trying to win for them something better than Charters, and to turn them back from riot which would only end in distrust and starvation. Real freedom from slavery to 'one's own stomach, one's own pocket, one's own hunger' comes from Jesus 'the poor Man, who died for poor men'. That May he confessed to the Chartists: 'We have used the Bible as if it were the special constable's handbook – an opium dose for keeping beasts of burden patient while they were being overloaded – a mere book to keep the poor in order.'[42] (There is no evidence that Marx's similar phraseology about religion was indebted to Kingsley.)

In 1920, Charles Raven described Kingsley's manifesto as the Church of England's 'first public act of atonement for a half-century of apostasy, of class prejudice and political sycophancy'.[43] Some Christian Socialist history has been written in that style of platform rhetoric. By contrast, Edward Norman in his fine study *The Victorian Christian Socialists* (1987) wrote of Maurice and his circle:

> . . . their 'Socialism' was not, by most available tests, either 'political' or 'Socialist' . . . surviving references to traditional social attitudes were thickly distributed within their thought. But for all that, the Victorian Christian Socialists produced a radical departure from the received attitudes of the Church . . . [44]

Here Norman implies that Marxism is the norm by which socialism is to be judged. But the multi-faceted history of Christian Socialism suggests that we need to diversify the term 'socialist' to include those who like Maurice, Charles Gore and Tony Blair claim a part in that tradition. It is time to recognize that there has often been more common ground between parties and traditions than partisan histories and politicians care to admit. In the Edwardian period, for example, Herbert Spencer thought 'New Liberalism' should be renamed 'New Toryism', presumably because of its paternalistic concept of the state. Maurice's own group was very diverse, united by their devotion to him, to the working class and the poor rather than by any ideology or political programme. Apart from Ludlow, they knew little of socialist thought. Based in London, they were far from the industrial north, which was so incomprehensible to southerners, as Mrs Gaskell pointed out in *North and South* (1855). Maurice held traditional views about social rank, monarchy and aristocracy and was opposed to unions. The workers should be given the vote only when they were educated. One of the prime functions of the group was to prepare them for political responsibility.

There are three main reasons why this group was, and continues to be important, despite the fact that it was so diverse, so middle class and so paternalistic. Firstly, by using the term 'Christian Socialist', they brought together two terms which were widely thought antagonistic in this country, and even more so on the continent. Maurice explained the term in 1850 as 'the only title which will define our object, and will commit us at once to the conflict we must engage in sooner or later with the unsocial Christians and the unchristian Socialists . . . our great desire is to Christianize Socialism'.[45] Secondly, they were the first Christian group to present a concerted attack on *laissez-faire* and to begin to sketch an alternative to it. As an undergraduate at Cambridge Maurice had defended Coleridge and Wordsworth against Utilitarian attacks. Maurice wrote in his first tract:

> The watchword of the Socialist is cooperation – the watchword of the Anti-socialist is competition. Anyone who recognizes the principle of cooperation as a stronger and truer principle than that of competition, has a right to the honour or disgrace of being called a Socialist.[46]

Thirdly the group is important because it has inspired Anglican and other Christian Socialists ever since.

The group can also be credited with tangible achievements. The Working Men's College, which opened in 1854, with Maurice as Principal, developed from classes held in 'The Hall of Association' – a significant title representing the antithesis of competition. When Maurice was dismissed from his Professorship at King's in 1853 because of his universalism, workers had expressed their hope that he might become Principal of a Working Men's College. Teaching was given voluntarily by priests, lawyers and artists. In the first term 140 enrolled, of whom half were working men. Maurice also was a pioneer in education for women and became the first Principal of Queen's College for women. Moreover, Maurice's group did much to promote the co-operative movement which had opened its first stores in 1844. Maurice believed that the movement would teach workers self-government, brotherhood, incorporate them into national life and eliminate industrial conflict. He discussed with workers the ideals of the common life in Acts, the monasteries and other groups. One of the group, E. V. Neale, put £60,000 into launching twelve co-operative workshops for various trades. The group was too diverse in outlook and aims to cohere and did not last beyond March 1855. Maurice turned from the co-operatives (which failed) to the educational work, which lasted. All but Kingsley retained something of their original vision.

Britain became more prosperous in the 1850s, 1860s and 1870s. The cry for a radical overhaul of society therefore died down. The group lacked economic credibility (apart from Ludlow). This disabled them from being effective proponents for Christian Socialism. Their simple moral contrast between cooperation (good) versus competition (bad) proved an enduring but flawed legacy. Yet at least they were not mediaevalists or ruralists. Maurice's most important legacy was his 'one city' theology with its insistence on Natural Law.[47] But he lacked a sense of both the inevitability and beneficial role of conflict in human affairs. A Platonist, he believed too readily that opposites could be reconciled. His consensualism expressed itself in his deep devotion to establishment, yet at a time when it was being eroded by pluralism. His positive theology of the state was significant at a time when its moral potential was being rediscovered. 'The State has been a great instrument, in God's hand, for preventing the mischiefs which might have accrued to the Church . . .'[48] By appealing to a God beyond religion; by beginning his exposition of Christianity with Creation, not like Evangelicals with the Fall; by seeing the church as a witness to the unity of all in Christ, whether people acknowledge it or not; by stressing that baptism and eucharist show that Christianity is a social faith: in all these ways he created a theology with profound political possibilities, which 'two cities' evangelicalism could never have. It is true that his understanding of the Trinity as including subordination, provided a basis for a hierarchical not an egalitarian society, yet his language about the universality of God and his love conveyed a yearning for equality.[49] At the end of *The Kingdom of Christ* (1838) he imagined a churchman in a grim manufacturing district. A church which was a tool of the aristocracy would have nothing to say. The Broad Churchman, eager to teach a reasonable gospel, would have something to offer. The Methodist or Evangelical would have more to offer – a message of salvation for perishing souls. But that was not enough:

> . . . men feel that they are not merely lost creatures; they look up to heaven above them, and ask whether it can be true that this is the whole account of their condition; that their sense of right and wrong, their cravings for fellowship . . . are all nothing.

If religion, people say, will give us no explanation of these feelings, then we will forsake it and go to Chartism or socialism. He presented a vision of an interdependent society in which the middle classes 'act upon the lower, so as to be their guides and not their tyrants', and in which the upper classes may be brought into a fruitful relation with the middle classes:

how each portion of the community may preserve its proper position to the rest, and may be fused together by the spiritual power which exists for each, the minister of all, the creature of none.[50]

Stewart Headlam, priest founder in 1877 of the Christian Socialist group the Guild of St Matthew, paid this tribute to Maurice:

> You, ladies and gentlemen, probably do not know what it is to have been delivered in the world of thought, emotion, imagination, from the belief that a large proportion of the human race are doomed to endless misery. You are freeborn – mainly through Maurice's work and courage.[51]

A. J. Scott (1805–66) provides an example from Presbyterianism of how the rejection of Calvinism and the adoption of universalism could lead to Christian Socialism.[52] In 1830, no longer willing to sign the Westminster Confession, he took up an independent ministry in London. He became a close friend of Maurice's and was greatly influenced by him. True society, he believed, existed only through cooperation. The greatest obstacle to this was selfishness which could not be overcome through economic change but through the widening of human sympathy, beginning in the family. He appealed for political parties to cooperate and to be prepared to question the status quo. 'God is the God of order, but not necessarily pledged to that particular form of order, by which your quiet and your wealth seem to you to be best secured.' Scott rejected Chartism as materialist and lacking a spiritual dimension. It was no use trying to control upper-class selfishness by encouraging the poor to make selfish demands. Instead, Scott supported Owen's cooperative experiments. Scott joined Maurice's circle the day after the Chartist demonstration. In 1857 he relinquished the Principalship of Owens College Manchester (later the university), and devoted more time to working-class education. He and his friends had founded a

Working Men's College in Manchester similar to the one
founded in London by Maurice.

Believing that each person had a spiritual conscience he criticized the Catholic tradition for setting the church, the sacraments
and the priesthood between the individual and God. His
Christian individualism differed markedly from Maurice's
Liberal Catholicism in which the corporate life of the church and
the sacraments provided models for his political thinking, though
Maurice was always finding ways to universalize the particular so
as to apply it to all humanity. But both were agreed about the
centrality of the incarnation and the universality of God's love.
Scott rejected the Calvinist view that human beings were 'wholly
defiled'. Rather they were viceroys of the world who should share
power fraternally with their fellows.

Mrs Gaskell

Foremost among Scott's friends were William Gaskell, Unitarian
minister in Manchester and his wife Elizabeth, the novelist. (Her
daughter married Scott Holland's cousin.) After the success of
her first novel *Mary Barton* (1848), she visited London and met
Dickens, Carlyle and F. D. Maurice who, like Thomas Hughes
and Kingsley, greatly admired this sympathetic portrayal of the
poverty and industrial strife in Manchester during the hungry
1840s. It was England's first mature social novel, and also shows
a good grasp of economic realities. The impetus for it arose from
a mill-worker who responded to her advice to be patient: 'Have ye
ever seen a child clemmed [starved] to death?' She wanted (she
wrote) to 'give some utterance to the agony which, from time to
time, convulses this dumb people'. Clearly she did not write for
the workers – they did not need her erudite footnotes explaining
their dialect – but to move others (like the manufacturers in her
husband's congregation) to compassion and action. (Some were
in fact outraged.) Ministers and members of Cross Street Chapel,
leaders of Manchester life, originated many social reforms in the
city. Unitarians were more inclined than Anglicans and Non-

conformists to ascribe disease (for example) to man-made causes than to divine punishment, and were therefore less fatalistic. The novel, implicitly based on the hymn to love in I Corinthians 13, offered a very different message from the *Communist Manifesto* published the same year.[53] She called on masters and men to unite in a common brotherhood, and on the well-off to look after the poor. Neither Barton, the trade unionist who murders, nor the hard-faced millowner whose son he murders, are presented as villains but as sinners in need of forgiveness. The main theme is the total lack of understanding shown by the well-off for the poor. Barton angrily asks: 'If I am out of work . . . does the rich man share his plenty with me, as he ought to do, if his religion wasn't a humbug?' (ch. I). The rich do not suffer from recessions like the poor. 'I never see the masters getting thin and haggard for want of food' (ch. XXXVII). Mrs Gaskell explained that it was easy for suffering workers to see legislators, magistrates, employers, even ministers of religion as 'their oppressors and enemies' (ch. VIII). Essentially good people were driven into tragedy by the environment. She (like Dickens) showed the middle-class failure to understand industrial conflict and working-class solidarity when she depicted unions as essentially oppressive. The novel ends with the heroine and her husband emigrating (a favourite solution to problems in Victorian novels and advocated by some Christian Socialists like Maurice, Hughes and Kingsley). The hope lies not in legislated reforms, but in mutual forgiveness and understanding between rich and poor. *North and South* (1855) offers a vision of social unity realized after many trials and much repentance.

The religion in these two novels certainly owes nothing to the doctrinal, sacramental and liturgical Catholicism urged by Maurice and later Anglican Socialists as the only basis for social action. Rather it is focussed on the Bible and Jesus, the poor man. Mrs Gaskell was correct. Most working-class religion was not sacramental but an ethical system supported by biblical stories and texts.

Dickens' *Hard Times* (1854) was a powerful but essentially

diagrammatic fable, protesting against the extinction of imaginative and instinctive life by utilitarianism and industrialism. It offered no solution. Its characteristic refrain was 'Tis a muddle'. Whereas Mrs Gaskell found hope within the people in the industrial system, Dickens had to go outside it to the circus to find authentic life. This type of anti-industrialism nourished socialist dreams of reviving Merrie England.

Christian responses to urban society

Mrs Gaskell advocated the translation of the rural tradition of *noblesse oblige* into urban life. So the previously tough-minded but now repentant manufacturer in *North and South* built a dining room for his men (whom he had once called 'hands') and ate there sometimes himself. New Lanark continued to inspire. Early in the century, the Ashworth brothers, both Quakers, built model workers' houses and schools near the Irwell, fined employees for shoddy work, gave rewards for good behaviour, evicted dirty tenants and controlled the workers' morals with constables, as at New Lanark. Edward Akroyd, an Anglican mill owner, built workers' cottages, a school, a library and a church at Copley near Halifax between 1847 and 1865, and created a similar development at Akroyden nearby. Titus Salt, a Congregationalist, was the first manufacturer to move his mill into the country where he created the village of Saltaire. It was like a squire's estate as everyone worked for Salt and wages were paid in tokens to be spent in the shops or exchanged at the bank. However, model villages were rare. In any case, both urban and rural paternalism could be stifling.[54] In 1888, the Congregationalist W. H. Lever began to construct Port Sunlight for his workers: 'our endeavour is to socialize and Christianize business relations and get back to the office, factory and workshop that close family brotherhood that existed in the good old days of hand labour.' It was his custom to read *A Christmas Carol* to his workers on Christmas Eve. Businessmen could be as nostalgic as socialists.[55]

The social thought and action of the churches developed

considerably between the first wave of Christian Socialism in the
1840s and the second wave in the 1880s. Much of this development was in a corporatist direction. James Fraser (Bishop of
Manchester 1870–85) was the first bishop to address a
Cooperative Congress. He mediated in industrial disputes and
defended the right of Joseph Arch and agricultural workers to
found a union. During a lockout he criticized the farmers and
defended the strikers. Arch, a Primitive Methodist, typified the
connection between class and denomination. He refused to
receive communion in the parish church because worshippers did
so by social class with the poor last. Most leaders of his union
were, like Arch, lay preachers. Nonconformity provided leadership in other unions. It created an ethos in which it was natural
for a meeting to begin with a hymn and a prayer. It was Cardinal
Manning's mediation in the 1889 Dock Strike which made his
social concern widely known, though most Roman Catholics were
uninterested in social questions. Friendly Societies, like unions,
were typical working-class institutions which combined self-
help with mutual support. Both church and chapel became keen
advocates of these Societies. *Self-Help* (1859) by Samuel Smiles
was avidly read by aspiring working people and thus helped to
form the ethos of the unions, Friendly Societies and Labour
movement.[56]

'The Civic Gospel' was developed in Birmingham between the
1850s and 1880s by Nonconformist ministers, particularly
George Dawson, a Unitarian, and R. W. Dale, a Congregationalist. When Joseph Chamberlain, who came from a Unitarian
family, became mayor in 1873 he drew upon this tradition which
had helped to make Birmingham a model for local democracy.
Dawson gave the inaugural address at the opening of the
Birmingham Free Library in 1866, emphasizing that it was a
Corporation Library:

> . . . the expression of a conviction on your part that a town like
> this exists for moral and intellectual purposes. It is a proclama-
> tion that a great community like this is not to be looked upon

as a fortuitous concourse of human atoms, or as a miserable knot of vipers struggling in a pot . . . It is a declaration that the Corporation of a great town like this has not done all its duty when it has put in action a set of ingenious contrivances for cleaning and lighting the streets . . .

He hoped that private ownership of great art and book collections was coming to an end through 'a holy Communism, a wise Socialism'. Dale believed that politics was a noble vocation:

Parliaments, town councils, judges, magistrates, have their place in the Divine order. The Christian man is not released from the obligations of citizenship; to him these obligations are strengthened by new sanctions . . . Paul describes the levying and collection of taxes as a divinely appointed function of the civil magistrate.

Elsewhere Dale praised Maurice for converting many Non-conformists to this view of politics. He criticized John Bright for not grasping the moral potential of state action.[57] It was not until 1905 when Charles Gore became Birmingham's first bishop that an Anglican radical voice was heard there. The civic gospel prepared the way for municipal socialism which was particularly valued by the Christian Socialists. But the power of the state was also growing, of which various Public Health Acts beginning in 1866 and the 1870 Education Act were examples. Politicians had to take working people into account after the 1867 and 1884 Reform Acts enfranchised more of them. The unions were given legal protection in Acts between 1871 and 1876.

Ruskin and Morris

A survey showed that the book which had most influenced the first twenty-nine Labour MPs elected in 1906 was *Unto This Last* (1862) by John Ruskin (1819–1900). It also laid the foundations of Attlee's socialism and transformed Gandhi's life. When

Maurice's Working Men's College opened in 1854 each student was given a reprint of a chapter of Ruskin's *Stones of Venice*. Ruskin lectured there for six years. Though Ruskin lost his evangelical faith, he remained an evangelist with all the strengths and weaknesses of evangelicalism – its urgency, its tendency to oversimplify, its pleasure in prophetic denunciation. Ruskin did not belong to the Christian Socialists and thought little of Maurice.[58] His frequent biblical references won him a hearing from the earnest. *Unto This Last* takes its title from Matthew 20.14. Ruskin was a Tory paternalist. The old and destitute should be provided with comfort and a home, but unemployed people should be compelled to train at government schools and then made to work. Political Economy was a delusion. The value of anything is intrinsic, determined by God, not by the market. His view that the professions represented the ideal in which personal gain is secondary to service of the community strongly attracted the clergy and middle-class ethical socialists.[59] Looking back nostalgically to pre-industrial society, he believed that mechanization alienated the worker from his work. A locomotive engineer who joined his St George's Company had to give up his job and take up hedging and ditching.[60]

William Morris (1834–96) developed Ruskin's thesis that mechanically produced goods were dead and deadening. Yet in his firm he was inevitably caught up in industrial and commercial life. He had to use machines to produce multiple copies. His life was cushioned by an annual dividend income of about £900 (£32,000 in current terms) a year. When in 1884 he accompanied members of the Social Democratic Federation to meet the Lancashire cotton strikers, it was the first time he had ever been involved with working people in the mass, the first time he had entered a worker's house.[61]

In 1891 he expressed his dream of society in *News from Nowhere* (Utopia). Parliament has become a dung market, but all are equal, and money, prisons, formal education and central government are abolished and the countryside reclaimed from pollution. For Morris, socialism was about community, as he wrote in *John Ball*: 'Fellowship is heaven, and lack of fellowship is hell.' Yet there was a gulf between himself and working people who wanted cheap mass-produced goods. A former kitchen-maid recalled how she slaved below stairs late at night and early in the morning to serve Morris and his friends upstairs who were discussing socialism.[62] Morris's influence on socialism was immense. Tawney's vision of a socialism not handed down by intellectuals but rising up from the people owed much to Morris. He taught Barbara Castle that socialism was not only about struggle but also about sensual fulfilment. The laconic Attlee eagerly quoted Morris's praise of fellowship. So does Blair. Harold Laski visiting Northumberland miners during the slump of the 1930s found copies of *John Ball* and *News from Nowhere* in house after house, even after most of the furniture had been sold off.[63]

The second wave of Christian Socialism

Why was there an upsurge in socialism in the 1880s of which the creation of the Fabian Society in 1884 and the Christian Social Union in 1889 were part? The 1860s and 1870s had been relatively prosperous, but there were serious recessions in the later 1870s and middle 1880s. The first Fabian Society pamphlet (1884) was entitled *Why are There so Many Poor?* Some like H. M. Hyndman, who in 1881 founded what became the Social Democratic Federation, believed that revolution would come in 1889. When it did not, he changed the date to 1900.

Christian Socialists urged that more of Labour's claims should be met to avert social breakdown. The unions had moved away from Owenite visions of self-sustaining communities towards state intervention, so tacitly accepted normal political processes. The desire for a force independent of the Liberals grew. By the 1890s working-class admiration for Gladstone was declining. In 1892 Keir Hardie became an independent Labour MP. The next year the Independent Labour Party was born in Bradford. Carlyle, Ruskin and Christianity had more influence upon it than Marx. The ILP felt like a religious crusade. Many of its members were rooted in Nonconformity. 'More inspiration for the work has been drawn from the teachings of Jesus than from any other source', claimed Hardie. However, Labour's relationship with Nonconformity was complex. For its first three years the ILP made the signing of the temperance pledge a condition of membership. But this was abolished in order to widen the membership to include public house culture. In 1891 the first of a number of Labour Churches were created. They arose partly out of a tension between aspiring Nonconformists who wanted their chapels to become more respectable, and Nonconformist socialists who criticized the chapels for not being committed to social change and, for being unsympathetic to union militancy. The ILP inaugural conference was held in a Labour Church Institute and 5000 delegates attended a Labour Church service. But the Labour Church movement was largely over by 1900. Its religion had become so attenuated that services seemed too like political meetings.[64]

The article on 'Political Economy' in the 1885 edition of the *Encyclopaedia Britannica* contended that *laissez-faire* was no longer sacrosanct. The standard economic textbook became Alfred Marshall's *Principles of Political Economy* (1890) which advocated state action – for example to promote working-class education. The New Liberals, who were to dominate the 1906 Liberal government, were prepared to use state and municipal power with a new boldness. H. H. Asquith had learned from his mentor T. H. Green the way in which 'the collective action of the community may and ought to be employed positively as well as negatively'.[65] The speeches at the annual Church Congresses of Anglican clergy and laity reflected the growing acceptance of collectivist solutions. A Committee of the 1888 Lambeth Conference of bishops from the world-wide Anglican Communion reported that there was no 'necessary contradiction' between socialism, interpreted broadly, and Christianity. It advocated cooperative schemes, not nationalization; urged the government to protect 'proletarians from the evil effects of unchecked competition', but proclaimed that 'the best help is self-help' through thrift and self-restraint; suggested ordinands should study economics; that clergy should establish friendly relations with socialists and learn 'how much of what is good and true in Socialism is to be found in the precepts of Christ'. A Committee of the 1897 Lambeth Conference said that Christian opinion 'ought to condemn the belief that economic conditions are to be left to the action of material causes and mechanical laws, uncontrolled by any moral responsibility'. Those unwilling to work should be disciplined by making work a condition of relief. The church should consider supporting stronger control over the housing of the poor and the minimizing of unemployment through Labour Bureaux, Conciliation Boards and public works.[66]

Many Nonconformists had once denied that the state had any right to provide education. They now accepted state provision and compulsory schooling. In *The Bitter Cry of Outcast London* (1883) Andrew Mearns, a Congregationalist, described the appalling living conditions in London. These, he believed, could not be overcome by voluntary action alone. Yet his pamphlet only stirred church opinion when his revelations about widespread sexual immorality were publicized. The resultant controversy helped to create the Royal Commission on the Housing of the Working Classes. In 1888, the Presbyterian minister Donald MacLeod showed why those who lived in one room were likely to be non-churchgoers, to have a high rate of drunkenness, poverty and mortality. Christians were realizing how determinative environment could be. In *Darkest England and the Way Out* (1890), William Booth, founder of the Salvation Army, prompted by his discovery that the very poor did not join it, devised a scheme whereby the poor could be trained to become industrious, and therefore more likely to respond to the gospel. He thus combined social concern with traditional evangelical emphases upon salvation and individual choice, horror at indiscriminate charity, dislike of urban life and belief in the restorative value of the small controlled group. He envisaged three separate colonies, one in the heart of the city to draw in the poor; those who responded well would be transferred to a farm colony; the best would found a new community overseas. He termed it 'The Great Machine'.[67]

As we have seen, Christians were often keen to commend cooperative schemes. They offered an alternative to the competitive spirit, did not threaten property and taught individual responsibility and thrift. A number of Victorian socialists rejected state action as the way to socialism and preferred voluntarism, self-help and mutual aid societies. By 1872 cooperative retail societies had over 300,000 members in England and Wales. Gladstone and Bright, when they argued for an extension of the franchise in 1866, adduced the movement as evidence of the large numbers of workers who had become responsible and thrifty. The movement owed more to E. V. Neale, one of Maurice's group, than to any other person. However, the Cooperative Wholesale Society transformed the movement into a business enterprise. All profits went to consumers, not workers. Idealists were elbowed out by businessmen. Workers had to strike and form unions to maintain wages and conditions. The failure of the movement to balance the needs of workers and consumers and to achieve active participation by either, was a serious blow to socialist ideals. Independent cooperative workshops faced extinction as the CWS opened establishments to compete with them. In the search for cheap goods the CWS even patronized sweatshops and probably did some sweating itself. Neale complained to the Second Cooperative Congress in 1870:

> The noble idea of regenerating society from top to bottom, by an effort springing from the united exertions of those whom it consigns to its lowest rooms, has given way to the idea of obtaining good articles at the cheapest possible price.[68]

Bishops at the 1897 Lambeth Conference were also very worried lest 'this great movement . . . should degenerate into a vast system of joint-stock shopkeeping or industry, conducted on selfish principles, with no dominant moral purpose pervading it . . . but aiming chiefly at large dividends'. They especially deplored the tendency to abandon profit-sharing.[69]

The settlements

The tradition of *noblesse oblige* continued, not least among the clergy. When *The Bitter Cry of Outcast London* appeared in 1883, Scott Holland, then a don at Christ Church, described how deeply it had touched Oxford.[70] One expression of this concern was the multiplication of university and public school settlements and missions, the first of which had been founded by Uppingham in 1869. By 1914 there were over forty settlements in working-class areas of the cities. Beatrice Webb described the development of a new sense of *social* sin and quoted from a lecture given in 1883 by the Balliol economics don Arnold Toynbee shortly before his death. He had been a disciple of T. H. Green. It included a confession to the workers, with echoes of Prayer Book language, that the middle classes had 'sinned against you grievously', offered charity instead of justice. But we (he said) are ready to change, to give up comfortable lives 'to devote our lives to your service', provided that you 'remember' that material civilization is 'not an end in itself'.[71] By 1900 the Oxford branch of the Christian Social Union was ranking Toynbee with Carlyle, Ruskin, Maurice and Kingsley in Leaflets 33 and 34 on Social Reformers. It quoted his remark that the first socialistic measures were initiated by Tory landowners, not by radicals.

In 1884 Toynbee Hall was founded in his memory through Samuel Barnett, Vicar of St Jude's Whitechapel, where Toynbee had lived latterly. Barnett, a liberal churchman, and another of Green's disciples, had ministered there since 1873. It was one of the poorest parishes in London, had virtually no middle class, and many Jews and Irish. Barnett was something of a saint with a keen social conscience. His clothes were always shabby because he had them run up by out-of-work tailors. Not many people came to church, so he devoted himself increasingly to bringing national life and culture to the people. The role of the church was 'to make men friends, to unite all classes in common aims'.[72] At first, Barnett was also deeply involved in the Charity Organisation Society, founded by Octavia Hill in 1869. COS visitors called on the poor to determine whether they were deserving or not, and how they might be helped, or helped to help themselves. The COS attempted to solve poverty by trying to recreate something of the old face-to-face parochial system of relief. In 1874 Barnett said 'Indiscriminate charity is among the curses of London . . . the poor starve because of the alms they receive.' Beatrice Webb, a COS visitor, with a Christian upbringing, wrote detachedly: 'it is distinctly *advantageous* for us to go amongst the poor . . . the study of their lives and surroundings give us the facts wherewith we can attempt to solve the social problems . . .' Form 28 warned her that 'Persons of drunken, immoral or idle habits cannot expect to be assisted unless they can satisfy the committee that they are really trying to reform.' The COS believed that poverty was caused by a failure in character. Document 6a stated that it was 'good for the poor' to meet all the ordinary crises of life such as sickness and old age from their own industry and thrift and not to rely on public or private charity. Otherwise they would make no effort to meet these themselves.[73] (There are echoes of COS principles in both Thatcherism and New Labour.) But, asked Beatrice Webb, is it so simple? What about a deserving woman with an undeserving husband? Was not the COS by discrediting almsgiving, contradicting the gospel? Mrs Barnett had a dream in which she was one of the undeserving poor. The Barnetts revolted against the COS in 1895 and argued that the state should provide for pensions and housing and make society more equal by redistributive taxation. 'God loveth a cheerful taxpayer', Barnett would say.[74]

Barnett's aims at Toynbee Hall were: to bring men from Oxford to acquaint future leaders with poverty and help create a national community across class divisions; to create in Whitechapel a collegiate community which would provide local people with a range of educational and vocational courses, and so help to train workers for leadership. Toynbee Hall established close relationships with the unions, several of which met there regularly. Barnett mediated in a number trade disputes. Scott Holland denied that it was 'an artificial importation of alien elements'; rather it 'gives back the very people *who alone can functionize on behalf of the body*' (my italics) Some modern commentators deride the settlements. Would it would have been better if the men had remained in their colleges? In fact Toynbee Hall did much to create a socially sensitive political leadership for the twentieth century. In 1913 when Barnett died, forty-four MPs, including Asquith, Balfour and MacDonald, paid tribute to his friendship and wisdom. Beveridge, Tawney and Attlee worked there. Stedman Jones remarks: 'Toynbee Hall has as much claim to be counted among the ancestors of the Labour Party as Methodism, Taff Vale or William Morris.'[75] Settlements attracted helpers from across the political spectrum. George Bell, a don at Christ Church from 1910 to 1914, a Christian Socialist, was secretary of the Oxford Settlements Committee. He first met the future Tory party chairman, Lord Woolton, as the warden of a Liverpool settlement when he took undergraduates there. We should also remember the long tradition of deferential working-class Tories who enjoyed being looked after in a secure hierarchy, like the butler in the film *Remains of the Day*. The people of Stepney were proud to have 'Major Attlee' as their mayor after the First World War, though his background (Haileybury and Oxford) was alien.

He had been converted to socialism through working at the Haileybury club for boys in Limehouse, with its motto 'Sursum Corda'. Women's colleges also founded settlements and missions. Lady Margaret Hall, which had been founded in 1878 by E. S. Talbot (later a contributor to *Lux Mundi*), in 1897 created a settlement in Kennington after its members had studied Booth's *In Darkest England*. Maude Royden of LMH, a millionaire's daughter, later a pioneering Anglican feminist, was moved towards socialism by settlement work. Toynbee Hall influenced Scott Lidgett, the founder of the Methodist Settlement in Bermondsey in 1890 where he ministered heroically for fifty-nine years. Though keen to use state action to deal with the drink trade, he remained anti-socialist.[76]

Settlements were usually less overtly religious than missions, and thus attractive to those whose faith was insecure, like the hero of *Robert Elsmere* (1888), the weighty novel by Mrs Humphry Ward. One of Green's disciples, Elsmere developed doubts, resigned his living and went to work in the East End. There he explained his ministry and his demythologized faith to the workers. His progressivist, immanentist and idealistic faith was widespread in Labour circles. Early this century it was preached by two famous Nonconformist socialist ministers, R. J. Campbell and D. R. Davies. In the end both found it too thin and became Anglican priests.

The churches and the workers

Only a minority of the workers were militant atheists. Most admired Christ and instinctively felt he was one of them, crucified by the religious and wealthy, and subsequently betrayed by the churches, and that he, like them, rejected 'organized religion' in favour of moral action. Most churches and chapels operated on a top-down basis, whether the clergy were Tories or socialists. Church life also reflected class divisions. In Portsmouth, until the 1920s, St Thomas's (now the Cathedral) had pew rents; there was another church in the parish for the poor. A mile away was St Agatha's, the Winchester College Mission founded in 1882. The poor were crammed into narrow streets. In 1885 Fr Robert Dolling arrived, a classic slum priest looking like a fat pork butcher. In his ten years he transformed the parish – a gymnasium to promote dancing and physical fitness, meals for children and old people, twelve almshouses, a communal meal for forty on Sundays at the parsonage at which Wykehamists, thieves, fallen clergy and MPs sat down together. When he supported Stewart Headlam and his socialist Guild of St Matthew it caused so much controversy in this conservative naval town that he offered to resign. Many of the slum priests came from gentry backgrounds, public schools and Oxbridge. Dolling was a socialist who found the Christian Social Union too mild, but far from shunning the privileged, Dolling used his Irish

charm and his Winchester and Cambridge connections to stir
their consciences and empty their pocket books. But when he left
in 1896 the parish never recovered. He had made it dependent on
him.[77] Wesleyan Methodism tried to reach the unchurched
through 'Central Halls', intended to look as unlike churches as
possible. By 1909 there were forty-one, attracting financial support from wealthy laypeople wanting the workers to be converted
and wooed away from atheistic socialism. All Central Halls did
social relief work. Yet they were no more successful than any
other churches at creating a working-class leadership. Most
workers who attended were reclassed sooner or later.[78]

Only the Roman Catholic Church had a substantial allegiance
of working people. They were associated with other churches and
chapels, but few actively belonged. But unlike Nonconformity
which gave great scope for lay leadership and the Church of
England in which lay responsibility was increasing, the Roman
Catholic Church was dominated by its clergy who maintained the
laity in their dependence. Its social conscience was expressed
through ameliorative pastoral work among its own poor, financed
by its aristocracy. Cardinal Manning was a Gladstonian Liberal
but supported trade unions, the extension of the franchise and
more state action on social issues. His views were more akin to
those held by leaders of other churches than of his own. He continued to exercise the social paternalism he had learned as an
Anglican priest. Above all he wanted to reassure the nation that
the Roman church was loyal and a-political. In 1890 he attacked
the gulf between 'the world of wealth and the world of want', but
his solution was simply to urge more charitable giving.
Manning's successor, Vaughan, was a strong Tory. Only one
bishop questioned the economic system in the way that by the
1880s was common among leaders of other churches.[79] Leo XIII's
encyclical *Rerum Novarum* (1891) represented a new beginning
for Roman Catholic social ethics after the negative attitude to
many features of the modern world of the *Syllabus of Errors*
(1864). It defended private property, rejected both *laissez-faire*
and socialism, favoured the corporate state and the right of work-

ers to join unions, but these had to be Catholic Associations (this led on the continent to a damaging split in the union movement). Left-leaning Roman Catholics called it 'The Workers Charter', but the atheist Robert Blatchford saw it as an attack on socialism and an attempt to help the poor without disturbing the rich. The Catholic Social Guild (1909) and the Catholic Workers College in Oxford (1921) both helped to spread the teaching of the encyclical. Gradually more Roman Catholics began to participate in the Labour movement.[80]

The Guild of St Matthew (1877) was probably the first socialist society in England, yet its creator Stewart Headlam was a priest educated at Eton and Cambridge with private means.[81] He enjoyed being impish. He argued that Eton was a home of social equality because no one asked who your father was. As a curate he got across the Bishop of London in 1878 by praising music halls, theatre, the ballet and appearing on a platform with a Fenian. The bishop withdrew his licence for some years, but Randall (later Archbishop) Davidson, a long-standing friend, secured his reinstatement in 1898. It is doubtful however that he wanted to be in mainstream church life.[82] The Guild was never large – membership in 1895 was only 364, of whom 99 were clergy. Its aims were to combat prejudice against the church; to stress the eucharist and Prayer Book teaching; 'to promote the study of social and political questions in the light of the Incarnation'. Its roots went back to a remarkable priest, Thomas Hancock, who influenced by Maurice preached socialism in the 1870s, and to slum priests who had a natural sympathy for the underdog.[83] One of them, Fr Stanton, on his deathbed left money for the 'undeserving poor'. The main influences on Headlam were: sacramental life and doctrine, Maurice and Henry George. The eucharist was 'the Great Emancipator's Supper'. Ruskin taught him the value of art and craftsmanship. Henry George (*Progress and Poverty*, 1880) persuaded him that a progressive tax on land would both restore the land to the people and provide considerable revenue. A Liberal Catholic, he welcomed *Lux Mundi* and hoped it would encourage people to read Maurice. An incarnationalist and immanentist, like Maurice, he believed that all were already in Christ, and so took a positive view of the secular. Secularists were nearer the kingdom than Moody and Sankey. 'It is because we are Communicants that we go to the Theatre' he would say.

Christ was 'the Carpenter of Nazareth, the Divine Revolutionist, the Emancipator of the Oppressed, the Founder of the Democratic Church'.[84]

But members were increasingly alienated by his obsession with the Land Tax, his advocacy of disestablishment and universal secular education and his support of Oscar Wilde during his trial in 1895 – Headlam paid half his bail of £5000. In 1909 Headlam, autocratic to the end, dissolved the Guild which had sadly declined. Despite its achievements it was defective in ways typical of many Christian Socialist groups. It lacked working-class members. It talked of democracy but allowed Headlam to be autocratic. Though he got himself elected to local government, he like Maurice and Hancock, stood aloof from the parties. He failed to recognize the significance of the ILP, despised Hardie and thought working people not ready for responsibility. Hardie himself commented:

> As a Scotsman and a Nonconformist, I well remember the shock it gave me that the leading member of the Guild divided his attention fairly evenly between socialism and the ballet.[85]

The changing attitudes to social questions in some parts of the church life during the last quarter of the nineteenth century interacted with changes in theology. Broadly, there was a shift from atonement to incarnation; from God's wrath to his love; from Jesus as Saviour to Jesus as human example; from transcendence to immanence; from awe to fellowship; from eschatology to the coming of the kingdom here and now. So Hugh Price Hughes declared in 1889: 'Every kindness that you show to the drunkards of the Regent Street slums . . . is a kindness shown to Jesus Christ.' A slum priest accused of forsaking the gospel for secular concerns replied: 'I speak out and fight about the drains because

I believe in the Incarnation.'[86] The recovery of the English carol in the Christmas services of lessons and carols, which began at Truro Cathedral in 1880, encouraged devotion to a vulnerable baby and mother. But of course, more conservative theology persisted in parts of all the churches and in the sects. However, by 1900 Christian Socialists were prominent in Anglicanism and Nonconformity, but not in Roman Catholicism. Church leaders realized that they should cultivate links with the emerging Labour movement and that Christian Socialists were useful bridge builders. Thus the militant atheism and anti-clericalism so common in continental socialism were rare in Britain.

There was no simple correspondence between theology and social ideology. The Liberal Catholicism of the *Lux Mundi* group offered the most obvious theological basis for Christian Socialism. Its image of incarnation as self-emptying moved many to minister to the poor. Baptism as entry into, and the eucharist as sharing in a democratic fellowship could be made vivid to ordinary parishioners. The common ground between Catholic Anglicans with their sacramental teaching and immanentist Nonconformists was that 'both regarded the material world as an object for sanctification' whereas evangelicalism treated the material and spiritual as antithetical. Yet there were Christians who believed in incarnation and sacraments who were not socialists, and socialists who rejected the Catholic tradition, such as the Baptist John Clifford and the Methodist Hugh Price Hughes.[87] Clifford came from a Chartist background, had worked a sixteen-hour day in a factory as a boy, waged passive resistance against the 1902 Education Act and opposed the Anglo-Boer War. Hughes came from a middle-class background and was an ardent imperialist. Both were progressivists. Clifford defined socialism as 'a pushing forward of the inner soul of humanity towards its predestined goal'. In January 1914 he predicted the end of 'Militarism' and 'Priestism', but in August supported the war because the 'progress of humanity' depended on it.[88] Both saw politics as an exhilarating moral crusade against evil. Victory was near. The Free Churches believed they would replace the Church of

England because they were more progressive and democratic. Ramsay MacDonald made a tactless bid in the 1924 election campaign for Free Church support. 'In the Labour Party, we have the spirit that used to animate your souls, widened, brightened, and heightened.'[89] But for many Free Church people Labour was tainted with rationalist utilitarianism. Labour also offended by holding Sunday election meetings. The Free Churches never allied themselves to Labour as they had to the Liberals, yet in many places the first Labour leaders had been Nonconformists. Free Church influence on the party can be also discerned 'in the stress on moral ends, the tendency to see the Labour party as a vehicle of righteousness' and its 'biblically-flavoured sense of moral outrage'.[90] But Nonconformity's rejection of Sunday leisure, drink and gambling distanced it from working-class culture. Perhaps one reason why Labour has been out of power for most of its existence is because in its formative years it was deeply influenced by Nonconformity, which was suspicious of power, and of those in power, and rarely close to those who wielded power. Many of the Anglo–Catholic socialists were likewise happiest in opposition to authority in church and state. Moral absolutes and righteous indignation are always easier to maintain in opposition.[91]

A. S. Peake, a young Primitive Methodist layman (later a famous biblical scholar) in 1883 went up to Oxford. The following year he wrote to his parents to quieten their anxieties about his socialist sympathies. He had been so moved by *The Bitter Cry of Outcast London* that though a classic Dissenter, he considered becoming an Anglican slum priest. He explained 'An Oxford socialist is one who takes a deep interest in the welfare of the people.' Christ would have been a socialist today. We cannot make people good by laws, but they can raise the moral condition of the people, lessen drinking and put people in better housing. Otherwise the people will rise and take their rights by force. So we must 'lend a hand to help the masses' to make them 'a God-fearing religious element of society'. After reading Booth's *In Darkest England* he wrote:

The poor are Christ's representatives. He has identified Himself everywhere with the down-trodden, the suffering and the outcast. Inasmuch as we do good to one of these we do it to Him. We serve God by helping our fellow. I feel intensely that privilege implies responsibility.[92]

Henry Scott Holland and the Christian Social Union

The Christian Social Union

The Christian Social Union (CSU) was launched at a meeting in June 1889 presided over by Henry Scott Holland, a Canon of St Paul's Cathedral.[1] More space will be given to the CSU than to other similar organizations, because the CSU is often under-estimated and misrepresented. Yet it attracted the largest number of members of any organization for social reform in the history of the Church of England, and created a tradition of social thought which continued long after its demise in 1919, a tradition which includes William Temple and R. H. Tawney – and arguably Tony Blair.

The roots of the CSU are in traditions and personalities we have already surveyed – Coleridge, Carlyle, Ruskin, Maurice, Headlam, T. H. Green, Arnold Toynbee and what emerged as the New Liberalism. Thus for example in 1893 all forty-four members of one CSU branch had read Ruskin's *Unto This Last*. The CSU was also a fruit of the Catholic Revival which, by rejecting Erastianism, had by this stage taught a significant number of leading Anglican priests that the church had the right and sometimes the duty to stand against the state. Holland was deeply influenced by T. H. Green, who without intending to, produced a philosophical foundation for the New Liberalism and for Anglican socialism. Green's political attitudes had been influenced by his uncle, a priest, who was a disciple of Maurice.

He believed that the state ought to promote the common good, but he was not a collectivist, and hoped that this would be achieved by local and voluntary action. However, Green taught that only in community could the individual find true significance and that the church and its gospel must advance social welfare and political justice. The divine meets human beings in all aspects of life, for God is immananent, within us.[2] Holland wrote that Green had 'taught us the reality of the co-operate life and the inspiration of the community. He gave us back the language of self-sacrifice, and taught us how we belonged to one another in the one life of organic humanity.' R. G. Collingwood, who began to read philosophy in Oxford in 1910, wrote: 'the philosophy of Green's school might be found from about 1880 to about 1910, penetrating and fertilising every part of the national life'.[3]

B. F. Westcott (Bishop of Durham 1890–1901) also exercised a considerable influence on the CSU, and became its first President. It was a sermon by him in 1868 when he was a master at Harrow which awoke a type of monastic vocation in Gore, then a boy of 15.[4] Holland in his mid-twenties spent part of the summer of 1872 reading under Westcott, whose theology resembled that of Maurice. Holland in 1875 joined a group of Liberal Catholic dons including Gore, who called themselves mockingly 'The Holy Party'. Several of them were contributors to *Lux Mundi* (1889) edited by Gore, the most creative theological symposium of the century. About 1879 when he was a don at Christ Church, Holland formed a small group to discuss social questions. Reading *Unto This Last* had a profound effect on them. As we have already seen, by the 1880s interest in socialism inside and outside the church was quickening. It was a major topic at the 1887, 1890 and 1895 Church Congresses. The 1888 Lambeth Conference encyclical warmly commended the study of it and was deeply concerned by 'excessive inequality in the distribution of this world's goods'.[5] Scott Holland, Stewart Headlam, H. C. Shuttleworth (both of the GSM) and H. H. Champion (a leading light in the SDF) addressed its committee, which was considering socialism. The CSU, inaugurated in June that year, regarded

the bishops' declarations on socialism at the 1888 Lambeth
Conference as its charter and their rejection of *laissez-faire* at the
1897 Lambeth Conference as an authoritative sanction for what it
was attempting. In July a small group under Gore's leadership
began the process of slow gestation which led to the founding of
the Community of the Resurrection in 1892 with Gore as
Superior. In November 1889, *Lux Mundi* was published. It was
the manifesto of Liberal Catholicism, a new mutation of
Tractarianism, which employed Greek patristic thought to enable
scientific and theological explorers to be regarded as potential
allies, whereas for Tractarians they were enemies to be fought.
Aubrey Moore in his essay argued that the Christian did not
simply either protest against or surrender to new truth but rather
used 'the method of assimilation'. Unlike *Essays and Reviews* it
included a chapter on 'Christianity and Politics' which urged
those with authority to use it for 'the common good', rejected
Erastianism, asserted the independence of the church and the
'inherently social nature' of human beings. Later, Gore became a
leading campaigner for more self-government of the church. In
an Appendix he urged the creation of applied ethics, attacked
an individualistic view of rights and advocated the creation of
an educated public opinion to bring pressure on the governing
classes.

The aims of the CSU were to make the Christian Law rule
social practice, to study how to apply Christianity to social and
economic life and to present Christ as King. Its Anglican and
eucharistic basis was shown by a rubric asking members to pray
for it at holy communion, particularly on or about the Epiphany,
Ascension and Michaelmas. By 1911 there were 68 branches in
England and affiliated societies in the United States, Canada,
South Africa and Australia. Whereas the GSM had never risen
above 400 or so members, by 1906 the CSU had 6,000 members.
Of course there were some, especially clergy, who belonged to
two or three groups at once, like the Revd James Morell, hero of
Shaw's *Candida* (1895) who had Maurice, George, *Fabian Essays*,
Morris and Marx on his bookshelves and was an active member

of both the GSM and CSU. Shaw based Morell on Shuttleworth and Headlam. Unlike the GSM the CSU was not Anglo Catholic, nor was it dominated by its leader. Some moved over from the GSM. Though the CSU's members were more diverse in churchmanship and politics than those of the GSM, its leaders like Holland, Gore, Percy Dearmer and John Carter were Catholic sacramentalists. Holland wanted the CSU to have a firm doctrinal basis and was determined to repel the 'Socialistic Nothingarian'.[6] Whereas Headlam and Hancock of the GSM lacked prominent roles in the church – and probably did not want them – Holland became Canon of St Paul's in 1884, and in 1895 Gore became Canon of Westminster and E. S. Talbot became Bishop of Rochester. So these three 'Luxites' (as they were known) were able to be in close touch with each other and with centres of political life. Between 1889 and 1913, sixteen out of the fifty-three new bishops were members of the CSU whereas only one member of the GSM (C. W. Stubbs) became a bishop. The GSM 'did not . . . suit our purposes', Gore remarked bluntly.[7] Holland and Gore probably thought the GSM too idiosyncratic and too suspicious of the normal political processes to have much influence in church or nation. Percy Widdrington, a priest member of the GSM (then of the Church Socialist League and later of the Christendom Group) described a divergence of ethos between the GSM and the CSU:

> . . . it passes my imagination to see Gore or even Holland at one of Headlam's Sunday night 'At Homes', surrounded by budding poets, painters, writers, actors and ladies of the ballet.[8]

The CSU functioned in part as a Fabian-type educational and research group. It provided its members with series of lectures and sermons, pamphlets and study guides on a wide range of subjects from the Poor Law to the trade unions. This was particularly important for those Christians who were deceived by the tradition of the Old Testament prophets into thinking that by

denouncing an evil something had been achieved.[9] By contrast
the CSU was down to earth. Businessmen were invited to meetings to discuss how they related their faith to the conduct of their
firm. The CSU undertook investigations into social problems,
and then presented the findings to the authorities or took action
itself. 'The object of the CSU is to talk with a view to action',
declared one pamphlet. It pointed out that when a particular
example of sweated labour was exposed, the wages of the women
were substantially raised by pressure from the consumers – in this
case public schools. In 1898 the London branch researched
the conditions of labour in the fish curing industry and in fruit
preserving factories and sent reports to the relevant Secretary
of State with proposals for remedial action. In 1901 the CSU
executive asked all branches to study local housing. The Oxford
branch produced a leaflet on 'The Housing Problem' which
summarized the issues. It suggested asking the Town Clerk for
information on insanitary property, advised a house-to-house
inspection in poor areas and provided a sample questionnaire on
the number of rooms, amount of rent, water supply, sanitation
etc. The results were to be sent to the Town Clerk, the Medical
Officer of Health or a sympathetic town councillor, or if necessary
to the press. The solution might be the creation of a housing
association. It concluded: 'The Housing Problem will hardly be
solved apart from further collective action on the part of the State
and of the Municipalities.' This was typical of the CSU, com-
bining Fabian style investigation, the encouragement of local
initiative and the blessing for collective action.

The CSU also acted as a pressure group on MPs. In 1900 the
CSU organized a public meeting on housing and persuaded
Herbert Asquith to chair it. That year the London executive held
meetings with interested MPs on social issues being considered
by parliament, and lobbied 173 MPs urging their support for the
Employment of Children Bill. In 1906 the CSU executive included the MPs Charles Masterman (Liberal), a friend of Gore,
and John Talbot (Tory), Bishop Talbot's brother. Working
through three MPs (Talbot, and H. J. Tennant and Sir Charles

Dilke, both Liberals) the CSU influenced the Factory and Work-shops Act (1901) and the Trade Boards Act (1909). The GSM never exercised this type of influence.[10]

The CSU envisaged society as a partnership in which con-sumers would exercise ethical discrimination in purchasing; management would cooperate for the common good; and the state or city would act to regulate conditions and in some cases provide services. The CSU assumed too easily that if everyone was pre-sented with the facts of injustice and inequality, they would have consciences to be quickened and be ready to act. It did not take enough account of vested interests skilled at defending empires, nor of the general human preference for inertia and the status quo. Preferential dealing and ethical consumption were crucial CSU principles. John Carter, a Canadian priest based at Pusey House, Oxford, a founding member of Gore's Community of the Resurrection, was the secretary of the CSU and editor of the academic CSU journal *Economic Review* 1891–1914. In his pam-phlet *Preferential Dealing* (1900) he quoted in the same passage from the 1897 Lambeth Conference and from CSU's favourite economist Alfred Marshall, another Balliol don, who had asked at the beginning of his *Principles of Economics* (1890): 'Why may we not outgrow the belief that poverty is necessary?'

> To quote the Lambeth Report on Industrial Problems:-
> 'A Christian community, as a whole, is morally responsible for the character of its own economic and social order, and for deciding to what extent matters affecting that order are to be left to individual initiative, and to the unregulated play of eco-nomic forces.' And economic science, having abandoned the old policy of *laissez-faire* has in this respect approximated to the Christian point of view. 'Public opinion', writes Professor Marshall, 'based on sound economics and just morality will, it may be hoped, become ever more and more the arbiter of the conditions of industry.'

It was not sufficient, Carter argued, for government to legislate or for unions to agitate. The public must be aroused to its responsibilities for determining the direction and conditions of industry. Again he quoted the Lambeth bishops. Christian opinion should 'condemn the belief that economic conditions are to be left to the action of material causes and mechanical laws, uncontrolled by any moral responsibility'. Carter claimed that in Oxford before the CSU published its approved list of firms, only eight printing firms accepted standard conditions, now there were twenty-one. The fundamental principle was that 'cheapness may be bought at too dear a price'.

The Oxford branch met local bakers and journeymen in 1897 and agreed to a schedule of maximum hours and minimum wages. Seeing Oxford undergraduates estimating the hours and wages of journeymen bakers who provided college bread, rather than simply taking the service for granted, was for Scott Holland a sign of real progress.[11] By 1900 the Leeds group listed 572 approved firms. By 1905 the Oxford list covered tailors, printers, shoe-makers, drapers and bookbinders. The CSU literature on prefer-ential dealing frequently quoted in support of its stand the 1897 Lambeth Conference Committee on Industrial Problems which had urged Christians to consider not only the cheapness of goods, but also the conditions under which they were produced, as well as the 1891 Fair Wages Resolution in the Commons. Members were asked to buy china and earthenware with leadless glaze, and a list of firms which supplied such goods was produced. The CSU's national campaign, helped by the Labour Churches, forced Midlands manufacturers to change their methods. Investors as well as consumers had moral responsibilities. A pam-phlet *About Investments* stated: 'A Christian investor is morally responsible for the manner in which his money is used' and should enquire whether interest rates were high because wages were low. *Trade Unions* (1899) urged the recognition of a mini-mum wage in all contracts by public bodies and municipalities, believing it would do much to eliminate sweating and make work-men more efficient.

In *Commercial Morality* (1904), Carter quoted Huxley's Romanes Lecture to refute the neo-Darwinian argument for *laissez-faire*: what is ethically best is the result of self-restraint, not of ruthless self-assertion; of cooperation, not of treading down competitors. But (wrote Carter) the cooperative system makes greater moral demands than is convenient for many. He quoted a survey which showed how difficult it was for businessmen to apply Christian principles in business. A follow-up pamphlet in 1905 with the same title, which Carter wrote with Holland, argued that some immoral practices in commerce could be dealt with by legislation, some by trade associations, others by consumers exercising their preferences. But those workers unable to rectify immoral practices should resign and the CSU should support and protect them. Too often it was said: 'I cannot morally face Communion, and keep my place in my shop or office.'

The CSU attracted an unusually wide range of churchmanship and political views which at first proved an asset but ultimately a problem. William Temple, more definitely socialist than the CSU, was chairman of the Oxford branch in 1906. In 1905 Hastings Rashdall and William Sanday were vice-presidents, though both were anti-collectivist. Rashdall had joined the CSU in 1890 when an Oxford fellow. From 1892 to 1910 he helped to edit the CSU's *Economic Review* and assisted with the revision of pamphlets. His parents had connections with land and banking. He believed that religion was about righteousness – hence his admiration for Gore, despite acute theological differences. But he was a Tory in politics, like many of the modernists[12] and opposed the growing tendency in the CSU and elsewhere to identify Christianity with collectivism, though he was in favour of the cooperative movement. Sanday also rejected the belief that applied Christianity meant government action. He argued (rather curiously for a modernist) that to yoke Christianity to a modern movement was to expose it to decay as time passed. He eventually resigned from the CSU.[13] L. T. Hobhouse, the leading academic exponent of New Liberalism, a friend of Gore's, a former worker at Toynbee Hall, influenced by Marshall, Green and Toynbee, was a much more typical CSU member. Staying at Toynbee Hall in 1889 during the Dock Strike, he had been deeply impressed by the workers' solidarity and discipline. He came to believe that socialism could be built upon what Liberalism had accomplished.[14] Gore was also close to Charles Masterman, the Liberal MP who lived with the poor of Camberwell for a time. He was related by marriage to E. S. Talbot, who was also a member. Other well-known names which appear in the lists of members are R. H. Tawney, Charles Raven (later a well-known theologian and pacifist) G. K. Chesterton and Percy Dearmer (editor of the *English Hymnal* and advocate of the 'English Use' in liturgy).

In 1890 Dearmer had to threaten to resign from the CSU unless women were allowed to join. Even after the First World War, the Labour Party still relegated women to a separate conference, though women did a lot of work at the local level.[15] What role did women play in Christian Socialism? Enid Stacy (1868–1903), a regular communicant at the Anglo-Catholic church of All Saints, Clifton, was brought into Christian Socialism by the Anglican layman E. D. Girdlestone. She lost her job as a teacher through supporting a strike of working girls in Bristol. But she joined the ILP National Administrative Council and lectured at the LSE and in the USA for the Fabians. In 1897 she married P. E. T. Widdrington, a priest member of the GSM. A remarkable personality, she died tragically early, aged thirty-five. The CSU itself included at least three important Anglican women leaders. Ruth Kenyon, daughter of a priest, in her early years was brought back to the Christian faith by Gore. She studied at the London School of Economics, became secretary and treasurer of the Hastings and St Leonard's CSU and later was active in the Church Socialist League, the Anglo-Catholic Schools of Sociology, the Christendom Group, the Labour Party and lived by the discipline of the the Fraternity of the Resurrection associated with CR. Gertrude Tuckwell, the secretary of the CSU Research Committee from 1898, was the daughter of a Christian Socialist priest and the niece of Sir Charles Dilke, the radical Liberal MP. She became aware of poverty through teaching in working-class areas, and then devoted herself to improving the conditions of women through parliament and the unions. She founded the

British section of the International Association for Labour Legislation in 1904 and became President of the Womens Trade Union League in 1905. She was devoted to Gore. Constance Smith, another priest's daughter, was an important member of the CSU Research Committee. She worked with Tuckwell particularly in the campaign against lead glaze, and was H .M. Deputy Chief Inspector of Factories 1921–25. One of the benefits of having Anglicans in the Christian social movement was that they often provided a wide range of political and social contacts.[16]

Where did the CSU stand? Carter explained the official line to the 1897 Church Congress:

> . . . the Christian Social Union does not propose to use partic-
> ular measures as tests of loyal membership . . . we are bound to
> remember that Christians as such should never be absolutely
> committed to any political or economic system . . . it should
> always be possible for a sincere Christian to be either a good
> Tory or a good Radical, or even an honest Socialist or a moral
> Individualist.[17]

In practice such neutrality proved elusive or even illusory and the CSU leadership and much of the activist membership came to support the collectivism of the New Liberals. But the 1906 Liberal government did not always live up to the CSU's expectations. This encouraged some to look towards Labour.

Gore always insisted that it was the Christian Social, not Social*ist* Union. Was that partly a matter of tactics to keep as many types of concerned Anglicans on board? When the ILP was founded in 1893, 'socialist' was not included in the name because it might put off the workers. The term was also omitted from the name of the Labour Party. To the conservative minded, the term 'socialism' meant free love, atheism, expropriation of private property, class hatred and violent revolution. Certainly the CSU included those like E. S. Talbot who described themselves as 'Conservative – with a bad conscience' yet passionately wanted 'a better distribution of wealth' and regarded slums as a 'curse'.[18]

But much CSU literature advocated that the needs of the community should more often take precedence over those of individuals.

Like 'Catholicism', 'socialism' can be defined narrowly or broadly. In this period it was often used broadly. Holland contended 'there is no private action that has not a social value'. Freeden comments: 'It was in this form that socialism penetrated the consciousness of the British intelligentsia.' Thus the traditional hostility to the state so characteristic of nineteenth-century liberalism was being replaced by a belief that the state could have a positive moral function. This was propagated by the New Liberals. Their four leading intellectuals, Graham Wallas, L. T. Hobhouse, J. A. Hobson and J. L. Hammond all had Anglican upbringings; all but Hobson were sons of clergy.[19] The Anglo-Boer war showed up Britain's inefficiency. Centralized social reconstruction attracted support across the party spectrum. This corporatism had very little room for the evangelical emphasis on the responsibility of individuals for their own lives. Westcott, Gore, Holland and Carter used both the language of, and the term, 'socialism'. Joseph Chamberlain in 1885 had declared of government attempts to fight social inequality: 'Of course it is Socialism . . . every kindly act of legislation by which the community has sought to discharge its responsibilities and its obligations to the poor is Socialism, but it is none the worse for that.' Sidney Webb in 1890 applied the term 'socialist' to nineteenth-century factory and health legislation. Hobhouse wrote: 'The ideas of Socialism, when translated into practical terms, coincide with the ideas to which Liberals are led when they seek to apply their principles of Liberty, Equality and the Common Good to the industrial life of our time . . . The political order must conform to the ethical idea of what is just.'[20]

To ask 'Was the CSU socialist?' forgets such broadly-based understandings of the term, and also that in the last hundred years and more, the lines between the parties have been often irregular and kaleidoscopic. So in the Edwardian period Labour was still partly sheltering under the Liberal wing. The 1945

Labour government took over the social consensus of the Coalition, which in turn built upon the social welfare provision and nationalizations of the Conservatives in the 1930s. In their turn the Conservatives of the 1950s continued much of the framework established by the Attlee government. Thatcherism shocked many people because it challenged the consensus which had continued in many areas of policy since late Victorian times. The Labour Party itself has always included those who defined their socialism as social reform rather than as class war. Early resolutions of the Labour Representation Committee carefully avoided committing its members to socialism or the class war. It was not until 1918 that the Party agreed to a programme of public ownership and even then some trade unionists consoled themselves with the belief that they could prevent it being carried out. Though until 1995 it was theoretically committed to Clause 4, it never attempted to put it into practice. The CSU, therefore, has a right to be included in the socialist tradition.

The CSU publications often recommended those of the Fabian Society. Equally the Fabian Society published tracts on Christian Socialism by Dearmer, Headlam and Clifford. Like the Fabians, the CSU believed in gradualness, not revolution, and offered social reform from above. Neither the GSM or the CSU tried to attract a working-class membership. Scott Holland went to Eton and Oxford; his father was wealthy enough not to have to do anything in particular. Charles Gore went to Harrow and Oxford; his father was nephew of the third Earl of Arran and his mother Countess of Kerry. E. S. Talbot went to Charterhouse and Oxford; he was the grandson of the second Earl Talbot; his wife was a Lyttelton whose brothers included a headmaster of Eton and a Colonial Secretary. Five of the six founding members of the Community of the Resurrection were members of the CSU, and most of them thought of it as a Christian Socialist community. Yet when CR moved in 1898 to the West Riding mill town of Mirfield to help bridge the gap between church and workers, the brethren lived in a large mansion built by the former President of the Mirfield Conservative Club, the wealthiest mill owner in the

district. When in 1902 CR bought the mansion and its nineteen
acres, all but £500 of the £5,000 price (say £242,000) was raised
from capital donated by five of the brethren.[21] The CSU's
Christian Socialism derived from Christian paternalism, as was
unequivocally exposed in a pamphlet *Socialism* (1905) published
by the Oxford branch. It argued that though few in England
would call themselves socialists,

> yet our factory laws, trade unions, co-operative societies,
> industrial partnerships, and our manifold and increasing devel-
> opments of municipal activities, bear unmistakable witness to
> the workings of a genuine socialistic spirit. In most countries,
> Socialism is a hostile movement of the lower classes against the
> upper; in England it is rather a benevolent movement of the
> upper classes towards the lower.

In most countries (it continued) socialism was anti-clerical; here
the growth of atheistical socialism had been prevented by
Christian Socialism. Of all social groups here the working people
were the most indifferent to socialism but they are 'being social-
ized from above, almost against their will' by 'unconscious
Socialists working socialistically' through their support of municipal enterprise.

To have Westcott, Bishop of the senior see of Durham, as
President 1889–1901 added prestige to the CSU. He was known
as something of a saint and for his successful mediation in
the Durham miners' strike of 1892. 'The one denial of Christ is
to leave him out of any sphere of life' he told C. F. Andrews,
later Anglican apostle to India and friend of Gandhi. Westcott
continued Maurice's incarnationalism. But by the time he died in
1901 the CSU was ready for Gore, a more overtly political
President. Westcott's noble, but opaque, language was reassuring
for some, obfuscating to others. In *Socialism*, a paper given to the
1890 Church Congress, he said that he was not going to discuss
any particular type of socialism – Owenite, Fabian or Marxist –
but its essential idea.

> Socialism is the opposite of Individualism . . . [which] regards
> humanity as made up of disconnected or warring atoms;
> Socialism regards it as an organic whole, a vital unity formed
> by the combination of contributory members mutually inter-
> dependent . . . The method of Socialism is co-operation, the
> method of Individualism is competition. The one regards
> working with man for a common end, the other regards
> working against man for private gain. The aim of Socialism is
> the fulfilment of service, the aim of Individualism is the attain-
> ment of some personal advantage, riches or place or fame . . .
> the central idea of Socialism . . . is the common well-being of
> all alike.

But 'equal development' did not involve equality but hallowed
individuality. Socialism did not commit anyone to 'one line of
action'. Westcott went on to expound an evolutionary and optimistic understanding of history. (By adopting such a view it was
possible to excuse the disagreeable features of the past because
they happened at a primitive stage of understanding. So then
change could be advocated without casting aspersions on the
divine government of past history. Some theologians had used a
similar approach to excuse 'barbarities' in the Old Testament.) So
Westcott contended that life had evolved from serfdom to wage
labour and that we must now move on to the next stage – a
society marked by the cooperation of each citizen.[22] (Sometimes
Tony Blair sounds as if he had read Westcott.)

In *The Christian Social Union* (1895) he said that human life
was not solitary but social. So-called economic laws described
what is, not what should be. At one time the abolition of slavery
had been regarded as incompatible with productivity. Though
the state must have a wider role, legislation 'is the last and not the
first thing in social reform'. In the meantime the CSU should
study, help to form opinion and bring classes together to
strengthen 'the sense of fellowship by mutual understanding'.[23]
In *The Christian Law* (1896) he showed his conservativism
by lamenting the destruction of the old employer-employee

relationships by industrialism. He deplored class antagonism and industrial strife.

> The [Christian Social] Union affirms a principle, enforces an obligation, confesses a Divine Presence. It has no programme of immediate reforms . . . it would be disastrous if the Union itself were to be identified with a party or with a class.

What was needed was 'fellowship'. 'The neglect of Lazarus by his rich neighbour was not less condemned because Lazarus was carried by angels into Abraham's bosom.'[24] Ruth Kenyon summed up his contribution:

> It was the teaching of 'solidarity', in an age still individualist, and of *Christus Consummator*, Christ the Fulfiller of every aspect of humanity, in an age which thought chiefly of *Christus Consolator*, the comforter of the sorrows of humanity.[25]

What other evidence do we have concerning the CSU's concept of socialism and the state? In order to rebut one of the regular and violent attacks by the Tory Hensley Henson (Bishop of Durham 1920–39) on the CSU, John Carter explained in 1896 that only four documents – two by Westcott, one by Holland and one by Gore – officially expressed the principles of the CSU, which were 'simply as such as should be readily recognized by every Churchman'. There was no specific programme. It included all shades of political opinion.[26] G. K. Chesterton, an early member, became a speaker and preacher for the CSU. In the 1890s he believed that Christianity and socialism resembled one another in three ways: both arose out of compassion, both identified the evil of society as covetousness, both wished to replace competition with bearing one another's burdens. But there were also great differences. The rich young man in the Gospels asked 'What shall I do?' His counterpart today says 'What will society do?' Christ said 'Sell all that thou hast and give to the poor.' Socialism says 'Elaborate a broad, noble and workable system.' (As Hastings pointed out when Chesterton became a Roman Catholic, he lost a lot of his prophetic insights about society.)[27]

After the death of Westcott and his replacement by Gore as President in 1901, New Liberalism became more dominant in the CSU and there was a growing conflict between those content with Westcott's generalities and those who, like Gore, wanted to identify the CSU with a more radical position. Some of the latter joined the Church Socialist League (CSL) when it was formed in 1906, including some Mirfield Fathers. F. L. Donaldson, vicar of St Mark's Leicester, who had moved from the GSM into the CSU, now also joined the CSL. In 1905 he led 440 unemployed men in a march to London. As they set off, supported by a crowd of 100,000, they sang 'Lead, kindly Light'. Archbishop Davidson with great insensitivity refused a deputation and said he had to spend sixteen or seventeen hours a day on immediate duties. This left insufficient time to study unemployment. Keir Hardie was scathing: 'a religion which demands 17 hours a day for organisation and leaves no time for a single thought about starving men, women and children has no message for this age'.[28]

A CSU plan of study, *Christianity and Socialism* (1908), showed how far the CSU had moved from its early professions of neutrality. 'The demand for socialism may be taken to represent a demand for the reconstruction of industrial society, based on a recognition of the evils of the present system, and the suggestion that it is lacking in moral principles.' Socialism had three possible meanings: cooperation was superior to competition – the priority of the interests of society over those of the individual; the progressive development of social control over industrial life; or in a strict sense, collective ownership. 'It will hardly be disputed' that the ethical principle of socialism was 'identical with that of Christianity'. It concluded with questions. What features of the existing social order should a Christian fight against? Is there a limitation to state control of society? Would socialism promote brotherly feeling?

The international Pan-Anglican Congress of 1908 discussed

socialism. The presence of the two Archbishops on the platform and the general drift of most of the speeches showed the influence of the CSU upon Anglican leaders. The chairman lamented the absence of industrial leaders; those attending were mainly clergy and academics. (This was a significant and widespread weakness of the Christian social movement.)

The preface to the Report was by T. C. Fry and John Carter, both of the CSU. They contended that socialism arose out of a great demand for justice. The first charge upon industry should be proper wages. No wonder that Lord William Cecil, Bishop of Exeter, said he felt out of place as a non-socialist. William Temple argued that Christianity was incompatible with un-limited competition. If human beings would give of their best only for self-interest, then Christ was wrong. He called for more 'collectivism' through nationalization. E. G. Selwyn (later Dean of Winchester) thought the Labour Party was animated by the spirit of Amos, Micah and Isaiah. The veteran J. M. Ludlow protested against 'any narrowing of the large word Socialism, which stood for the faith that brought men together in one common force – the faith of Frederick Maurice'. Donaldson produced his famous slogan 'Christianity was the religion of which Socialism was the practice'. Gertrude Tuckwell, who on behalf of the CSU had helped to organize the Sweated Industries Exhibition of 1906, in a paper on sweating, pleaded for priests to turn from 'barren theological casuistry' to understand the struggles of working people and the poor. In another paper, Scott Holland asserted that since capital was 'congealed Labour' created by a web of cooperative endeavour, it was right to control it publicly. H. B. Lees-Smith (also a member of the CSU and later a Labour Minister) stood up for the unions – they maintained the balance of power in industry, provided expertise in negotiations, schooled members for leadership and acted as Friendly Societies. Donaldson pleaded that employment should be stimulated in recessions; the unemployed should be given financial help for training, to move house or to emigrate. W. Cunningham,[29] Archdeacon of Ely, the Cambridge economist, a friend of both

Green and Toynbee, was a critic of *laissez-faire*, but objected to the CSU because he believed that moral duties could not be compelled through state action. Older economics relied on self-interest, but modern economics recognized an interplay of motives. Christian ministers did not have a commission to rearrange the distribution of goods or to be industrial arbiters. Gore described various forms of socialism – those which made the state supreme over even the family, religion, science, art; those which proposed equality of wages and education disregarding the need for exceptional people. But the socialism upon which much current legislation was based arose from a demand for justice like that of the prophets. Clement Rogers thought socialism would harm the poor, by making people permanently dependent. The Anglo-Catholic leader Arnold Pinchard of the CSU argued that the church was an example of collective ownership. It held all its spiritual possessions in trust and then distributed the sacraments freely, so all were brothers at the altar.[30]

The CSU successfully penetrated the church's leadership. In the Lords debate on Lloyd George's People's Budget in November 1909, all the three bishops (Gore, Percival and Lang) who spoke in favour were members of the CSU. In the debate on 22 November, Gore argued that improvement to social conditions would result from 'an immense increase of public expenditure'. He supported taxes on unearned increment on land. 'I can conceive no kind of tax which is more just or more necessary.' Taxation was 'the true means of re-distributing the proceeds of industry in a more just and equitable manner by taxing the rich, for public works particularly, for the benefit of the poor'. He supported the Budget because it went some way towards the equalization of the burden of taxation upon rich and poor. Another example of the dominance of the CSU in this period was that all the bishops on the 1907 Canterbury Convocation Committee on 'The Moral Witness of the Church on Economic Subjects' were members. It was convened by Gore. It advocated a 'living wage' as the first charge on industry. This was to become a theme of Christian social thought during the next thirty years. A report on the same subject to the 1908 Lambeth Conference extensively quoted this Convocation Committee Report and recommended CSU book lists. The influence of the CSU spread into the parishes through *The English Hymnal* (1906). This was the first Anglican hymn-book to include hymns about the social gospel, including Scott Holland's 'Judge Eternal'. It was also the first to omit the verse

> The rich man in his castle,
> The poor man at his gate,
> God made them, high or lowly,
> And ordered their estate

from Mrs Alexander's hymn 'All things bright and beautiful'. *The English Hymnal* was edited by Percy Dearmer, a leading member of the CSU.

To what biblical and theological basis did members of the CSU (and Christian Socialists generally) appeal? Certain biblical passages were common currency throughout the Labour movement except for militant atheists. Even in the late 1940s (as I remember) it was still quite natural for James Griffiths, a Labour Minister, to open a meeting of Manchester Fabians on land taxation with 'The earth is the Lord's, and the fullness thereof' (Ps. 24). In a booklet in a series edited by Fr Paul Bull at Mirfield (*c.*1908) F. L. Donaldson of the CSU and the CSL focussed on texts about fraternity and unity – 'Be ye not called Rabbi . . . all ye are brethren' (Matt. 23.8); 'that they may be one' (John 17.11); 'one body' (I Cor. 12.12); 'there can be no male or female, for ye are all one man in Christ Jesus' (Gal. 3.28). He also quoted warnings against riches (Luke 12.15f., 16.19f.; Mark 10.23; Matt. 6.28, 16.26) and from James 5.4 which denounced employers for not paying proper wages. Like other Anglican socialists, he argued that the equality of all in baptism and at the eucharist provided a model for society. For Conrad Noel and others, the doctrine of the Trinity proclaimed 'a social God' in whom, as the Athanasian Creed insisted, all three persons were equal.[31]

From Maurice onwards, Christian Socialists increasingly cited the eucharist as an example of Christian society. Headlam said that all, including secularists, could worship Christ in the eucharist as 'the social and political Emancipator' who sympathized with the outcast and denounced the respectable.[32] Some priests promoted the eucharist as the main Sunday service because it exemplified Christian Socialism. The first parish eucharist (in the modern sense) was probably inaugurated in Stepney by Walter Frere about 1890, a year after the founding of CSU of which he was a member.[33] Two years later he became a founding member of CR which deepened his Christian Socialism. As its Superior he presided over the meetings at Mirfield in 1906 and 1907 between church and Labour leaders. (Frere became Bishop of Truro and a leading liturgist.)[34] Anglican socialists found support from other aspects of the liturgy. 'The Lord's Prayer is confessedly socialistic,' claimed Donaldson. 'No individualism is therein found.' Others, notably Thomas Hancock of the GSM, like Kingsley in *Yeast*, expounded the *Magnificat* as a revolutionary hymn.[35] But both Anglo-Catholic and Non-conformist socialists preached the story of Jesus the worker born of poor parents and put to death by the political and religious establishment. Hugh Price Hughes, like other Christian Socialists, believed that it was possible to create the kingdom of God on earth. Percy Dearmer maintained that baptism made us members of the fellowship of the church and sharers in the communion of saints; the doctrine of the resurrection of the body impelled us to fight against disease; six of the commandments were about our duties to our neighbours.[36] Paul Stacy, a West Riding priest, a friend of CR, whose sister had supported a strike of women workers in Bristol, put it succinctly: 'The Catholic Faith is Socialist from the Font to Paradise.' Headlam contended that the *Catechism*, by speaking of 'that state of life, unto which it *shall* please God to call you' taught that people can be called from one state to another. Some Anglicans, like Conrad Noel, quoted the teaching of some of the Early Fathers, as well as the Bible and liturgy, to support their case.[37]

Nonconformist socialists did not argue their case from the sacraments, liturgy and the Fathers, but focussed on Jesus. In 1905 Philip Snowden (a Labour MP from 1906) addressed the ordinands at Mirfield, invited by Fr Paul Bull CR, a passionate socialist. Because Snowden and Bull shared a socialist faith this made Snowden, though he was from a Methodist background, acceptable in that stronghold of Catholic orthodoxy. His ILP tract *The Christ that is to Be* (1903) is characteristic of Non-conformist ethical socialism in the progressivism of its title, its immanentism, its rejection of the church's priesthood and 'pagan Creeds' and its admiration for the teaching of Christ. Snowden contended that everyone could believe this, including atheists and agnostics, because it was common to all religions and moralities and commended sacrifice, love, association, cooperation, 'saving one's life in the common life'. As Leonard Smith points out, this was a skilful attempt to win the support of Nonconformity by including both the terminology and ideas which would appeal to traditional Evangelicals but also to the near-agnostics on its fringes.[38] R. J. Campbell's *New Theology* (1907) demonstrated what happened when Nonconformist theology was adapted to socialism through an extreme form of immanentism: 'Go with J. Keir Hardie to the House of Commons, and listen to his pleading for justice to his order, and you see the Atonement.'[39] (The Cowley Fathers' library classified the book under 'Controversy (Heresy)'.) In 1915, Gore, his one-time mentor, who had written a powerful refutation of the book, received him back into the Church of England and the following year ordained him.

Tories and old style Liberals among the CSU members became increasingly alarmed by the apparent swing of the CSU towards socialism. On the other hand, though it was warm towards the unions ('the workmen's dyke') and rejected the Wage Fund theory, it was too wedded to consensualism as the essence of Christianity to take sides with Labour. Only William Temple among its leading members did that. The theologian Hastings Rashdall protested that harmony was impossible if non-socialists in the CSU were treated as sub-Christian. William Sanday, another conservative member, resigned in 1906 and W. R. Inge left a little later. In 1908, twenty-four CSU members joined a number of clergy in signing a Liverpool Clarion Club Manifesto which called for public ownership. Henson led the protests. Some more withdrew. On the other hand, James Adderley resigned from the executive because it was not socialist enough.[40] In 1905 Keir Hardie appealed to clergy for help in the forthcoming General Election. In 1906 he addressed a gathering of clergy and Labour leaders at Mirfield. One consequence was the establishment in 1906 of the more militant Church Socialist League, supported by leading CR brethren. The CSL created a home for those Anglican socialists who were discontented with the CSU. That year 165 Anglican clergy, including fourteen of the CR brethren, signed a Public Address congratulating the Labour Party on its electoral success. Gore had already had doubts about the CSU in 1906. In 1911 he resigned as President believing that it should be wound up, and a new start made after a lapse of three years or so. There seemed no way of resolving the division between those who saw the CSU's purpose as impartial research and education, and those who saw it as a political society for the Christian Left.[41]

During the war it went into hibernation. Yet 'Christianity and Industrial Problems' (1919), one of the follow-up reports after the National Mission (1916) from what was known as the 'Fifth Committee', has been described as 'the outstanding expression of Christian social thought about post-war society'.[42] The Fifth Committee was dominated by the CSU – Bishops Gore, Kempthorne, Woods and Talbot; R. H. Tawney and other friends of Gore such as Albert Mansbridge, George Lansbury and George Bell. The 1920 Lambeth Conference Committee on Social and Industrial Problems echoed the penitence expressed by Gore and the CSU for the church's failures to uphold a social application of the gospel. In 1920 the CSU merged with the Navvy Mission to form the Industrial Christian Fellowship (ICF). Its hopes echoed those of the bishops at the 1920 Lambeth Conference: 'We believe that God wills fellowship.' But these hopes were shipwrecked by the 1926 General Strike. Like the CSU, the ICF was unwilling to recognize that the powerful will not normally surrender power without conflict. It placed too much faith in a transformation of human nature through the ideal of work and industry as public service. Like the CSU, its social ethics were largely produced by clergy who do not to have to compete for work, never experience unemployment or the class struggle. The continuing influence of the CSU was also evident in COPEC (Conference on Christian Politics, Economics and Citizenship) in 1924. Former members of the CSU played important roles: Temple presided over the 1500 delegates; Gore, Raven and Tawney also made significant contributions.[43]

How should the CSU be assessed? It was the first Christian organization in Britain for study and action on social questions which attracted a sizeable and influential membership. When it was founded, a considerable proportion of the population identified socialism with anarchy, free love and revolution. The CSU and other Christian Socialist groups did something to dispel that myth by the end of the First World War, and strengthened links between the churches and Labour. So even Conrad Noel, a flamboyant priest and socialist, who could be pretty scathing about the CSU, claimed optimistically:

> But whatever be its defects it has convinced a large mass of English church-goers of the importance of social questions. It has persuaded them that the Christian religion essentially involves social righteousness in some form or other.

Ruth Kenyon said in 1932 that the CSU had achieved two things. It had changed the minds of a whole generation of ordinands at Oxford and to a lesser extent at Cambridge. It had created a nucleus of lay people with a social conscience. Jones pointed out that the annual meetings of the Church Congresses in the 1870s ignored economic and social questions, whereas those up to the First World War were dominated by them.[44]

So at least some Christians learned that the church was not an end in itself but was meant to be a sign and servant of the kingdom. The method of the CSU which aimed to study social problems without partisanship and then to set forth options for action became a standard method for the Church of England. If the CSU affected the church, it also, as we saw, led to some political action. Sidney Webb regarded Christian Socialists as allies and praised the CSU among other societies. Another sphere of CSU's activity was the creation by some branches of settlements and the purchase and repair of workers' cottages. In London the CSU sponsored the Maurice Hostel as a centre for social work, lectures and clubs which in 1908 sent 1300 children on holiday. The CSU also influenced the creation of other similar organizations: the Friends' Social Union (1904), the Wesleyan Union for Social Service (1905) and the [Roman] Catholic Social Guild (1909).[45]

But the CSU had obvious weaknesses and limitations. Its purely Anglican membership was a limitation, but the lack of ecumenical cooperation on social questions made this inevitable. So, as we saw above, each church had its own organization. Because the CSU aimed to educate a wide variety of Anglican opinion, it was insufficiently focussed to be a successful pressure group. Its greatest limitation (like that of the GSM) was its lack of working-class membership. A half-hearted attempt to recruit workers in 1898 lasted only a year.[46] Moreover, the CSU had no roots in the industrial north. Though it campaigned on behalf of the workers and the poor, it did not participate in their characteristic organs – the unions and the Labour Party. Judith Pinnington claims that the press was noticeably reluctant to report the CSU or anything progressive or positive about the Church of England and preferred to concentrate on ritual controversies. She asserts that Roman Catholic social concerns got a consistently better press. She argues that while the CSU often received a courteous hearing from government ministers, this led to little action. In 1912 the CSU *Commonwealth* seemed 'heartily sick that it had ever appeared to endorse the Liberal administration . . . despite its setting up in 1908 an office close to the Houses of Parliament, it remained psychologically "outside".'[47]

In 1921 Gore looked back on the CSU and drew attention to its failures. Even allowing for Gore's tendency to gloom, they seem largely valid:

> It had not succeeded in stirring-up what it believes to be the right spirit in the mass of those who preach in the pulpits or sit in the pews of the Anglican churches.

The church remained a body which 'as a whole the social reformer or the Labour man regards as something which is alien to his ends and aims'. It also failed to raise up a sufficient body of Anglican trade unionists to make 'any effective impression on the Labour movement as a whole'. During the First World War, Fr Keble Talbot CR, one of Bishop Talbot's sons, and Scott Holland's godson, discovered as an army chaplain that the ordinary soldier did not believe in mystical and sacramental Christianity. He asked: 'is that to be despised or accounted irreligious which shows itself supremely in action'? Yet Holland's Christianity and that of many of the CSU clergy was precisely of that mystical and sacramental type which was alien to the stoutly Protestant and moralist character of working-class religion.[48]

Henry Scott Holland (1847–1918)

Scott Holland, the founder of the CSU, was successively a don at Christ Church Oxford (1871–84), a Canon at St Paul's (1884–1910) and Regius Professor of Divinity at Oxford (1910–18).[49] His character was complex. On the one hand he was the boyish enthusiast. Someone recalled a reading-party with him:

> How he tore down the grass hill to the little river, in the fresh sunlight of Sunday morning, on the way to early service, and took the stepping-stones two at a bound.

His jocular Dickensian style celebrated the oddness and romance of life. Yet faced with moral turpitude, this most affirmative of priests could show a Tractarian sternness, as Fr Waggett SSJE remembered:

> No man could be more tender with those who failed and stumbled . . . But speak a word in the sense that the failure did not matter, that failure might not be failure, that transgression might do no harm, that one might in some degree unclasp the armour of holiness or put aside a demand of the great law; and there was a new note in Holland's voice.[50]

A celibate, he had to struggle to sanctify his passion for close friendships. For some years he used the scourge.[51] Cosmo Gordon Lang, as Bishop of Stepney, went to him for confession and remembered him not only as 'the most delightful of companions' but also his times of stress and depression. Holland was probably the only person to know those two enigmas, Lang and Gore, through and through. Gore was fiercely independent, a loner, yet he said of Holland, his closest friend, when he died:

> For the last forty years and more, there was no question, speculative or practical, which has presented itself to my mind, on which I have not found myself asking 'What will Holland say?' and been disposed to feel that I must be wrong, if I turned out to be thinking differently from him.

Walter Carey (onetime Bishop of Bloemfontein) wrote that Holland, like Dolling and Stanton, represented 'a new type of priest – evangelical, catholic, social reformer'.[52] Holland was also a great preacher and orator who could hold people spellbound.

His tutor at Eton, William Johnson, an economist and historian, had also taught Headlam. Johnson was a friend of Maurice and Kingsley. At Oxford, the chief intellectual influence on Holland was that of T. H. Green. He belonged to Green's inner circle of students. He gratefully acknowledged his debt to Green in a letter after his ordination in 1872, though Green was very Protestant and far from orthodox. In reply Green begged Holland not 'to substitute, for the moral presence of God in the Church, a miraculous and mystical one' and warned him against 'Sacerdotalism and Sacramentalism'. He had been disturbed when their mutual friend Gerard Manley Hopkins had become a Jesuit. For Green true moral citizenship was superior to the search for saintliness; monasticism rested upon a false antithesis between church and world, religious and secular. Later, Holland recalled that Green had 'charged us with the democratic ardour which made him always the active champion of the poor and the preacher of the obligations of citizenship'. So Holland came to believe with Gore that true religion must issue in social righteousness and be expressed in community.[53]

Like Gore, Holland was a Liberal Catholic, committed to orthodoxy, yet also to the reform of the church and society. He was convinced, like Headlam, that true Christian thinking about society must be done theologically. His approach to the world was not negative and pessimistic. Rather he looked for its transfiguration. So he was critical of Campbell's 'New Theology' as a mismatch between theology and politics, because Campbell was a socialist politically but an individualist theologically.[54] But of course the relation between theological and political stances is not that simple. Campbell's theology, like his socialism, derived from his progressivist modernism. 'Campbell saw himself as a leader in this great movement of liberation and renewal.'[55] In fact his theology fitted the progressivist and modernist socialism of the Edwardian period better than a theology like that of Gore who refused to see history as a simple record of progress and who saw all human achievement as flawed by sin.

Romantic and artistic, Holland recoiled from rationalism and Utilitarianism. As an undergraduate he had found Jowett's moralistic sermons in Balliol chapel deeply unsatisfying. He had learned the importance of the imagination through his love of art and music and from Wordsworth, Keble, Ruskin and J. S. Mill's *Autobiography*. His Oxford Group on Politics, Economics, Socialism, Ethics and Christianity (PESEK) read *Unto this Last* together in the late 1870s:

Ruskin showed Holland and the others that political economy could be a truly humane science taking into account man's spiritual nature, instead of merely basing itself on the iron-clad laws of the market place . . . that man's economic behaviour was in fact governed by his interior and moral character as well as his external and material situation; that the poor need justice rather than almsgiving; and that cooperation rather than competition is the law of life.

Holland once remarked: 'Imagine putting up a stained glass window to Faith, Hope, and Political Economy.'[56]

Though he did not propose a wholesale change in the existing economic system and did not contest the economic theory of the day as expressed by Alfred Marshall, he argued that economic relationships could and should be moralized and brought under political control. He thought that most church people oscillated between a-moral economics and individualistic pietism:

We live as shuttlecocks, banded about between our political economy and our Christian morality. We go a certain distance with the science, and then, when things get ugly and squeeze, we suddenly introduce moral considerations, and human kindness, and charity. And then, again, this seems weak and we pull up short and go back to tough economic principle. So we live in miserable double-mindedness.[57]

In a sermon of 1884 he drew attention to 'the familiar and most wicked phrase "A company has no conscience"'. As a result 'we sin through becoming the tools of a system'. In another sermon of 1895 he concluded that while many exercise a sensitive morality at home, they lacked a morality in public life. Hence when the National Mission was held in 1916 he urged that repentance should be made for 'corporate' as well as personal sin.[58]

His remedies for society were twofold. The consumer could and should exercise a moral influence on the market and the workers' conditions through preferential dealing. Workers should be protected through legislation which ensured a minimum wage and other benefits; trade unions could also act as safeguards for workers' rights.[59]

In *Our Neighbours* (1911), a handbook for the CSU, Holland drew together many of his favourite themes. The CSU, he claimed, was 'but a typical incident in a general movement of mind' prepared for by Ruskin and Carlyle. We had learned from Huxley that social progress meant putting a check on the cosmic process. We needed to redefine 'neighbour'. Neighbours are not necessarily friends, but people in the social network who enable you to live, eat and work. The CSU existed to educate the church's conscience. So it had to be within the church to be able to demand from communicants that social service to which their communion pledged them. 'The CSU is, then, the company of all conscience-stricken Churchmen, who have lost their Neighbours, and cannot tell where to find them.'[60] Those who think that competition is all-pervasive forget the daily unseen cooperation which is the basis of state and city alike. Unlike many socialists, Holland was not a ruralist. 'The Town is the expression of our love for one another.'[61] Nor had he sympathy for anarchistic socialism. We look to the municipality to provide wash-houses, baths, pure milk, health visitors, town planning, housing, rent control, transport, parks, infirmaries, asylums, education and medical care for children. 'The Municipality is sacred to us. It is our only instrument by which to fulfil the Commandment of our Lord – "You shall love your neighbour as yourself".'[62]

But we have obligations to neighbours beyond the locality – we are intertwined nationally and internationally. Only the state can control social and industrial practices across the country and help to create international control too. For in factory and other legislation we have already asserted the right of the state to intervene.

The State must take up our task of neighbourly responsibility, or it can never be taken up at all. 'But this is Socialism', you cry. Exactly. This is the irresistible verity on which Socialism has seized.[63]

But this does not mean that the state should do all that 'Economic Socialists' want it to do. We cannot make people good by legislation, but they 'can be helped, invited, encouraged, impelled' through changes in their environment. 'Law, then, spells not coercion, but liberty.' It is our 'friend' and 'embodies for the worker the care and responsibility which the whole nation recognizes and undertakes on his behalf'. It is individualism not law which destroys independence:

> 'Somebody has thought of me.' So says the Factory girl, as she looks up at the printed Regulations . . . by authority of the Home Office . . . 'Somebody cares for me.' So says the poor battered woman, making nails and chains at Cradley Heath . . . I voted them in. They are my Government. They stand for me. They appeal to me. They take their authority from me.

Holland rebutted the charge of creating a grandmotherly state, pointing out that law in a democracy originated with the people. So (in a phrase for which he became famous) every workman is himself 'his own grandmother'.[64] He could sound Hegelian, as is clear in the following passage which Preston rightly says conveys 'a rather optimistic view of a conflict-free community':

> Capital and Labour should be but two sides to a single fact . . . They need not be in opposition, but only in antithesis . . . For industry is Fellowship. It is not a blind collision of opposing interests.

Some of Holland's statements celebrating the state could sound totalitarian. But towards the end of his life he came round to Figgis' concept of the state as a community of communities. In a lecture in December 1914 on Figgis' *Churches and the Modern State* (1913), Holland said that the war had made the book even more significant: 'we are face to face with the notion of an absolute State that sweeps up all individual liberty'. Individuals are social beings, but the state is 'too huge, too remote, too abstract to allow us to find freedom in it'. So we must develop smaller, intermediate communities. He saw no future in the solutions of Belloc and Chesterton, but warmed towards syndicalism.[65]

Holland grounded his communalism and his conviction that the state should respect the lives of individuals in his beliefs about Trinity, church and sacraments. Church and eucharist are signs of the social unity which God wills. Like Maurice, Holland believed that all are redeemed by Christ whether they realize it or not.[66] Thus one of the purposes of the church was to uncover the activity of God in the secular world. Doctrine was vital to social ethics:

> . . . we have steadily voted against the tradition that to be a social reformer you must be shadowy in your creed . . . To care about drains was supposed to mean that you sat loose to the Creed; and we have upheld the counter-position all these years, that the more you believe in the Incarnation the more you care about drains.[67]

Whereas Gore believed that the church should be a highly disciplined body with higher boundary walls, Holland was concerned that this would reserve it for the good or elect. But he did believe that the church had become too identified with the status quo and needed reform, a more democratic form of government, should ordain working people, and give a greater role to women as churchwardens and deaconesses, for example. By the turn of the century he supported disestablishment, too. The sacraments also spoke to Holland of socialism.[68] The brotherhood of the eucharist pointed towards a reordered society. He criticized those who crowded in 'to take of the food, to feed on the glory, to yield their souls to the Hush and the Holy'. They indulged their individualistic pietism, but totally neglected their social responsibility.[69]

But did Holland know anything first-hand of the workers about whom he campaigned? He empathized with other people, but he came from a privileged background, and when he died, his estate was over £21,000 (£417,000 in today's terms). He lived in prestigious places and spacious houses. But he was in regular touch with Labour leaders. Ramsay MacDonald wrote 'Labour Notes' in the CSU *Commonwealth* for some time. Holland was the favourite preacher for workers' services at St Paul's. He preached to the 1882 Cooperative Congress. Remarkably for someone from his background, he understood the concept of workers' solidarity during the 1889 Dock Strike:

> We have a natural pity for those men who are willing . . . to go back to work for any wage that they can get . . . But do not let our pity blind us to the fact that such men are the despair of British industry . . . Let us make clear that our moral judgment goes wholly against them – goes to those who look around and ahead, and understand their social responsibilities; and are loyal to the brotherhood of labour, and to the law of sacrifice for others' good . . . Here, with these, are the forces which give us hope in the future of our industrial classes.[70]

He had studied Booth's *Life and Labour of the People in London* (1902–3). But he also had some direct contact with the workers. Though his idea of a group of Oxford men living in community at Hoxton came to nothing, in 1884 he was one of those behind the creation of Oxford House in Bethnal Green, which was more of a church mission than Toynbee Hall. (James Adderley, later founder of the Franciscan-style Society of the Divine Compassion, and a strong Christian Socialist, was Head of Oxford House 1884–85.) Holland founded the CSU Maurice Hostel and settlement in a desolate area of Hoxton in 1898. His particular concern was the work of the church in the inner city. He wrote to a curate to say how glad he was that he was beginning his ministry not in a rural parish but in Hoxton (which he depicted ingenuously):

> There is something seething in the London slums which it will take all our energies to 'grapple with' . . . Hid away at Oxford,

the fullness of the new life is a mystery to one . . . you must see
actual living, actual dying, actual sinning, real good hearty vice,
naked sin . . . [71]

In 1873 he undertook a mission in Hoxton in Passiontide and
Holy Week which included street preaching. After another
London mission in 1876 he wrote with naive relish:

I did enjoy my glimpse of rough London thoroughly – that
thrilling sight of the black and brutal streets reeling with
drunkards, and ringing with foul words, and filthy with
degradation – and the little sudden blaze of light and colour
and warmth in the crowded shed . . . the contrast with our rich
solemn days, our comfortable Common Rooms, and steady
ease . . . [72]

Donaldson, the priest who had marched with the unemployed
from Leicester to London, one of Holland's friends, remarked
after his death that for all his head-knowledge of Labour, he was
always on the outside looking in. The truth of this remark was
illustrated by Holland's romantic picture of British troops in Le
Havre whom he visited in 1915. He thought them a 'perpetual joy
. . . clean, fresh, upright . . . never insolent, or rowdy . . . really
noble to look at'.[73]

Like other Christian Socialists from the upper classes, he felt a
deep sense of responsibility for the plight of the poor.
Commenting on the Poor Law Report of 1909, he rejected the
belief that poverty was caused by personal moral failure:

It is no fault of theirs. It is much more likely to be ours: we
have housed them in slums, and taken their mothers from them
to toil in our factories: and have given them no chance of sweet
air, and clean habits, and leisure . . . We are under obligation to
them in reparation for our misdoings, we must ease their days:
for Christ's sake, we must cherish their ills. We owe them honour, because they are poor, and weak, and helpless.[74]

The type of poverty in modern society was not the poverty blessed by Christ, for it 'tends only to maim and stunt and discredit and degrade'.[75] Fundamental changes in society were needed, not charity. However, he was ambivalent about the emerging Labour Party. In 1896 he appealed to Labour to trust churchmen. They had much in common. They had both discovered that individuals could only realize themselves in corporate fellowship – Holland referred here to effects of the Catholic revival in the Church of England. Labour would grasp its need of the church when 'the weight of inherited evil' impeded the creation of a new society. In 1897 he and other liberal churchmen berated the Liberal Party for its lack of sympathy to Labour. Holland believed that the conversion of individuals was still important for Socialism made high moral demands:

> Socialism is not a Political System that can be planted down anywhere, or can be voted into action tomorrow. It is an Ideal towards which we are to work, which we shall realize step by step, as we advance spiritually, in the apprehension of our civic obligations, and in our love for the brotherhood, and in our victory over ourselves.

Unlike Gore, he sometimes wrote as though progress was inevitable. The First World War was a shock to his evolutionary optimism. He wrote in September 1914: 'I could not have believed that man could be so diabolical.'[76]

John Heidt sums up the achievements of Holland and the CSU:

> . . . by the First World War England was virtually unique in being the one country where many people did not think that Christianity and Socialism were necessarily incompatible. This was largely due to the work of Holland together with Charles Gore, B. F. Westcott and other associates, and the major vehicles for the public proclamation of their views were the Christian Social Union and *Commonwealth*.[77]

3

Charles Gore

Charles Gore (1853–1932) was successively Bishop of Worcester, Birmingham and Oxford.[1] He was related to many of the Whig families of England. Like the Whigs, Gore was an outsider-insider. He was a loner, conscious of being different from the rest of his family. When he was Bishop of Oxford, to the scandal of some, he made friends with his bohemian neighbour Lady Ottoline Morrell. He often told her that he also had felt 'outside the herd' from his schooldays. He is the most fascinating and most influential bishop of the twentieth-century Church of England. Geoffrey Nuttall, though a quintessential Non-conformist, and then fiercely anti-Anglo-Catholic, heard him lecture when a young man, and realized that for the first time he was listening to a great man.

Gore was liable to glooms about himself, the church and society. He tried to deal with his tempestuous emotions by repression and detachment, but got exasperated and sometimes lost his temper. He had no intimates. He could not respond even to Scott Holland, his dearest friend, with the same open emotion Holland showed to him. Though he preached and worked for brotherhood and community in the nation and the world, his self-isolation meant that he could never immerse himself in the communal life of the Community of the Resurrection he had founded in 1892. He withdrew when appointed a bishop in 1901. Yet he continued to live austerely. He refused as Bishop of Worcester to live at Hartlebury Castle. When Bishop of Oxford his bedroom was almost bare, except for an old iron bedstead, a chest of drawers, a prayer desk and a tin bath. There was no carpet. The Whig tradition into which he was born, his belief in incarnation as self-emptying (*kenosis*, Phil. 2.6–8) and his own sense of being an outsider, made him take up the cause of the underdog – the workers (he wanted CR to move to the industrial north); the Boers (he condemned the British concentration camps in 1901); the Welsh (he supported Welsh disestablishment); Conscientious Objectors (though he was not a pacifist). Yet his startling and sometimes savage comments both amused people and kept them at a distance. Gore, discussing the labour demonstrations in London in 1887 remarked: 'It's a pity that they did not loot the West End.' His actual contacts with working people were occasional rather than regular. Early on, a tour of Oxfordshire villages in the company of Joseph Arch introduced him to rural poverty. Realizing he knew little of the lives of ordinary people after he was priested in 1878, he went for three months as a curate to a parish in Bootle in 1879, and in 1880 and in following years spent his summer vacations as a curate in Toxteth. But when CR moved to the small parish of Radley in 1893 and he was an incumbent for the first time, he found parish life and ordinary people beyond him and he broke down for this and other reasons. In 1903 as the new Bishop of Worcester he went to institute a vicar in a poor area of Birmingham. He caused astonishment by deciding to stay not with the curate or churchwarden but with a bricklayer. But for much of the rest of his life his contacts with working people were confined to meetings with Labour leaders. Gore's desire for the church to be disciplined, self-governing and fraternal rather than a loosely defined institution compromised by its state connection, may have owed something to his unease with democracy and the crowd as well as to his theology derived from the Old Testament prophets and New Testament images of the disciples as leaven and salt. A Bournemouth parish priest complained to Gore about the conventionality of its churchgoing. 'Nothing seems to prevent them coming to church,' he said. 'Have you ever tried preaching the Gospel?' Gore asked. Gore was complex, compassionate, stoical, frightening, sad, humourous, stern: very different from the more light-hearted, more optimistic and less agonized Holland.

When Gore was a boy of fifteen at Harrow, he was profoundly influenced by a sermon preached by Westcott (then an assistant master) in which he called for the creation of a modern version of the disciplined life lived by Benedict and others – 'social evils must be met by social organization'. Gore was also influenced by Westcott's teaching that the gospel was relevant to every aspect of life and that humanity was one. But whereas Westcott's socialism did not emerge until the 1880s, already in the late 1860s and early 1870s Gore at Harrow and Balliol was a radical. In 1872 he developed a great admiration for the efforts of Joseph Arch, the Primitive Methodist, to create a union for agricultural workers. In 1921 preaching at Bradford on Industrial Sunday he revealed: 'There was a time when he himself was profoundly disgusted with the Church and the squirearchy – in the days when he knew Joseph Arch.'² In his first term as Principal of Pusey House in 1884, he aroused a storm by inviting Stewart Headlam to address a meeting of the GSM there. In 1889, a few months after the formation of the CSU, Gore created further controversy by giving hospitality at Pusey House to Ben Tillett, leader of the recent dock strike. At the subsequent public meeting Gore praised 'the self-sacrifice' of the stevedores for striking in sympathy, and said that in the Labour movement led by such men as Lansbury and Hardie, he saw a righteous claim for 'justice not charity'. In 1893 Gore chaired a meeting at which Tom Mann, another leader of the strike and a founding member of the SDF, explained trade unions to undergraduates. Gore was convinced that the passion for social justice in the Labour movement at its best showed that it was moved by the Spirit of God.

Gore was convinced that the workers were alienated from Christianity, not because of intellectual difficulties or problems about the Bible, but because they did not find in the churches the fruit they had a right to expect. At the end of his early statement *The Social Doctrine of the Sermon on the Mount* (1892) he told the CSU:

The moment has come for the Church, and more particularly the Church of England, to put social morality, Christian living, in the forefront of its effort . . . We try too much to 'get people to come to church'. We want, on the other hand . . . to consolidate Christian moral opinion in each district of Church life . . .

Gore thought that paying the market price for clothes and ordering them in good time was on the same level as saying one's prayers, reading the Bible and receiving holy communion. Though Gore said he was little influenced by Maurice, he had imbibed Whig paternalism and Tractarian moralism. His moralism was evidenced by his constant references to J.B. Seeley's *Ecce Homo* (1865) which Shaftesbury described as 'the most pestilential book ever vomited, I think, from the jaws of hell'. Its depiction of Christ's real humanity and as moral teacher was a revelation to Gore. He ranked the book with Kingsley and Maurice as the three main influences which led people into the settlement movement, social reform and the CSU. (Barnett had also been deeply moved by it.) Seeley had written (ch. XIII) that Christ had founded a 'universal society' and urged upon its members 'a life strictly social and civic'. Gore also acknowledged the influence upon him of Carlyle, Ruskin and Green in his early days. But Gore was never a disciple of Green like Holland, nor indeed of anyone else.

Fundamental to Gore's Christian Socialism was his kenotic interpretation of the incarnation. This 'humiliation' and 'self-limitation' of Christ had a profound moral significance for him. He wrote in 1891:

St Paul . . . teaches us that the right way to understand the action of God in the Incarnation is to contemplate it morally. It is an act of moral self-denial such as can be an example to us men in our efforts at sympathy and self-sacrifice.

State socialism was a threat to liberty.

But there is another sort of socialism, wholly voluntary . . .
which the Incarnation seems, beyond all question, to bring
with it. There exists what can rightly be called a Christian
socialism, by the very fact that the law of brotherhood is the
law of Christ.[3]

We owe (he regularly asserted) to the Old Testament prophets
our sense of the indissoluble union of religion and morality, for
'there is nothing He really demands of men but righteousness'.[4]
So when he celebrated the eucharist he always insisted on including the Ten Commandments instead of the shorter less
moralistic alternatives favoured by Anglo-Catholics. He used
adjectives which conveyed his moral passion: 'tremendous', 'hor-
rible', 'fearful'. Jesus, he asserted, was not a mystic. His prayer
consisted mainly of petition. So we should 'ask for all that makes
men effective agents of the kingdom of God with its ethical
character'. 'Always He is plainly on the side of the humble and
poor.' Though he demanded renunciation of worldly values he
was not an ascetic. Salvation was essentially social; the church was
a brotherhood transcending all human distinctions. So if, for
example, an employee is dimissed for loyalty to principle, the
CSU should support him.[5]

But Gore also wanted a disciplined church, shorn of half-
believers, modernists and the ill-disciplined. Christianity should
be 'a spiritual aristocracy' (a revealing phrase). He did not seem
to realize that the Labour movement's concern for brotherhood
and justice derived from what E. S. Talbot called 'diffusive
Christianity'. For Gore, baptism was incorporation into a community and the eucharist was 'the sacrament of fraternity'. CR
was founded to reproduce the life of Acts 2.42–44 as an example
to society of community. Throughout his life, Gore idealized the
early church.[6] He passionately believed that change could only
come from the disciplined few. He pointed to what had been
wrought by the Tractarian minority. A small number of really
committed Christians could also transform society.

His views on the church and society were classically expressed in a sermon to the 1906 Church Congress on 'The Church and the Poor' – 'the cry of a permanently troubled conscience which cannot see its way'. The early church, he said, spoke for the poor and associated wealth with 'tyranny and wrong'. But today the church was not in touch with the mass of the labouring people, because it was 'the church of the rich rather than of the poor – of Capital rather than of Labour'. The church must rid itself of the administration of poor relief; artisans must be given a much greater role in church government; the clergy must bring out 'the social teaching of the sacraments' and work for social justice; 'we must dissociate the clergy from being identified with the wealthier classes'.[7]

He had a much more acute awareness of original sin than Holland and many contemporary social reformers. Human plans could be shipwrecked on the rocks of human sin: 'no step could be made in legislation unless there was, corresponding to that, an advance in the character of the people which could be appealed to'. Human nature 'presents in great measure a scene of moral ruin', so Christ comes 'not merely to consummate an order but to restore it, not to accomplish only, but to redeem'. Thus a Christian who devotes himself to bettering social conditions, as his brother's keeper, will eventually discover that though much improvement can be wrought through laws, 'the heart of the matter lies in character . . . in jealousy, in suspicion, in self-assertion, in lust, in dishonesty . . . in a word in sin'.[8]

Gore promoted the extension of the franchise to women both in state and church elections and believed that democracy was the will of God for his day, but he had doubts. Jesus dreaded the idea of 'public opinion as the guardian of the moral standard' and had 'a profound contempt for majorities'. To be leaven, salt, light, a city set on a hill, the 'Commonwealth' of Jesus had to be 'in marked separation from the surrounding world'. 'The Church must always be saying those unpleasant things that strike upon the conscience and check the first enthusiasm.' He was critical of claims of human progress. 'Progress in Christianity is always a reversion to an original and perfect type.' The word which 'most forcibly characterises man's spiritual history . . . is not progress, but recovery, or redemption'. Evolution was 'as compatible with retrogression as with progress'.[9]

Gore expressed his political commitments, as we have seen, in part through the CSU. In line with CSU principles, when he was a Canon of Westminster, he bought shares in a London store to be able to protest at a shareholder's meeting about the oppression of its employees. He addressed Cooperative Congresses and patronized Cooperative shops. When he became Bishop of Worcester he outraged local traders by immediately joining the local Cooperative Society and addressing a Cooperative meeting. But he had to admit that he had been obliged to send some Coop boots back three times. He added wryly: 'the wicked shops are best'. He supported the movement because it distributed wealth more widely, helped the weak and educated the consumer in responsibility.

Unlike Westcott and Price Hughes who supported imperialism and the Anglo-Boer war, Gore, like Holland, was a critic of both. During the First World War, like Holland, Temple and Bell he swam against the nationalist tide and tried to maintain a sense of the Catholic church transcending national boundaries and hatreds. He regularly prodded the Labour movement about its failure to apply the principles of equality and justice to race relations that they desired to see in national life.[10]

He was a leading supporter within the CSU for industrial legislation, such as the Factory Bill of 1901. As Bishop of Birmingham he was passionately concerned for housing reform and town planning; he intervened in strikes; he supported union rights, collective bargaining and the Trade Boards Bill of 1909 to ensure minimum wages in certain industries where sweating was common. When in 1911 a Reading firm sacked nearly one hundred of its employees who had wanted to create a union, Gore was indignant, sent a subscription to a fund for those dismissed, announced he would attend a protest meeting in the town and set up an investigation into working-class conditions there. As we saw in the last chapter, he strongly supported Lloyd George's 'People's Budget' of 1909.[11]

Like Temple and Tawney, he took an active role in the WEA. Indeed it had been founded in 1903 by Albert Mansbridge after hearing Gore preach in the Abbey. He was immensely pleased when in 1903–4 CR established a scheme for a total of five years of free training for ordinands from poor homes at the CR university hostel in Leeds and at the theological college at Mirfield. In the Lords on 24 July 1907 he caused consternation in Oxford and Cambridge by proposing (at Temple's suggestion) a Royal Commission on the two universities. They had always trained the governing classes, he said, but now the workers were part of the governing classes. Yet the universities had become 'a playground for the sons of the wealthier classes'. Once again Gore was asking the well-to-do to shoulder their moral obligations to the rest of society.

Though he was wary of anything which threatened Catholic principles, he was very ready to cooperate with the Free Churches on social questions. He became President of the interdenominational Council for Witness on Social Questions when it was founded in 1913. Its first act, influenced by him, was to issue a manifesto advocating a minimum wage. He admired Nonconformity for its social and political dissent. Its very existence was a constant reminder for Gore of Anglican failure. In his Primary Charge of 1904 as Bishop of Worcester he remarked: 'The history of religion in Birmingham since the seventeenth century is very largely the history of Nonconformist activity and influence.'[12] Politically he was more at home with its radical Nonconformists than with its Tory Anglicans.

When he resigned as Bishop of Oxford in 1919 he gave as one of his reasons his desire to join the Labour Party. It is not known whether he ever did. He did not join 510 Anglican priests of England, Wales and Scotland who in 1923 signed a memorial to Ramsay MacDonald and the Labour MPs congratulating them on becoming the official Opposition and offered their support. Though no bishop signed it, F. R. Barry and Walter Frere who became bishops a little later did so. In retirement, freed from the constraints of office, Gore regularly participated in political debate and activity.

In 1919 he joined Arthur Henderson (Methodist) and George Lansbury (Anglican) in a conference on 'The Religion of Labour'. He said that the spirit of the Labour Movement might be summed up in the cry 'Not charity but justice'. He asked whether in that cry there was a religion which could be made explicit and therefore more influential. The real source of brotherhood was belief in God. 'Can we rally the Labour Movement to the recognition of the moral sovereignty of Jesus Christ?' He wished the large number of Christians who believed in the Labour Movement could be organised to make explicit the crucial importance of religious belief as the basis for human solidarity.[13]

What did Gore mean by 'Christian Socialism'?[14] He had much less knowledge of the classical socialist writers than Headlam, but he referred to the researches of the Webbs and social histories by his friends J. L. and Barbara Hammond and R. H. Tawney. Like other members of the CSU he cited the works of the foremost economist of the day Alfred Marshall, Professor of Economics at Cambridge, as an example of the current more collectivist approach to social problems. Gore was as *dirigiste* in some of his social solutions as in his attempts to discipline the clergy. So he advocated detention for the 'feeble-minded' and for the 'workshy' as well as unemployment insurance. If he quoted I Corinthians 12 on the care of the members of the body for one another, he also cited II Thessalonians, 3.10 'if any would not work, neither should he eat'. *Laissez-faire* (he asserted) by proclaiming that acquisitiveness was the dominant motive for society was 'anti-Christian', a denial of 'Thou shalt love thy neighbour as thyself'. He paraphrased *Unto this Last* in his declaration that the riches of the nation did not lie in the quantity of its commodities, but in the number of people who were living healthy happy lives.[15] By contrast with *laissez-faire* individualism, Christian ethics were social and were concerned with the good of all, yet also must take eschatology and the provisionality of human history into account. He was nervous of using the term 'socialism' because it often meant the supremacy of the state. But for him the term meant that all people were of equal worth and that the welfare of the community should take precedence over individual gain. He was attracted to the cooperative ideal and self-determining small groups – hence his interest in Guild Socialism, though he doubted its practicability. He had a temperamental dislike of large organizations and impersonal cities. He did not want CR to become so big that its members no longer knew one another intimately. Yet he was also clear that there could be no return to the Middle Ages – not least because 'mediaeval sociology' postulated a united Christendom. He wrote in 1918 that the war had illustrated the way in which a communal cause could evoke self-forgetting sacrifice, service and cooperation, morally superior to a competitive society.[16]

Though he supported state and municipal action to remedy social ills, he always emphasized that the conversion of the heart was fundamental. 'The secret of redemption is within.' He warned that socialism might 'represent nothing more than the instinct, the unregenerate, uncleansed instinct of a class that is discontented'. If a socialist state came into existence, Christians would need to be vigilant – there could be sweating just as well in a state industry or a cooperative undertaking. A socialist society would make greater moral demands than most of its advocates realize. 'It may be true that "collectivism" would remove many of the temptations to selfishness . . . but it will substitute other temptations quite as perilous.'[17]

In a paper for the 1908 Pan-Anglican Congress, he declared: 'The socialistic movement is based upon a great demand for justice . . . The indictment of our present social organisation is indeed overwhelming.' Identifying himself with the Old Testament prophets he called the church to penitence and reparation:

> . . . it should make a tremendous act of penitence for having failed so long and on so wide a scale to behave as the champion of the oppressed and the weak . . . for having so often been on

the wrong side. And the penitence must lead to reparation while there is yet time, ere the well-merited judgements of God take all weapons of social influence out of our hands.

He denounced *laissez-faire* as a self-enclosed system which had attempted to exclude God and had listened more to economists than to the prophets or Christ. He was determined that socialism should not become a self-contained and self-satisfied secular system. 'Human affairs are not governed by mechanical laws, and do not move towards necessarily determined conclusions.'[18]

He repudiated utopianism because he was too aware of the all-pervasiveness of sin. Dreams of a 'fresh start' were in vain, but mere 'ambulance work' was not enough. A system that produced huge discrepancies of poverty and wealth 'stands condemned in the sight of our Lord', he told the Birmingham Diocesan Conference in 1907. He advocated more education, the raising of the school age, provision of open spaces, removal of slums and town planning. This was of course a programme of social reforms, but not revolution. In 1927 he was still advocating what had been essentially the CSU method:

> There must be thirty or forty or a hundred in every town, who are both believers in the Name of Jesus as the true redeemer of man, and are also sure that this redemption requires for its free course social and industrial reform and reconstruction of a radical kind. Let them get themselves organised and active, so that they can become known and recognised locally, and even, if necessary, feared in municipal life.

A revolution was indeed required but only through 'gradual and peaceful means'.[19]

What was Gore's attitude to property? In his introduction to *Property* (1913) he wrote that while we are all 'in the bonds of an organised system of property' we lack a common mind about it. He approved of Hobhouse's distinction between property 'for use' and property 'for power'. In our society, he said, vast numbers of people cannot realize themselves for they are treated as 'hands'. Something had gone badly wrong. The case for redistributive measures was that fulfilment of life was more important than 'rights of property'. The early church taught that property was to be held for the common good: 'there is no legitimate claim which property can make against what appears to be the welfare of the State . . . individualism in property has overdone itself . . . it is working disastrous havoc'. On various occasions he stressed that private ownership of property was essential if individuality was to be preserved, but it must be earned by work. He condemned the 'workshy' whether rich or poor. After the First World War he contemplated the possibility of nationalization of some basic industries with equanimity, for the rights of property were never absolute. But he preferred co-partnership which would give workers a stake in a common enterprise. They would work harder, industry would become a service to the consumer and a few individuals would no longer amass large fortunes. He also commended the traditional concept of Christian stewardship and greatly admired the model village of Bourneville. Gore was a great friend of George Cadbury and joked that when the Church of England cast him out he would become a Quaker. He paid tribute to squires and owners of property who were 'impregnated with the noble sense of what the responsibility of their position means'. Yet he insisted:

> The 'rights of property', what does it mean? Nothing in the world but the selfishness of those who have, and because they have want to stick to what they have . . . The Church can never ally itself with the right of property.

Again he pointed out:

> . . . it is society which has enabled men to acquire and to hold wealth, and society has therefore the power to lay its hand upon it when the individual claims to use it for the damage of the whole body . . .

Consequently he thought the land tax in the 1909 Budget admirable. The CR brethren pooled all their resources, but retained control of whatever capital they possessed (but not its income). When Gore left to become a bishop he gave CR the right to all the royalties of the books he had written during his membership. To help to fund the new see of Birmingham (which was carved out of his Worcester diocese) he resigned £500 from his see and gave £10,000, a bequest from his mother, to endow it.[20]

As an undergraduate in the early 1870s he had defended trade unions in the Oxford Union and continued to defend their role in safeguarding the interests of their members. In 1913 he told a congregation of striking tram workers in Oxford that while he was not going to express an opinion about the dispute, he believed that 'the cheapest labour was not the best or the most profitable' and that the principle of unionism was 'thoroughly Christian' and had been 'an incalculable boon' to industry. In this case he recommended arbitration. But Gore refused to idealize working people. He told a meeting of trade unionists called by the ICF in 1920 that great interests, ecclesiastical, political and financial had conspired together to silence the carpenter of Nazareth – a popular version among working people. But he pointed out that the common people who had heard him gladly also deserted him and asked 'how did the other carpenters, and the rest of the work-ing people treat Him? . . . Now you understand why . . . there is hardly any feature in history so disappointing as democratic revolutions.'[21]

Gore approached the question of industrial conflict with greater *Realpolitik* than most Christian leaders, for he frankly rec-ognized the benefits won by working-class militancy. At an ICF meeting in 1921 G. A. Studdert Kennedy, the former chaplain, now the chief ICF missioner, proposed conciliation and arbitra-tion as the only Christian answer to industrial strife. Gore proposed an amendment which recognized the role of the strike in uplifting the workers. Gore wrote in a 1926 COPEC pamphlet:

. . . the vast majority of men and women are born and die exploited for the advantage of the minority . . . If the position of this vast majority has been gradually improving during the last hundred years, that has been because they have, in a measure successfully, combined to rebel against their slavery in its extremer forms, aided no doubt by the assistance of some merciful and rational men of the privileged classes, but relying in the main on their own efforts, and fighting continually against the organised resistance of the mass of the well-to-do.

In the past, the middle class had been forced to revolt against the aristocracy. The General Strike and the coal strike were part of a long reaction against the established industrial system.[22]

Gore was a member of the Standing Conference of the Christian Churches on the Coal Dispute. It also included Temple, other bishops and Free Church leaders. This attempted to mediate, much to the fury of conservative members of the churches. In 1926, Dean Inge, with upper-class spleen, characterized two types of the supporters of this effort at mediation: 'obvious time-servers, who will have their reward when the Socialists come in to power' and 'the new type of parson, sprung from the ranks and soured by poverty and thwarted social ambition'. During the General Strike, Archbishop Davidson of Canterbury intervened after being prodded by bishops, Free Churchmen and the ICF and issued an Appeal on 7 May signed also by Cardinal Bourne, the President of the Free Church Council and others. The Appeal concluded with three practical proposals. The government-controlled BBC and *British Gazette* refused to publish it. This gave it notoriety. It reached the public through the TUC newspaper *The British Worker* and through other means. However, on 9 May, Cardinal Bourne condemned the General Strike, alarmed by the possibility of losing some of his flock to socialism and impelled by that instinctive Roman Catholic fear of being accused of disloyalty. The strike was (he declared) 'a direct challenge to a lawfully constituted authority . . . a sin against the obedience we owe to God . . . and against the charity and brotherly love which are due to our brethren'. This outraged Roman Catholic trade unionists who since *Rerum Novarum* had thought their church recognized union rights. So, by accident, the cautious Davidson for a brief moment was praised (or reviled) as 'the workers' friend'.[23]

In reality, the General Strike and the inability of church leaders to understand it was the nemesis of much that the churches, not least the Church of England, had done during and after the war, for example through the Fifth Committee, ICF and COPEC to reassure Labour and the workers of their sympathetic support. The parliamentary opposition to the Trade Disputes Bill of 1927 imposing restrictions on the unions was led by the Anglo-Catholic Socialist, Sir Henry Slesser, the former Labour Solicitor-General. But some Christians, hitherto sympathetic to Labour, had been scared by the exhibition of union militancy and supported the new restrictions. Free Church people had known where to stand on Victorian and Edwardian issues like Non-conformist disabilities, disestablishment in Wales, temperance, church schools. But they (like most other Christians) were baffled by the new economic issues, strikes and class conflict. Calls for Christian reconciliation were fruitless. In some chapels a gulf opened between the two sides to the conflict which never healed. The Free Churches now split three ways between the three parties. The General Strike, the collapse of Labour in 1931 and the formation of a National government increased Conservative support among Free Church people.[24]

Hensley Henson, Bishop of Durham, who had become a patrician Tory individualist, used the General Strike as yet another stick to beat Gore (once his mentor and colleague), Temple, Anglo-Catholicism and Christian Socialism. It was no accident, he wrote, that 'our leading Christian Socialists are also prominent as Anglo-Catholics' for they looked to the Middle Ages in religion and economics. He quoted approvingly Sir Josiah Stamp, the Methodist industrialist and chairman of the LMS Railway, on the need for cool heads not warm hearts in confronting the vagaries of markets and currencies and other economic problems. Appeals for universal brotherhood faded on the lips when faced with the helplessness of religion to solve such questions, Stamp believed. Henson commented: 'The world is a sterner place to live in than it is pleasant to remember, and we forget its sternness at our peril.' He blamed idealistic church leaders for misleading the religious public with false economics and for courting Labour, and thus encouraging its demands. Victorian Christian Socialism, reinforced by COPEC, had led to the 'unfortunate intervention' of clergy in the coal stoppage. He attacked churchmen and politicians for admiring working-class solidarity in the General Strike, though it had been created by 'brutal coercion' and 'terrorism', and had led to the breaking of contracts. 'The familiar economic issues of industrial conflict . . . are questions which do not obviously or necessarily involve any Christian principle, and need not wound any Christian conscience.' The 'highest service which religion can render to the victims of the economic process is to strengthen character . . .'[25]

Gore believed that it was morally necessary to interfere with the markets. He recognized that mediaeval attempts to define a just price and to suppress usury were not feasible in modern economies. But he and the CSU advocated paying higher prices for goods produced by firms which provided better conditions. That the first charge upon industry should be a 'living wage' was one of Gore's constant demands, reiterated in church reports, and supported by Gore's friend L. T. Hobhouse in his influential book *Liberalism* (1911). To those who like Henson objected, Gore pointed to the fact that many wages were determined by collective bargaining or Wage Boards, and not by supply and demand.[26] The concept of a living or minimum wage had originated in church circles in the Canterbury Convocation Report *The Moral Witness of the Church on Economic Subjects* (1907) produced by a committee chaired by Gore. The report of the Fifth Committee in 1918 and the 1920 Lambeth Conference Committee on the Church and Industrial Problems both reiterated the case for a living wage. But, as Oliver points out, the church did not suggest how this might be economically feasible. In 1922, the Federation of British Industries campaigned to reduce wages and argued that they should be fixed at a level industry could bear. The bishops were silent, despite urgings from the Church Socialist League to respond. Gore, however, continued to press for a living wage.[27]

For Gore, poverty was not inevitable. The churches ought to have been fighting for justice, for good housing, for good drains, and for good wages but instead had relied on the evils of charity and indiscriminate giving. Throughout his life he practised what he considered the right type of giving to those in need. When he was a bishop he set aside £1000 for this purpose annually. Charitable giving by the churches had encouraged people to view them as places from which to cadge. Christians rather ought to give as citizens. We should pay higher taxes readily instead of loathing them.

Gore had a high valuation of the city, indebted to examples both from Greece and Birmingham. Gore thought it deplorable (as would have Aristotle) when people said they enjoyed London because they could do what they pleased. In Greek as in mediaeval times, a conception of 'corporate life and corporate responsibility was realized'. But in London, life was individualistic. So when he was enthroned in Birmingham in 1905, and entered upon his most fulfilled episcopate, he spoke of his pride in his city bishopric, for very much of what was best in world history and religion was bound up in the life of cities. London was too big to be a city. Birmingham was full of 'corporate feeling' and took pride in its heroes.[28] Was his concept of the corporate city state compatible with his suspicion of establishment and his desire for the church to stand over against society as a pure and disciplined remnant? Gore's hymns of praise to the city echo those of Holland, but are in stark contrast with the nostalgic ruralism of many socialists.

Though, as we saw earlier, Gore had rejected that belief in an automatic progress, so characteristic of late Victorian socialists, Christian and non-Christian, and took sin seriously, he did at times use the language of Green's Hegelianism. So when in 1898 he argued for a considerable degree of self-government for the church and for the full participation of lay people (including women) in its new bodies, in part he justified this change because it reflected the transition from feudalism and aristocracy to democracy in society. He looked back to Maurice and Kingsley and celebrated a line of continuing advance in social Christianity, however incomplete or faltering. He celebrated the great progress in social welfare in 1911 from the Wages Board to unemployment benefit. Like his beloved Old Testament prophets and the Deuteronomic writers Gore read history moralistically. Hence he was attracted to the kind of crusading history with heroes and villains written by his friends J. L. and Barbara Hammond, both of whom came from clerical homes. When *Religion and the Rise of Capitalism* appeared in 1926, Gore welcomed it as supplying evidence for the church's failures he had so often castigated. He commented that Tawney 'has for the first time in English, told us truly, in a well-documented record, how this all came about'. Yet that year (1926), 37 years after the foundation of the CSU, he had still to lament that most congregations 'still largely consist of members of the comfortable classes whose chief anxiety is that they and their successors and their like should remain comfortable'.[29]

Large numbers of people, clergy and laypeople, including seminal figures like Tawney, Temple and Bell, derived much of their understanding of the church's role in society from Gore. In the 1920s, John Groser, the East End Christian Socialist priest, in conflict with the diocese of London for his political views and actions, consulted Gore who advised him to continue his struggle and not to give in. In 1939, Trevor Huddleston went to Mirfield to join the Community of the Resurrection inspired by Gore, its founder and its Christian Socialist tradition. After the Anglo-Boer war it was Gore who urged CR to go to South Africa. It started work in 1903 and up to 1977 trained most of its black ordinands, including Desmond Tutu. So there is a direct line between Gore and Tutu which runs through the work of CR and Huddleston in South Africa. When Huddleston went to be a bishop in Tanzania in 1960, CR gave him Gore's pectoral cross, which he said inspired him with strength and courage. The young Michael Ramsey read the life of Archbishop Davidson and was depressed by the politicking. He read Prestige's life of Gore and was inspired.

4

R. H. Tawney

R. H. Tawney (1880–1962) was nurtured within the CSU tradition, but also grew beyond it. He was a close friend and disciple
of Gore, but unlike Gore and Holland was a layman. Though not
an economist, Tawney knew more about economics, economic
history and political life than either Gore or Holland. But he came
from a very similar background – he was educated at Rugby and
Balliol and was an Anglican. Born in Calcutta at the height of
Empire – his father was part of the Indian Educational Service –
he met William Temple on his first day at Rugby. Tawney
disliked its conventional life. Its formal religion conveyed
the impression that the events of the gospel had 'all happened on
a Sunday'. He went up to Balliol in 1899. Temple followed him a
year later. Senior to both was William Beveridge. Later Temple
married Tawney to Beveridge's sister. Barnett of Toynbee Hall
preached. Tawney always dissented from conventional norms
when principle demanded it. So he refused to proceed to his
MA because this was obtained merely by the payment of a fee.
Yet throughout his life he retained many of the characteristics of
the Edwardian gentleman.

The Master of Balliol, Edward Caird, a moral philosopher with
a social conscience, urged Tawney and Beveridge to discover why
poverty existed alongside wealth and to do something about it.
Beveridge became sub-warden of Toynbee Hall in 1903. Tawney
joined the CSU and after graduation went to live at Toynbee
Hall from 1903 to 1906 and for part of 1908 and 1913. 'The
Oxford ideal of a gentleman in Tawney's youth enjoined a moral

character and outlook which preferred public service to private commerce, asceticism to social display.'[1] He thought Toynbee Hall too paternalistic and early on he rejected both evangelism and philanthropy as solutions to the problems of society.[2] He looked instead to ethical socialism. Later on in life he concluded that state action alone could not solve social problems, for the state was composed of individuals whose attitudes might need to change. Early on, however, in *The Acquisitive Society* (1921) he naively thought that after nationalization '*it would be reasonable* to ask that the miners should set a much needed example to the business community by refusing to extort better terms for themselves at the expense of the public' (my italics). In the latter part of his life he worried that so little had been done to change the character and motivation of the people, and wondered whether the Labour movement really wanted to revolt against capitalism.[3]

In 1905 he joined the executive of the WEA and dedicated himself to it for the next forty-two years. It had been founded by Mansbridge under Gore's influence. Temple was President 1908–24. Tawney was President 1928–45. It was through Tawney's years of tutorial work with the WEA that he began really to know working people – or rather that elite which was willing and able to study. In 1953 he said that he had received the best part of his education when, as a WEA tutor he 'underwent, week by week, a series of friendly, but effective deflations' at the hands of his students. He regarded education not as a middle-class conveyance of culture but as preparing working people for power: 'in the WEA Tawney's egalitarian Anglicanism found its most complete expression.' The WEA and the LSE, which he joined later, were free from that hierarchy and conventionality which he found so stifling in Oxford. But by 1948 he was deeply saddened that fewer and fewer workers were joining classes.[4]

Theologically Tawney owed much to Gore – his attraction to the alleged purity and discipline of the pre-Constantinian church, his contempt for establishment, his expectation that the church should nevertheless be able to bring about the moralization of the economic, industrial and commercial life of the nation. He believed that the revolt of ordinary people against capitalism was fundamentally ethical. Like Gore he was a moralist and inter- preted history in the light of a pre-conceived moral scheme. His diagnosis was that modern society was morally sick. The title of the first form of his famous 1921 book was 'The Sickness of an Acquistive Society'. He wrote about 'the disease of inequality'. For Tawney, the fundamental problem was that there was no longer an agreed common body of social ethics, as he believed there once had been. Capitalism was morally wrong because it treated human beings as means not ends. He was scathing when the left dismissed honesty and good faith as 'bourgeois morality' – 'as though virtues ceased to be virtues when practised . . . by the middle classes'. Tawney offered 'a secular version of the Fall . . . in which commercial forces accomplish the destruction of com- munal solidarities, and society as a spiritual organism gives way to the notion of society as an economic machine'.[5] Like Gore, he lived austerely – despite or because of his wife's extravagance. Kingsley Martin joked that Tawney wrote *The Acquisitive Society* and his wife illustrated it. Temple was invited to stay overnight. After a while Tawney rummaged behind some books and pro- duced some cold mutton cutlets. Temple's bed was two rugs on a bench inside a bow window and during the night this aroused the suspicions of a passing policeman.

Much that was theologically important to Gore, Holland and Temple was of less interest to Tawney, who, as we shall see, concentrated on certain key doctrines. Though he disliked religiosity he was for a time a Lay Reader. Throughout his life he went to church frequently if not regularly. Biblical moral judg- ments and allusions to the Authorized Version characterized all his writings, but references to the doctrinal basis of his assertions were less frequent. Perhaps he did not want to divide his audi- ence; perhaps he dreaded appearing evangelistic. It was not until his *Commonplace Book* was published posthumously in 1972 that the doctrinal basis of his religious and political faith became indisputable. So in 1958 a humanist like Raymond Williams in *Culture and Society* could present Tawney's thought without reference to its Christian basis. Yet it was this which delivered him from the utopianism which characterized so much socialism. As Raphael Samuels remarked, 'his Christianity gave him a sense of the totality of social relations – including their psychic roots – which a Marxist might well envy; and it saved him from triumphalism'.[6] He wrote in 1912 that he was beginning to realize 'the extraordinary truth and subtlety of religious dogmas' which he had scoffed at as an undergraduate.

> 'Original sin' – that what goodness we have reached is a house built on piles driven into black slime and always slipping down into it unless we are building day and night. 'Grace' – that wickedness in oneself is not overcome by willing . . .

'The Christian religion is for bad people like me,' he would say. However, while no change of system could remove 'the egotism, greed, or quarrelsomeness of human nature', it could create 'an environment in which these are not the qualities which are encouraged'. He explained the connection between belief in God and belief in humanity. 'What is wrong with the modern world is that having ceased to believe in the greatness of God, and therefore the infinite smallness (or greatness – the same thing!) of *man*, it has to invent or emphasize distinctions between *men*.' Yet Tawney also held on to another Christian doctrine so central to Gore and *Lux Mundi*: that human beings are made in the image of God. So in the First World War he confessed to his shame that he had enjoyed taking aim and killing Germans. It made him feel 'like a merry mischievous ape tearing up the image of God'.[7]

He thought the Benthamite principle of the greatest happiness of the greatest number morally defective. It could justify, for example, the ruthless exploitation of a small backward race if that produced greater wealth for a white nation. When we condemn slavery, sweating and the exploitation of a weak race by a conqueror, even though these may be convenient to the majority, we do so because each human being has 'supreme value'. Tawney, like Holland and Gore, wanted to moralize economics, for it was:

simply one branch of conduct . . . no consideration of expediency can justify the oppression of one by another. But to believe that it is necessary to believe in God . . . The social order is judged and condemned by a power transcending it.[8]

Central to Tawney's socialism (as it was for Morris, Gore, Holland and many others) was 'fellowship'. He cited Morris' aphorism 'fellowship is heaven, and lack of fellowship is death'. Socialism promoted true community and a shared culture, whereas capitalism, by its belief in hierarchy, acquisitiveness, competition and inequality destroyed fellowship. He quoted an attack upon the unfettered play of economic self-interest from Robert Crowley who belonged to Hugh Latimer's radical 'Commonwealth Men' of the sixteenth century:

> . . . men that live as thoughe there were no God at all, men that would have all in their owne handes, men that would leave nothynge for others, men that would be alone on the earth, men that bee never satisfied.

Capitalism taught people to judge life solely by economic criteria, Tawney believed, and instanced a Cabinet minister who had claimed that 'the greatness of this country depends upon the value of its exports'. Capitalism was based on the premise that 'man's self-love is God's Providence', and thus created acquisitive societies. It encouraged avarice:

> No one has any business to expect to be paid 'what he is worth', for what he is worth is a matter between his own soul and God. What he has a right to demand . . . is enough to enable him to perform his work.

Compromise 'between the Church of Christ and the idolatry of wealth' was as impossible as it was 'between the Church and State idolatry of the Roman Empire'.[9]

Tawney repeatedly asserted, and documented in *Religion and the Rise of Capitalism* (1926), that the church which had once set forth moral criteria for economic life, under the pressure of capitalist individualism encouraged by some Reformation groups, increasingly confined itself to private behaviour. In it he made one of his most famous statements: 'The social teaching of the Church had ceased to count because the Church itself had ceased to think.' Edward Norman has described *Religion and the Rise of Capitalism* as 'the most systematic and most well-known statement' of how the transition from mediaeval teaching to modern individualism occurred.[10]

Like others in the CSU tradition he rejected the Evangelicals' solution: 'In my experience those who say that what they desire is a change of heart usually means that they object to a change of anything else.'[11] Though he was attracted to the Webbs, his Christianity led him to believe that Benthamite fact-gathering by itself was not enough. People needed moral principles. It was his Christian belief and his rejection of utilitarianism which prevented him from being deluded by the Soviet Union, as they were. He regarded Communism as both oppressive and dishonest. In 1949, he derided British Communist leaders as 'elderly cynics, jumping backwards and forwards through hoops with a docility that would sicken a self-respecting poodle . . . The pretence that a despotism is not a despotism, but the servant of the people, the proletariat . . . is the stalest trick of tyranny . . .'[12]

Like Gore, he was highly critical of the Church of England for being 'a class institution, making respectful salaams to property and gentility, and with too little faith in its own creed to call a spade a spade in the vulgar manner of the New Testament'. During the First World War, refusing a commission, he served as a sergeant. In 1916, recovering from wounds after the battle of the Somme, he was visited in hospital by Gore. Gore told the Matron that he had one of the most valuable lives in England under her care. After he had left, she hastened to Tawney's bedside and upbraided him, 'Why ever didn't you tell us you were a gentleman?'[13]

Tawney was drawn into church affairs. He supported his old

friend Temple when in 1917 he launched a campaign for greater self-government for the church. He served on the Archbishop's Fifth Committee on Christianity and Industrial Problems which reported in 1918. He was involved in the inter-denominational Conference on Christian Politics, Economics and Citizenship (COPEC) which Temple chaired in 1924. Its section on 'Industry and Property', of which he was a member, was deeply indebted to his *Acquisitive Society*. He also attended the Conference of the International Missionary Council in 1928 and the Oxford ecumenical Conference on Church, Community and State in 1937. But by then he was becoming fed up with the churches because they prevaricated about capitalism. However, in the latter part of his life he resumed more frequent attendance at church.

Tawney was not happy about the idea of 'Christian Socialism'. Christian values, he believed, were to leaven the political order, but the kingdom of God could not be equated with one particular political system. To blend Christianity and socialism might (he considered) imperil the distinctiveness of each and make it more difficult for the ordinary person ('Henry Dubb' as he called him) to rebel against either or both. 'In the interminable case of *Dubb v. Superior Persons and Co.*, whether Christians, Capitalists or Communists, I am an unrepentant Dubbite.'[14]

He was always suspicious of those who would tidy everyone into a neat utopia, of those who regarded human history 'as a more sober, sedate, respectable, less tragic, sublime, disreputable and desperate, affair than it seems to me'. So he rejected utopianism and a romantic view of politics. The modification of society was 'an arduous business' which takes 'years of dull drudgery . . . the formulation, rejection and re-formulation of provisional solutions' which can be applied to 'the rough-and-tumble of an imperfect world'. Unlike many middle- and upper-class socialists he did not idealize working-class people.

A capitalist combine can practise corporate selfishness, but so can a trade union. If a condition of something approaching full employment were established, both the power and the respon-

sibilities of Organised Labour would be greatly increased. It
might abuse the former and ignore the latter.

He hoped that Christians might agree upon four principles in
social policy: there was a duty to secure the good life for the whole
of the rising generation; class poisons national life; it is harmful
for an excessive power to be wielded by a small number of
people; there must be a new attitude to property – certain major
industries should be publicly owned, but private possessions
should be owned on a larger scale by more people.[15]

Tawney joined the ILP in 1909 and the Labour Party in 1918
and remained a member for the rest of his life. His feet were kept
firmly on the ground through his participation in humdrum political life. Early in the century he was involved in the creation of
Trade Boards which ensured minimum standards in certain
industries. He was a notable member of the Sankey Commission
on the mines (1919) and keenly observed the class prejudices of
some of its members and witnesses. He drafted the 1928 and 1934
Labour Party manifestos and stood for Parliament four times.
Just as his religious allegiance led not only to national and international activities, but also to commitment to his local parish
church, so even at eighty he was discussing the party constitution
with his local ward as well as with Hugh Gaitskell, the then
leader. He preferred to talk of the Labour Movement rather than
the Labour Party as that had a more dynamic ring.

The two World Wars had a profound influence on Tawney. To
him both demonstrated how in a crisis, planning took over from
the market and the nation was bound together by a common purpose. 'What matters to a health of a society is the objective
towards which its face is set . . .' The wars taught him that
society ought not to allow sectional loyalties towards (say) unions
or churches to override the common good. The First World War
proved to him the value of 'Henry Dubb'. He remembered during the battle of the Somme advancing with a comrade who was
suddenly killed: 'the kindest and bravest of friends, whom no
weariness could discourage or danger daunt, a brick-layer by

trade, but one who could turn his hand to anything, the man of whom of all others I would choose to have beside me at a pinch'. In the Second World War not only did he enthusiastically join the Home Guard, but was drawn by Labour, now sharing government, into a political role. Unlike many socialists he rejected pacifism as utopian. In the 1920s when he was in the history faculty at the LSE, he continued to wear his ancient, dirty, torn sergeant's tunic – an example not only of his frugality, but also a parable of the way the war continued to hold him in its grasp with its comradeship. In wartime, Tawney was fascinated to note that the fighting machines were called 'services' and that *'esprit de corps* is the foundation of efficiency'. So when he argued that industry should regard itself as a service and a profession, he pointed out that in an emergency one had to rely on 'the professional zeal of the navy and nothing else'.[16]

What did Tawney mean by socialism? His socialism had definitely British roots. He drew upon William Lovett, the Chartist and his belief in the need for the working class to develop political independence; upon Robert Owen's communal gospel; upon Matthew Arnold's concern for social unity; upon John Ruskin's teaching that the function of the manufacturer is no more to work for profit than a priest's function is to earn his stipend; upon Gore (to whom he dedicated *Religion and the Rise of Capitalism*); and upon Temple. Biblical allusions and quotations are woven into the texture of his writings, which made them less accessible to a later agnostic generation. The humanist Raymond Williams criticized him for cultivating a 'filigree' style in order to woo his opponents. Terrill comments that Tawney's style conveys 'a feeling for the dignity of man, the moral unity of things, the seriousness of man's condition and his relationships, the hollowness of privilege and pomposity'. For Tawney being a socialist was not a simple matter of proclaiming certain political opinions, but meant embodying socialism in an appropriate style of life and language.[17]

He loathed any concentration of power – and therefore all forms of totalitarianism. He proclaimed a very Anglican belief in the dispersal of power. He rejected all forms of paternalism, including socialist paternalism. The socialist society envisaged by ordinary people

> is not a herd of tame, well-nourished animals, with wise keepers in command. It is a community of responsible men and women working without fear for common ends, all of whom can grow to their full stature . . . and since virtue should not be too austere – have their fling when they feel like it.[18]

This is an idiosyncratic blend of Ephesians 4.13–15 and libertarianism. Through the WEA, Tawney was aware that the Labour Party was not only the party of nationalization but also a remarkable apparatus of collective self-help from unions, cooperatives, chapels, pubs, burial clubs to Friendly Societies. Tawney described the ways in which capitalism had broken down the networks and small democracies of local communities. In his early days he was attracted to Guild Socialism. William Morris' vision of self-governing workers caught Tawney's imagination as it did the imaginations of other socialists of that period. But trade unions could become narrow minded, conservative and 'suspicious of innovations which might prejudice the vested interests of their members'.[19] Like Gore, he was sceptical about establishment and regarded the Church of England as an example of the deadening effects of state management. 'How syndicalist management fosters corporate selfishness is shown by the bar and by Oxford and Cambridge.' He cherished groups which nourished fellowship and were microcosms of the more fraternal society which he longed for:

> All decent people are at heart conservatives, in the sense of desiring to conserve the human associations, loyalties, affections, pious bonds between man and man which express a man's personality and become at once a sheltering nest for his spirit and a kind of watch-tower from which he may see visions of a more spacious and bountiful land.[20]

'The silly business of "honours"' was an obstacle to fellowship. Tawney contemptuously refused honours for himself. When MacDonald offered him a peerage in 1933 he replied 'Thank you for your letter. What harm have I ever done to the Labour Party? Yours sincerely. R. H. Tawney.' Honours created the kind of deference he loathed: 'To kick over an idol, you must first get off your knees.' A society in which 2% of the population of Great Britain took nearly one quarter of the natural output of wealth made fellowship impossible. Truly reciprocal relationships could not happen between thoroughly unequal people.[21] Rather, inequality fostered resentment and strife. To make efficiency the main criterion could also militate against fellowship and justice:

> People often argue that the industrial system is justified by its 'efficiency'. But this [is] the shallowest of claptrap. For what is at issue is not whether it is efficient, but whether it is just.

In addition, 'the denial that industry has any end or purpose other than the satisfaction of those engaged in it . . . produces industrial warfare . . . as an inevitable result'. Each group believes it has a right to what it can get, and since income is limited, when one group loses, another gains and there is 'no method other than mutual self-assertion' to determine incomes.

> A well-conducted family does not, when in low water, encourage some of its members to grab all they can, while leaving others to go short. On the contrary, it endeavours to ensure that its diminished resources shall be used to the best advantage in the interests of all. A nation, in so far as it is Christian, will observe the same rule.[22]

Lurking just below many of Tawney's assertions about fellowship, as here, one can discern the influence of I Corinthians 12 so important to Christian Socialists with its image of the body where every part has a function and where the body prospers by mutual inter-dependence and fellowship. This was a theme particularly close to the heart of Gore. But Tawney did not glorify the state. British Socialism, he argued, 'has not deified the state, but, while extending its sphere of action, has continued to see it, not as a master, but as a serviceable drudge'. The test of a policy was whether it served the good of the whole nation. He, like many of his generation, still believed that Christian values were widely accepted. He prized too highly the notion of the common good and a common purpose (which he valued so much in war-time) ever to embrace pluralism. He praised Elizabethan England for being both 'surprisingly homogeneous' and 'loosely knit' and 'decentralized'. He wrote towards the end of *The Acquisitive Society*:

> Such a philosophy implies that society is not an economic mechanism, but a community of wills which are often discordant, but which are capable of being inspired by devotion to common ends. It is, therefore, a religious one, and, if it is true, the proper bodies to propagate it are the Christian Churches.[23]

How did he understand equality? 'The inequality which Tawney denounced was', he considered, 'the product of specifically capitalist social organisation.' He did not advocate equal incomes but believed that differences of income would cease to count if all shared a common education and community: 'diversities must be based, not on the accident of class, income, sex, colour or nationality, but on the real requirements of the different members of the human family'. No society would ever attain complete equality; what mattered was that it should be 'sincerely sought'. What was crucial was that the essentials of life should be paid for by redistributive taxation. He believed that the worst inequalities would disappear if everyone were to be reared in healthy conditions, given a good education up to the age of sixteen, knew that employment lay ahead and that there was protection against the risks of life. 'Differences of remuneration between different individuals might remain; contrasts between the civilisation of different classes would vanish.' Equality meant 'the deliberate acceptance of social restraints on individual expansion . . . freedom for the pike is death for the minnows'. Equality also involved limitations on the absolute rights of private property. Nationalization was only one type of public ownership and was not an end in itself. It could be used, for example, to remove 'the dead hand of private ownership'. He attacked public schools as 'an educational monstrosity and a grave national misfortune' which did more to perpetuate the division of the nation than any other single factor. Fundamental to Tawney was his belief that there was a common humanity created by God, each member of which is of equal worth.

> . . . it is the mark of a civilized society to aim at eliminating such inequalities as have their source, not in individual differences, but in its own organization, and that individual differences, which are a source of social energy, are more likely to ripen and find expression if social inequalities are, as far as practicable, diminished.

In later life he was thankful to see a growth of equality and decline of deference under the 1945 Labour Government. 'At least shopkeepers are less polite', he exclaimed with satisfaction.[24]

In 1949 he defined his hope for society:

> A society which values public welfare above private display; which, though relatively poor, makes the first charge on its small resources the establishment for all of the conditions for a vigorous and self-respecting existence; which gives a high place among those conditions to the activity of the spirit . . . which holds that the most important aspect of human beings is not the external differences of income and circumstance which divide them, but the common humanity which unites them, and which strives, therefore, to reduce such differences to the position of insignificance that rightly belongs to them – such a society may be far from what it should be, but it has, at least, set its face towards the light.[25]

Tawney has inspired much admiration and affection. The 'Thomas More of the twentieth century', Adrian Hastings has called him. (Thomas More is now commemorated in the Calendar of the Church of England. Perhaps Tawney should also be added? It would be instructive for a politician to be included.) Hugh Gaitskell said at the memorial service: 'I think he was the best man I have ever known. The quality of his goodness was such that it never embarrassed you.' Someone said to Archbishop Temple: 'What we need are more men like Tawney.' Temple replied, 'There are no men like Tawney.' R. H. Preston remembered him in Bloomsbury: 'He had an unselfconscious goodness which taught me much about the graces of a Christian character.' Dennis and Halsey have written:

> Through his life and writings, Tawney offered socialists a code of personal conduct which dismisses the acquisitive scramble for money and peerages as vulgar trivialities, set its face against the whole degrading cult of individualistic materialism, and enjoins service and humility as active principles of man's relations to his fellows.[26]

Religion and the Rise of Capitalism had an enormous influence. It was hailed by Gore and other Christian Socialists as historical evidence for the case they had often argued: that the Post-Reformation church, because of its individualistic view of the gospel, had failed the people in their transition to an industrial society.

In the 1960s and 1970s, Tawney's ethical socialism was widely rejected by Marxists and hedonists or removed from its Christian roots. There are elements in Tawney's message which have dated or are difficult or impossible to apply in a global market. A total refusal to be acquisitive would put others out of work. But one cannot re-read *The Acquisitive Society* without realizing that there is a whole strand of ethical socialism which has been lost. In the 1940s it was patriotic to restrain consumerism first to win the war, and then to promote exports after it was over. 'Make-do-and mend' became a way of life. But today warnings against acquisitiveness ('a man's life consisteth not in the abundance of the things which he possesseth' Luke 12.15) have disappeared from not only platforms but also pulpits.

Tawney's interpretation of history has been severely criticized as inaccurate and tendentious. Atherton accused him of misinterpreting the history of Christian thought:

> He did this by overemphasising the value of the mediaeval hegemony of Church and theology over economic life, by rejecting Christian contributions to the growing independence of economics and politics in the eighteenth and early nineteenth centuries.

He failed to come to terms with 'the emergence of disciplines like economics with their high degree of relative autonomy'.[27] Certainly Tawney overestimated the degree to which the churches could influence society. He did not anticipate the growth of pluralism in Britain. It is notable that he was happiest in war-time when the nation shared a common purpose, discipline and ideology. He, like Gore, hoped that the church would renew its effectiveness by rediscovering social Christianity. He continued to assume a residual Christianity in the population. He would have found it impossible to envisage a situation where the Conservative Party would collapse in farce when the Prime Minister, John Major, proclaimed a return to basic moral values, because society could no longer agree what these might be. Though Tawney also appealed to a generalized humanism, it was more dependent on Christian faith than he realized.[28] Much of his writing was an appeal to religious values and authority which, as society became more secular, could ultimately only have meaning for a Christian audience. His style also, particularly in his earlier writing, with its biblical and classical allusions, assumed both Christendom and a certain sophistication.

Martin Wiener accused Tawney of stoking up Christian distaste for commerce and industry. G. R. Elton, the historian, described *Religion and the Rise of Capitalism* as 'one of the most harmful books written in the years between the wars', because it taught that the greatness of the country was based on 'money-grubbing wickedness'. It also (he wrote) 'greatly assisted in the decline of Protestant self-confidence and the consequent revival of Roman Catholicism'. Some recent revisionist histories of social thought, some of them seeking for the Christian roots of the New Right, have challenged both Tawney's history and his admiration of the collective.[29]

Preston argued that Tawney was misled theologically by Gore and overlooked the eschatological background to (for example) the Sermon on the Mount. This Gore believed could simply be adapted to create a new social order. Preston also contended that Gore and Tawney did not realize that the church, faced with a social problem, was part of the problem and not merely the cure. He also criticized Tawney for neglecting the positive role of self-interest and profit. Preston, writing in 1966, cavilled at those who only participate in politics 'if they identify a devil with horns and hoofs to oppose'. He added:

> The recovery of a greater eschatological role in theology . . . has destroyed the utopian element in the socialist case . . . Awareness of this in theological circles is undoubtedly the main reason why the Christian socialist movement has run into the sand.[30]

As Kenneth Leech and others have pointed out, there is a surprising gap in Tawney's account of the world. Despite his colonial upbringing he neglected the Third World and issues of race about which Temple and Oldham were more percipient.[31]

There was also a nostalgic thread in Tawney's thought. Like the Christendom writers he looked back to the mediaeval world when the church laid down the law for society. He shared the Victorian's faith in institutions like the WEA and the Labour Party, and despite caveats, shared much of their belief in the onward march of humanity.

'Casino capitalism pushed back the hope of a society united by the service of its members to the common weal.' So commented Dennis and Halsey on Thatcherism. Leaders of the churches at the time criticized the inherent appeal to consumerism and acquisitiveness in Sunday shopping and the National Lottery. New Labour has accepted both. Dennis and Halsey lament the passing of a tradition of Victorian seriousness of which Tawney was an exemplar:

> Men like Aneurin Bevan, who had spent his time away from work, 'reading everything he could lay his hands on' from the Tredegar Workmen's Library, did not live to see the great working-class libraries of Wales sold to Americans in job lots to make room for snooker tables and one-arm bandits.[32]

Almost saintly in his selflessness, he could have hardly have anticipated (despite premonitions) that degree of myopia and sectarianism which afflicted the unions in the 1970s – and under a Labour government! He underestimated the elements of irrationality, self-sabotage and chaos in human life. Having seen the devastation wrought by unrestrained markets, he did not realize that the market could locate and meet need more quickly and accurately than a command economy. He failed to show how a socialist economy could actually work. What hints he provided about that, were all within a national, not an international, economic system as we have it today. Anthony Wright asks where Henry Dubb is today – and indeed where Mrs Dubb or Ms Dubb might be, the women who are so absent from Tawney's writings.[33]

It is sad, but symptomatic, that Tawney, this great and moving Christian Socialist, is mentioned only in passing by Andrew Thorpe in his *A History of the British Labour Party* (1997). But there are signs that Tawney's moralism is now once more becoming important for the Left. There can certainly be no recovery of Christian Socialism which ignores Tawney.

5

William Temple

William Temple (1881–1944) was born when his father Frederick Temple was Bishop of Exeter. In 1885 Frederick became Bishop of London and in 1897 Archbishop of Canterbury. William's mother, Beatrice Lascelles, unlike his father, was socially well-connected as daughter of a younger son of the Earl of Harewood. Through his mother, William was related to Gore whose sister married a member of the Lascelles family. At Rugby he imbibed the tradition of an inclusive ecclesiology and a concern for society which went back to Thomas Arnold. At Balliol, with his friends Tawney and Beveridge, he learned a social application of Christianity from T. H. Green and Edward Caird, the Master. Temple was also linked to Beveridge and Tawney through Toynbee Hall which he visited. Hastings comments on the life-long friendship between Temple and Tawney:

> Tawney quietly provided Temple with solid meat to undergird his social enthusiasms (though Temple certainly dodged some of it – particularly Tawney's preoccupation with equality); Temple provided Tawney with an immensely valuable link to ecclesiastical leadership.

In 1914 Temple dedicated a book to Gore 'from whom I have learnt more than any other now living of the spirit of Christianity, and to whom more than any other (despite great differences) I owe my degree of apprehension of its truth'. Gore's Liberal Catholicism now joined Idealism as a major influence on Temple.[1]

At Oxford he joined the CSU. Later he became chairman of the Westminster branch and married Frances Anson, its secretary. In 1907 he helped the CSU to mount a Sweated Industries Exhibition at Oxford. Scott Holland taught him about the organic nature of the Catholic faith. Ordained to an Oxford Fellowship in 1908, he did not serve a curacy. He had hardly ever spoken to a member of the working classes, apart from butlers and servants in his father's palaces or Oxford colleges, until he joined the WEA in 1905 through Tawney. For some time he imagined that all workers were like those in the WEA. In 1908 he became president. He went on to be Headmaster of Repton, believing naively that he could reform a public school. After four years he moved on to St James's, Piccadilly, from which he resigned in 1917 to give full-time leadership to the Life and Liberty Movement – 'Gore's crowd' as Henson called it. During the war he was one of the clergy who kept his head and refused to indulge in that vicarious bellicosity common among some clergy who were sensitive about their non-combatant status. But by devoting himself to the campaign for church reform, Temple missed the opportunity to share with men of his age the crucial experience of the war. His *Mens Creatrix* (1917), which acknowledged indebtedness to St John, Plato and Browning, was an oddly Victorian book to appear in the year of Passchendaele. If he had been a chaplain in the trenches it would have benefited the church more than the new system of church government of 1919 which he did so much to inaugurate. Oswin Creighton, son of a former Bishop of London, was one of those perceptive chaplains who were agonized by the gulf between the church and the trenches. In 1918, shortly before he was killed, he described how he had spent one afternoon and evening in drenching rain, helping to load up ambulances with the wounded and dying. 'Then I get a memorandum from Life and Liberty asking what the men are thinking about the self-government of the Church.'[2]

From childhood, Temple had felt a sympathy for the underdog, but his temperamental optimism and philosophic consensualism made him a reformer rather than a revolutionary. In 1908 he wrote in the CSU *Economic Review*: 'The alternative stands before us – Socialism or Heresy', and warned that to ignore Labour would be 'to incur the guilt of final and complete apostasy, of renunciation of Christ, and of blasphemy against the Holy Spirit'. The same year he delivered his socialist message to the Pan-Anglican Congress. He was at the heart of the war-time National Mission, which he emphasized was about corporate not just individual repentance. His appointment as Bishop of Manchester in 1921 was part of a somewhat leftwards shift in the episcopate under the influence of the CSU and the war.[3]

In 1919 Temple began a process of trying to re-educate clergy and laity to accept a social interpretation of Christianity. Commissions were created which produced twelve volumes covering every aspect of society and 200,000 questionnaires were despatched. For example, the Commission which produced the report *Industry and Property* was chaired by Constance Smith and included Tawney, two MPs, five company managers or directors and two trade unionists among its twenty-nine members. The chapter on finance had been drafted by a banker, an accountant, a merchant, a stockbroker and a civil servant. Its recommendations followed the CSU-Tawney-Gore tradition. The process of consultation and study culminated in 1924 in COPEC (Conference on Christian Politics, Economics and Citizenship) held in Birmingham with 1500 delegates under Temple's chairmanship. It was ecumenical, but at the last moment the Roman Catholics withdrew. There were messages from the King, the Prime Minister (MacDonald), Asquith and Baldwin. Temple had condensed his social thought into four principles – freedom, fellowship, service and sacrifice, and explained to the delegates: 'Our aim therefore must be to work out the primary principles of the Gospel into those secondary principles which may make effective guides to action . . .' Here Temple was feeling after what became known as 'middle axioms'. The preparatory work and the conference itself were impressive, but there was lamentably little follow-up. COPEC grew out of the war-time conviction that there must be a new church for a new nation. But by the time of the conference, the Liberals had split, Labour was weak and inexperienced, the Conservatives were growing more hostile towards the unions and unemployment and industrial conflict had returned. The idealism which had urged the classes to work together for a new just order was evaporating. So the large number of COPEC resolutions on the living wage, full employment, shared management of industry, more even distribution of wealth and the supremacy of the motive of service soon began to look empty.[4]

By creating COPEC, Temple by-passed the Church Assembly and the other organs, formed in 1919, which he had worked so hard to bring into being. The attitudes at COPEC represented only a minority of clerical and lay opinion, and even that minority was divided about crucial issues like pacifism and remedies for unemployment. In reality, the churches were controlled by people of a very different hue. For example, the House of Laity of the Church Assembly was basically controlled by the Cecil family and their relatives which ensured Tory hegemony.[5] In 1928 Archbishop Davidson was replaced by Lang who had lost his early social idealism and had become a snob. After he became Archbishop of York in 1908 he never entered a shop again.

The increasing industrial conflict of the 1920s culminating in the General Strike (as we saw in chapter 3) exposed the facile optimism of COPEC and the ICF and their belief that there was an underlying industrial consensus which could be fairly easily uncovered. It was this belief in the possibility of a conflict-free world which fed pacifism and appeasement on the international scene. Temple's role in the rather naive work of the Standing Conference of the Christian Churches on the Coal Dispute and in COPEC were among the factors which made him the dominant figure not only of the Church of England but also of English Christianity by the time he became Archbishop of York in 1929.[6]

Temple was becoming more specific in his social prescriptions. In 1934 he appealed to the government to use any Budget surplus to restore the cuts in unemployment benefit and not to reduce taxation, and to the public to write to their MPs to support this.

The Chancellor, Neville Chamberlain, told Temple that if he had confined himself to expressing 'his strong sense of the suffering and hardship which were being endured . . . he would have had everybody with him'. But he complained that he had made practical suggestions, a further step which he obviously thought illegitimate. He advised MPs to take no notice of any such letters they received.[7] During his time at York his attitude to unemployment changed. At first he was chiefly concerned with the misery it caused and with palliative measures like the creation of clubs. But increasingly he was determined to get to the root of the problem. In 1936 the Pilgrim Trust agreed to finance a thorough investigation (an approach pioneered by the CSU). The result was a 450-page book, *Men Without Work* (1938), prepared by a group of which Temple was chairman, based on evidence from field workers in areas of high unemployment. It was well received in Whitehall and the church gained a better reputation for social and economic competence. The preparations for the international Oxford Conference on Church, Community and State brought Temple into touch with a wider range of Christians. By 1938–39 Temple acknowledged that his social and theological outlook was changing, partly under the impact of the prolonged international crisis, partly influenced by the Oxford Conference which brought Temple, Tawney, J. H. Oldham and Reinhold Niebuhr together. The Conference criticized capitalism for encouraging acquisitiveness, inequalities, irresponsible economic power and for frustrating Christian discipleship.[8]

Niebuhr, the American theologian who so influenced Temple and many others, believed that human beings could deal with their problems if they forsook illusions and took sin seriously. Perfect peace and brotherhood would never be realized this side of the eschaton. Meanwhile man

must content himself with a more modest goal. His concern for some centuries to come is not the creation of an ideal society in which there will be uncoerced and perfect peace and justice, but a society in which there will be enough justice, and in which coercion will be sufficiently non-violent to prevent his common enterprise from issuing into complete disaster.[9]

From 1938, Temple increasingly used neo-orthodox theological language, but as refugee German pastors perceived, Anglican theology (including that of Temple) remained strongly incarnational.[10] Ulrich Simon, of Jewish parentage, fled to England in 1933 where he was baptized, confirmed and ordained into the Church of England. Many of his relations perished in concentration camps. He admired Temple but was also critical: 'Temple was not demonic and did not know experientially the dark side of human nature.'[11] Niebuhr gave Temple a greater awareness of eschatology, but its influence did not go very deep. Temple wrote in 1939 that we should not 'try to "make sense" of everything; we shall openly proclaim that most things as they are have no sense in them at all'. Again he said in 1942 that the world did not exist as a rational whole; it was like a drama in which 'the full meaning of the first scene only becomes apparent with the final curtain'. Niebuhr also convinced him that 'the primary form of Love in social organization is Justice'. He wrote in 1944: 'Our problem is to envisage the task in a largely alien world', but he acted as though Christendom and the Church of England were still powerful realities and could reshape society after the war. Because he trusted that the state would continue to diffuse Christianity through its schools, he failed to press for the maintenance of a large church stake in the schools system. Rather he accepted its diminution. The year he died, he was predicting a post-Christendom church. It is doubtful whether he could have ever accepted such a revolution in his outlook.[12] Temple remains therefore an ambiguous figure. So, for example, despite his neo-orthodox language, he happily articulated the optimistic consensus about post-war society in *Christianity and Social Order* (1942). This was a restatement of his faith in top-down social policy.

In a series of broadcast addresses in 1940 with the significant title 'The Hope of a New World', Temple reiterated the message of the Christendom Group: 'The root of the trouble is that we

have deserted the natural order.' He favoured some state ownership (as with the Post Office), but state management involved
bureaucracy which could become as 'stifling to free personality
as grinding competition', but he supported 'a vast extension of
public control of private enterprise'. He recalled 'the economic
teaching of the Bible' that the purchase of land in perpetuity is
forbidden, for it belongs to God. He rejected land nationalization,
believed that rural landlords had many social functions and
should not be subject to death duties. But (surprisingly) he considered the social function of the urban landlord 'less evident' and
that the shareholder had no social function at all. He proposed the
revival of the Law of Jubilee whereby once every fifty years the
original equal distribution of land would be restored. This could
be achieved by shares repayable by a certain date; invested
capital might lose a proportion of its value each year until extin-
guished; or inheritance might be curtailed by drastic death duties.
(Did Temple think that investment would be supplied through
taxation? How did he imagine that the church could be financed
through such a system?) He supported worker participation in
industrial management and criticized Labour for its reluctance to
accept it.[13]

Early on in the war, Prebendary Kirk, Director of the ICF,
conceived the idea of a conference on post-war reconstruction.
Temple in 1941 declared that the church must be ready with 'its
system of principles' for the vastly transformed society he anticipated.[14] But he still assumed the persistence of establishment and
Christendom. The Malvern Conference of 1941 which resulted
was intended to be a 'grand gesture of faith and hope' at the
height of the war,[15] but was regarded by some participants as a
shambles. Whereas one paper was omitted from the report
because it could not be made 'suitable for publication', Donald
MacKinnon's paper – the only real theological challenge of the
conference – was too dense and idiosyncratic. The conference
was dominated by the traditionalist Christendom Group anxious
to propagate its ideas. The occasion was entirely Anglican,
whereas COPEC had been ecumenical. About four hundred

clergy and laity and fifteen bishops attended.[16] The speakers included Dorothy Sayers, T. S. Eliot, V. A. Demant, Sir Richard Acland and John Middleton Murray. Temple in his chairman's opening address commended 'middle axioms' as a way of connecting ultimate principles with 'the complexities of actual historical situations in which action had to be taken'. He acknowledged that most of the delegates came from one school of thought (i.e. the Christendom Group) because 'there is no single body of thought in the Church of England which is at once so extensive . . . and coherent'. But their attitude of 'dilettante disdain' (Kent) to modern society was very different from Temple's earnest attempts to grapple with it. His approach to social questions was based on Natural Theology. Without it, little could be said. Therefore he rejected the Lutheran separation of the spheres of church and state. 'It is easy to see how Luther prepared the way for Hitler.' He commended Niebuhr because his 'whole mind is possessed by the sense of that aboriginal sin which consists in . . . claiming in effect to be the God of his own world'.[17] MacKinnon rejected scornfully any easy-going Christian social outlook which blessed the status quo by appealing to creation and incarnation. 'The Incarnation is not the disclosing of certain universal cosmical principles . . .' Acland and Kenneth Ingram expounded collectivism. One of the preparatory questions Acland and others asked was:

> As Christians gather round the Communion table, all are equal as brothers and no distinctions are made; but as soon as they leave the church doors they are back in a world riddled with distinctions of every kind. What lies at the root of these distinctions?

Ingram concluded that it was the profit motive which led to chaos and war and proposed that groups of Christian propagandists should evangelize England for the social gospel. 'Their habit would be a pull-over and flannel trousers.' Leslie Hunter, the radical Bishop of Sheffield, proposed greater equality in clergy stipends as a witness against the profit motive.[18] (Roger Lloyd, Canon of Winchester and church historian had argued in 1940 that the 'Socialist revolution' in the state should be paralleled in the church with more or less equal salaries for all clergy, including bishops.)[19] V. A. Demant, the best thinker in the Christendom Group, contended that all problems stemmed from the breakdown of Christendom. The restoration of a Christian style of economy involved 'The Dethronement of Trader Man':

> The future of England both in war and in reconstruction depends upon fostering those pre-capitalist elements in English life which the war has stung into throwing off the hold which the trader spirit has got upon them.

A new reverence for the earth must be recovered, now being devastated by urbanization. Middleton Murray imagined the clergy leading a recolonization of rural areas, to create 'new and healthy tissue . . . to reanimate the social body'.[20]

It was not really a conference at all, but a series of rapidly fired-off papers. Acland's identification of Christianity with collectivism dominated the proceedings. The final statement declared that there were 'stumbling blocks' in society which made it harder for people to live Christian lives. The private ownership of 'the principal industrial resources of the community . . . *may* be such a stumbling block' (my italics). Temple would have preferred 'is' to 'may'. When Temple put his summary of the Conference to the floor, the church historian Alec Vidler retorted: 'I dissent from every word of it.'[21]

Temple afterwards acknowledged that there had been some chaos and that the programme had been too crowded. He celebrated three beneficial social changes between the wars, in penal reform, education and housing, and that the church had been 'solidly behind' them. Malvern (he said) had been different from COPEC: there was more belief that the evils of society arose from deserting the 'ascertainable order for society'; there was more concern for reform of church and worship – we should recover the eucharist as the offering of ourselves and our products; sweating had disappeared; union rights were recognized; but the monetary system had yet to be reformed. COPEC was now forgotten, but Malvern put the church on the map for many people. We needed to be reminded of the great tradition – Maurice, Kingsley, Westcott, Gore and Scott Holland.[22]

R. H. Preston in 1942 questioned the use of Natural Law by Temple and Demant. He accused most of the members of the Christendom Group of an 'ignorance of economics'. More recently Suggate contended that 'the deduction of a Christian sociology from dogma eclipsed empirical factors'; that 'the discipline of economics was treated with disdain or handled with incompetence'; that there was also a 'mismatch' between the ideas of the Christendom Group and what was 'feasible in an industrialized and half-secularised Britain'. Yet literature about the conference sold hugely. Temple followed it up with small day conferences to which he gathered representatives of various professions for dialogue with him, by a series of speeches round the country and by his *Christianity and Social Order* (1942).[23] The campaign opened at the Albert Hall in September 1942 when nearly 9000 people heard Temple, Garbett and Cripps speak. It was extensively reported. The popular *Sunday Pictorial* devoted a whole page to it on 27 September: 'the Church has jumped into the ring and the militant cry of two Archbishops cannot be stifled.' Temple re-asserted the right of the church 'to declare its judgement upon social facts and social movements and to lay down principles which should govern the ordering of society', for human lives were 'social through and through'. The church had to challenge the existing order about 'the broken fellowship of our national life' caused by poverty and unemployment. Profit had its right place, but 'that is not the first place'. He granted that people were not always going to act from motives of public service, but argued that we should 'secure that private interest becomes subservient to the public good', for example about the use of land. If it had been possible to establish property rights in air, then someone would have done it, and 'he would demand of us that we should pay him if we wanted to breathe what he called *his* air'. But no external changes to structures could by themselves produce fellowship. In a collectivized society the lust for power could replace the lust for wealth.[24]

At the Birmingham meeting in the series in November 1942 Temple contended that efficiency was 'immensely important', but in second not first place. Echoing Ruskin and Tawney, he said that the criterion for any economic system was not whether it produced greater output but whether it produced a better type of life and relationships. 'If we begin to think that the pursuit of economic wealth is a reasonable aim for a human being to set before himself as an end, everything will go wrong.' At Leicester in February 1943 he commended planning as the way to secure freedom from 'the irresistible pressure of blind forces'. (What would Temple have made of chaos theory?) He repudiated atomism and praised community. He spoke to the Bank Officers' Guild in February 1943 about usury and the just price. Speculation in foreign currencies should be prohibited because money was a medium of exchange, not a commodity. The concept of the just price rejected the idea that prices should be regulated primarily by supply and demand. He attacked the idea of a world bank which, without a world government, would be answerable to no one; it could produce labour flexibility across the world, but only by 'treating human beings primarily as instruments of production'.[25]

Temple's social thought found its final expression in *Christianity and Social Order*, published as a Penguin Special in 1942. It sold 139,000 copies because, as he said in 1943, 'Everyone is planning the good world which we hope to see when the war is over.'[26] He had consulted both Tawney and Keynes about the text. Despite all his efforts and those of Gore and the CSU tradition to educate Anglicans and the general public in social Christianity, he rightly felt he had to devote over a third of the book to answering the question 'What right has the church to interfere?' This section relied on Tawney's *Religion and the Rise of Capitalism*, which in turn owed much to Gore and Victorian

critics of post-Reformation individualism. The church, he believed, must respond to economic and social issues not only
because it had done so in the past, but because the sufferings of
those in bad conditions should win Christian sympathy; because
the social system created not only the context in which we live but
also expressed our values; because the system was unjust; because
of the church's commission to articulate and bring people back to
the Natural Order. While the church cannot corporately commit
itself to 'any particular policy', it should call its members to act as
Christian citizens. This might lead them (for example) to ask for
their rates to be increased to remedy bad housing, or that a
restoration of cuts in unemployment benefit should take precedence over any reduction in income tax. Temple added blandly:
'It is very seldom that Christianity offers a solution of practical
problems; what it can do is to lift the parties to a level of thought
and feeling at which the problem disappears.'27

In chapter 4, Temple turned to the primary social principles
which the church must announce. The first requirement of any
social system was that it should provide security against murder,
robbery and starvation. Christianity's awareness of original sin
should deliver it from utopianism. Only God known in Christ
could deliver human beings from self-centredness. (Temple's
christocentrism did not fit with his Natural Theology.) Because
human beings were self-centred

a statesman who supposes that a mass of citizens can be
governed without appeal to their self-interest is living in
dreamland and is a public menace. The art of government in
fact is the art of so ordering life that self-interest prompts what
justice demands.28

This was one of the most important lessons he learned from
Niebuhr.

In chapter 5, he drew upon the Anglican pluralist J. N. Figgis
(to be considered in our next chapter). Temple declared that freedom was the goal of politics, that human beings fulfil themselves

through intermediate communities, so the state becomes a community of communities. Showing himself aware of papal teaching, he commended *Rerum Novarum* and *Quadragesimo Anno* for promoting subsidiarity. In chapter 6 he made clear that Natural Law was crucial to his Christian ethics:

> In practice, the Natural Order or Natural Law is discovered partly by observing the generally accepted standards of judgement and partly by consideration of the proper functions of whatever is the subject of enquiry.[29]

Christian tradition also offers other principles: the family as the primary social unit; the sanctity of personality; the principle of fellowship.

He concluded with six objectives for society (1) 'Every child should find itself a member of a family housed with decency and dignity . . .' and (2) 'should have the opportunity of an education till years of maturity . . .' (3) Every citizen should have income adequate to maintain home and family and should (4) have a voice in the conduct of his business or industry and (5) have sufficient leisure with two days of rest in seven and holidays with pay and (6) have liberty of worship, speech etc. But he added that 'there is no hope of establishing a more Christian order except through the labour and sacrifice of those in whom the Spirit of Christ is alive' – again he suddenly and awkwardly switched to evangelism.[30]

Temple had been unsure whether to include the Appendix 'A Suggested Programme' in which he set out political proposals based on the book. Both Keynes and Tawney told him it would make the book more realistic. He felt it important (like Gore) to disavow socialism, adding: 'Socialism is a vague term, and in one sense we are committed to Socialism already', for example in planning. He was realistic about the role of self-interest in society. The art of government is not to devise what would be the best system for saints to work, but 'to secure that the lower motives actually found among men prompt that conduct which the higher motives demand'. So he had specific proposals for advancing towards his six objectives including Regional Commissioners for Housing; family allowances; public works in reserve to counter unemployment; planning agencies; a five-day week; regional devolution; measures to reduce a distinct share-holding class (maximum rate for dividends, withering capital); reform of banking; probable public ownership for urban land. The book ended with one of his evangelistic gestures: 'If we have to choose between making men Christian and making the social order more Christian, we must choose the former.'[31]

It is vital to realize that Temple was not an isolated social prophet, but one who articulated and did much to consolidate the social consensus. Temple was too much an insider, too much a product of powerful institutions in church and state, ever to be a radical prophet against them. When it came to the crunch over bombing policy, he went on trusting government assurances. It was the shy Bishop Bell, not the voluble Temple, who was willing to stand alone and face obloquy by opposing obliteration bombing.[32] Bell was the more distinctly modern figure. While Temple still quoted the Victorian bombast of Browning, Bell commissioned T. S. Eliot to write what became *Murder in the Cathedral*. Paul Addison, in *The Road to 1945* (1977), described the gradual shift from Baldwin's consensus to Attlee's. By the end of the 1930s, a programme of social reform was widely agreed among leaders of opinion, even though the Tory government regarded it as too socialistic. The evacuation of children at the beginning of the war and the bombing dramatically revealed the two halves of the nation to each other. Neville Chamberlain, who had been Minister of Health in the 1920s, wrote after the evacuation that he had never known that some of his fellow countrymen lived in such bad conditions. He pledged himself to help them in future. Labour held key home ministries. The war brought the whole economy under the control of the state. After Dunkirk a leader in *The Times* of 1 July 1940 declared: 'The new order cannot be based on the preservation of privilege, whether be that of a country, of a class, of an individual.' Anglo–Soviet friendship was now patriotic. I remember as a schoolboy in about 1942 listening to a lecture with the whole school by someone from the Ministry of Information. He extolled the virtues of the communist social system for putting public before private interest. The Beveridge Report was almost universally welcomed in 1942. The BBC broadcast details of it in twenty-two languages. The population enjoyed the new type of British films which were now being made which at last depicted the lives of ordinary people sympathetically. The film script of the novel *Love on the Dole* about unemployment had been banned by censors in 1936 because it was thought politically controversial. It was screened for the first time in 1941 and concluded with a pledge by A. V. Alexander, a Labour minister, that unemployment would never return.

On 21 December 1940, *The Times* printed a letter from the two Archbishops, Cardinal Hinsley and the Free Church Moderator supporting the Pope's Five Peace Points and adding five standards from the Oxford Conference on equality, education, the family, work and the resources of the earth. During the war the Balliol triumvirate of Temple, Tawney and Beveridge came into their own. Beveridge broadly agreed with *The Times* letter. Temple chaired the meeting in 1943 when Beveridge expounded his *Report*, and Temple defended it against right-wing critics who wrote to him.[33] It was Temple who had coined the term 'welfare state' in the fourth of his Scott Holland lectures, *Christianity and the State* (1928), which were dedicated to Tawney.

Temple was a Christian Socialist within the CSU tradition. What were the main sources of his political outlook?

The first source was his Christian faith. 'The suffering caused by existing evils makes a claim upon our sympathy which the Christian heart and conscience cannot ignore.' In a sermon in 1919 on the parable of the sheep and the goats (Matt. 25) he said:

Of what avail is it that I glorify [Christ] in his sanctuary or adore him in the Blessed Sacrament, if when I meet him in the street I turn away from him, or if I leave him to languish in the prison? . . . It is Christ who pines when the poor are hungry; Christ who is repulsed when strangers are not welcome . . .

This traditional theme of sacramental socialism was made famous by Bishop Frank Weston in his challenge to the 1923 Anglo-Catholic Congress: 'You cannot claim to worship Jesus in the Tabernacle, if you do not pity Jesus in the slum . . .' Temple, an incarnationalist and immanentist in the *Lux Mundi* tradition, was also quick, especially in his early days, to identify secular movements as expressions of the Spirit.[34]

Second, Temple began as a philosophical idealist and was always a Platonist. Therefore he was always liable to float above the particulars, the conflicts and the contradictions of human life into abstract phraseology, though he later moved towards critical realism and latterly Thomism. But he remained deeply indebted to Green and Hegel. Alan Suggate writes:

> Temple's inheritance gave him a disposition to believe that reality could be rationally comprehended and to take an optimistic view of man and social institutions . . . He assumed that it was possible to decide what was good in various positions and to effect a synthesis; that the interests of the individual and society were capable of harmony.[35]

Niebuhr's influence did not fundamentally alter his cast of mind which was unable (for example) to go down into the pit of despair and tragedy with MacKinnon at Malvern. Niebuhr's theology arose out of the experience of industrial conflict in Detroit. All Temple's ministry was among those at the high tables of life.

Third, Temple was influenced by the social moralism, anti-capitalism and anti-industrialism of Victorian writers like Carlyle and Ruskin, and despite caveats remained ill-at-ease with markets, competition, profit, efficiency, wealth. Competition (he wrote in 1912) 'is simply organized selfishness'. Yet he came to recognize that there was no simple way of translating Christ's teaching and example into political action – hence his consistent rejection of pacifism which, together with his appeal to Natural Law, Hastings regards as his two most prophetic features.[36]

Fourth, he had been influenced by the Christendom Group,

especially by the writings of V. A. Demant – hence the prominent role he gave to it at Malvern. The writings of the Group about Natural Order (a term he preferred to Natural Law) attracted him as the only sure basis on which to ground a critique of society and of government in a context of pluralism. But did Temple, daily surrounded by the inheritance of Christendom, forget how dependent Natural Law is upon Christian faith and its allies? Our much more pluralist and secular society makes an appeal to Natural Law noticeably more difficult.[37]

During the war it was widely believed in church circles (and encouraged by Allied propaganda) that the continental churches were vigorous agents of anti-Nazi resistance.[38] So it seemed obvious that Christianity should be the basis of post-war European society. 'No permanent peace is possible in Europe unless the principles of the Christian religion are made the foundation of national policy and of all social life,' declared Temple and the other religious leaders in their letter to *The Times* of 21 December 1940. It was no use, said *The Times* on 17 February 1940, fighting 'to safeguard religion against attack from without if we allow it to be starved by neglect from within'. 'Christianity as the Basis of Reconstruction' was the title of one of the chapters in George Bell's *Christianity and World Order* (1940): 'Christianity is not just one among many systems of morality or one among a number of religions . . . it is a revelation . . . absolute above all others.' Temple was working hard to create a reformed church with a radical social gospel to promote a united society in England (?Britain) based on a shared faith and values. Schools, he believed, should offer both individual development and a sense of world fellowship: 'There is only one candidate for this double function: it is Christianity.' Thus a radical social policy was to service essentially conservative ends. Temple did not anticipate how pluralist post-war Britain would become.[39]

Temple's concept of 'middle axioms' is one of his most enduring and controversial legacies. He defined them as 'maxims for conduct which mediate between the fundamental principles and the tangle of particular problems'. Obviously Christian leaders who seek to persuade politicians and the public of the validity of a Christian ethic cannot appeal to its theological basis as authority, but must find ways of giving it a wider appeal. They were first put forward by J. H. Oldham at the Oxford Conference. Since Temple, R. H. Preston has been their chief exponent. He writes about the need to seek a consensus of those with relevant experience about the broad moral issues and the general direction of social change. However, the Christian faith transcends 'any particular policies'. Middle axioms 'are not concerned with universal situations but current ones . . . We have to get to grips with the data of our own day . . .'. Alan Suggate agrees that because the churches have been too deductive in their ethics, 'it is best to start from the empirical'. Charles Villa-Vicencio of Cape Town University commends the use of middle axioms to South African Christians as they move from a theology of liberation to one of reconstruction.[40]

On the other hand, Stanley Hauerwas writes of 'the narrative character' of Christian convictions, and Chris Bryant regards axioms as 'too unbending, too static for the Christian Gospel' and points out that Jesus told stories and acted them out. So, he might have added, did the Old Testament. Nathan told King David the story of the ewe lamb. This so deeply engaged him that he unwittingly condemned himself for his own adultery (II Sam. 12). But David and Nathan shared a common faith, a common culture. Duncan Forrester is concerned that the inter-disciplinary approach to ethical issues may leave the theologian as a neutral holder of the ring, awed by the experts. It is in attempting to act out the gospel that we discover what it is.[41]

Reading Temple we become conscious of how much has changed since he died. Yet up to 1979, he embodied the war-time consensus. Edward Heath wrote a commendatory Foreword for a new edition of *Christianity and Social Order* published in 1976, the year after he lost the leadership of the Conservative Party to Margaret Thatcher. The revolutionary changes she made to her party, combined with Tony Blair's equally dramatic changes to Labour, have left Temple's politics remote from both parties.

Though Blair claims Temple as a decisive influence at Oxford, he has rejected significant elements in the Temple tradition, not least its top-down statism. A series of lectures in 1994 on Temple listed other changes since his death: a confident pluralism has developed in which no 'facts' are 'universal and privileged'; both Empire and Soviet systems have disappeared; power has shifted to the markets and the transnationals, not least through globalization; faith in state planning has declined; completely new styles of industrial enterprise ('virtual' companies) have developed. Thus achieving a more just society is now a much more complex process than was realized during and immediately after the war, when unemployment seemed finally to have been vanquished.[42]

Temple's serene and untroubled faith also makes him remote. His detachment could be chilling as when he wrote to a mother who had lost a son in the First World War. He had officiated at his funeral. She had left the grave distressed. He wrote to her that for him a funeral was not a parting. 'I feel that this way of thinking and feeling saves much pain . . .' Vidler remarked, 'Temple does not disturb and shake your mind, baffle and bewilder you, at once repel and draw you, as the great theologians do.' He noted how little there was about the Passion in Temple's writings.[43] John Atherton writes of 'the unwarranted elevation of Temple to a position of unchallenged eminence in British Christian social thought'. He regards Preston's contribution as superior. Frank Field accuses Temple of having damaged the Left by an optimistic view of human nature; of not knowing where power lay; of being a conciliator who wanted to make omlettes without breaking eggs (whereas 'all political strategies end in failure'); of failing to recognize the value of the market. Temple and Christian Socialism had made 'pariahs of practically the whole entrepreneurial class'. From the Right, Corelli Barnett blames Temple and others for persuading Britain to prefer a self-indulgent welfare state to the austerity which would have produced economic recovery. Barnett, like Wiener, pillories churchmen, including Temple, for abetting the decline of the industrial spirit through their distaste for commerce and capitalism.[44]

Yet Temple inspired adulation. G. B. Shaw said: 'To a man of my generation, an Archbishop of Temple's enlightenment was a realized impossibility.' John Kent, in a recent critical re-appraisal, describes him of having made the concept of greater equality more acceptable to the churchgoers and 'created a modern tradition of Anglican interventionism' which has been sustained. His death moved ordinary people in a way the death of no modern Archbishop has done before or since. Two office cleaners boarded a bus. One looked at the paper and said in a shocked voice, '*Our* Archbishop is dead.'[45]

Temple remains the one ecclesiastical leader this century who is mentioned in most secular histories of his period. More insti-tutions and churches are called after him than after any other twentieth-century figure. In the 1980s, when many church lead-ers were at odds with Thatcherism, they looked back to Temple and were heartened and tried to keep alive that vision of the com-mon good which they had learned from him. The reports *Faith in the City* (1985) and *Unemployment and the Future of Work* (1997) were clearly in the CSU-Temple tradition. One thinks of CSU's research projects about social problems and of the group which Temple chaired which produced *Men without Work* in 1938. Some Evangelicals have been uneasy about the deep involvement of Bishop David Sheppard in the production of these two reports of 1985 and 1997 and the political character of his ministry. They believe that a bishop like Sheppard from the evangelical tradition should be primarily concerned with what they term 'evan-gelism'.[46] Both reports, like the tradition from which they came, were too ready to assume that facts and values had only to be stated cogently for them to be accepted by politicians. Both reports went well beyond the statement of middle axioms to detailed practical proposals. Both, like the Christian Socialist tradition, to which they are to some extent indebted, have been criticized for their over-optimistic expectation of the results of state action and their tendency to treat people as wholly depend-ent victims in need of rescue from outside.

In the 1930s and 1940s, despite all the efforts of the CSU, Scott

Holland, Gore and Temple, the Church of England depended on one man – Temple – to articulate Christian attitudes to society. Yet he hardly spoke for the majority of the bishops or the clergy, let alone the laity. But by the 1980s the Church of England could rely on Boards of Social Responsibility at diocesan and national levels to monitor social problems and to act about them. So the characteristic statement of Anglican opinion about society in the 1980s was not a book by the Archbishop of Canterbury, as it had been in 1942, but *Faith in the City*, a report commissioned by him which fed into the decision-making bodies of the church at national and diocesan levels. Boards of Social Responsibility (like their equivalents in other churches) may convince or only reach a minority of churchgoers, but as statutory bodies they have a much greater scope for influence and action than voluntary bodies like the CSU or individuals like Scott Holland. If one person more than any other is responsible for this change, that person is William Temple.

6

The Search for Community

Human beings search for community because they are lonely. Or they look back to some past age when supposedly people lived in harmonious community. Or they look forward passionately to a new society in which God, human beings and the created order will be in harmony with one another. In the nineteenth century the more industrialized and unified Britain became, the more people longed for the supposed beauty and hierarchical stability of the villages, though arcadianism had existed long before industrialism. We have seen how Robert Owen and other benevolent manufacturers, like urban squires, built model villages for their workers. Both clergy and Chartists tried to alleviate rural poverty by providing allotments and small-holdings. A group of Anglicans proposed in mid-century the creation of a number of self-supporting villages, superintended by the church. Though this idea foundered, much of the support transferred to the promotion of the settlement of the Canterbury district in New Zealand under the auspices of the Church of England. Emigration was encouraged by clergy, including some Christian Socialists, partly for economic reasons, but there was always the hope that a new and more just society could be created in a new land.[1] For many Anglicans the village parish represented the pastoral ideal. The evangelical Church Pastoral Aid Society, which raised money for urban clergy, depicted a mediaeval village church on its magazine cover. When in 1836 the Church of England created its first new diocese since the sixteenth century, its cathedral and bishop were situated not in the industrial centres of Leeds or Bradford, but in the ancient market town of Ripon. Though Nonconformity was strongest in the industrial north, it regularly claimed that its purest and most typical expression was to be found in its village chapels.[2]

In the nineteenth and twentieth centuries, there was a widespread growth of associational groups as urban areas became more vast and impersonal. The chapels offered more face-to-face relationships than did the Anglican or Roman churches, but also acted as community centres for those who attended only for chapel anniversaries and Sunday school prize-givings. Some of the new Anglican theological colleges offered an experience of close community life, based on Oxbridge collegiate life and monasticism. Clergy then tried (often unsuccessfully) to reproduce this communal life in their parishes. Anglicans were becoming more associational by the second half of the century. By the 1870s parish priests were beginning to count the committed, to define them as regular communicants and to gather them into groups. The Catholic revival and the Parish Communion movement by the turn of the century were just beginning the slow process of transforming heterogeneous congregations into eucharistic communities.[3] The revival of Religious Orders in mid-century showed the determination of some Anglicans to create counter-cultural communities and to recreate the intense fellowship, shared possessions and corporate worship of Acts. The SSM and CR founded theological colleges at Kelham and Mirfield. Both had a particularly intense communal life. But revealingly, Mirfield whose monks were mostly upper class and whose students included some from the middle classes, produced many more political priests and bishops than Kelham, whose monks and students were more working class.[4]

George Orwell wrote of 'the dream of a just society which seems to haunt the human imagination' which might be called the Kingdom of Heaven, a classless society or a past Golden Age. The nineteenth century has been termed the most utopian century of modern times. Owen not only created New Lanark, he also established in 1824 'New Harmony' in Indiana, an ideal community of shared property and mutual kindness. It soon fell apart. Thomas Hughes, the Christian Socialist, created in Tennessee in 1880 a community for 'gentlemen and ladies', based on Rugby School, for those ready for manual labour and for the rural life which was passing away. It collapsed after a few years. People looked back to Eden, to Plato's *Republic*, to More's *Utopia*. They looked forward with Isaiah to a new order on earth, or with Revelation to a new society after much violent conflict. The socialist society was the nineteenth-century dream of utopia, of reason, justice and progress, inspired by a mixture of Christianity and the Enlightenment. This dream flourished despite the failure of the French Revolution to live up to its ideals. Is it true that 'without the presence of Christianity as a widely-shared system of beliefs, utopia loses its heart'? Or is Christianity fundamentally anti-utopian, as Augustine and Niebuhr contended?[5]

We move on to consider some twentieth-century examples of how individuals and groups interpreted community, and in some cases created community.

The first is the Anglican pluralist John Neville Figgis (1866–1919).[6] He was the son of J. B. Figgis ('Figgis of Brighton'), a leading minister of the Countess of Huntingdon's Connexion. During his time as an undergraduate at St Catharine's College, Cambridge, and later as a lecturer, he was influenced by three contrasting academics. The anti-clerical Professor F. W. Maitland awoke in him a love of the Middle Ages. The Roman Catholic historian Lord Acton pointed him towards a Liberal Catholicism which valued freedom and was suspicious of centralized power. Mandell Creighton, later Bishop of London, drew him to Anglicanism. But like his mother, Figgis suffered from uncertain mental health and at the end of his fourth year he broke down and had to withdraw for a time. He was ordained in the Church of England in 1894. After a curacy he returned to Cambridge, but in 1901 suffered another breakdown. Advised to give up academic work, he took a College living in Dorset where he served for five years. He arrived a semi-agnostic, but was gradually converted by the faith of the people and of his assistant priest and became a Liberal Catholic in the Gore tradition.

It was while seeing one of Shaw's plays that he decided that he should test his vocation to the monastic life with CR at Mirfield. In his writings he often praised Shaw for his attacks on mammon. He wrote to a friend in 1907:

> I am going to Mirfield because I have more and more come to see that if we want people to think we are sincere in Christianity, it is desirable to live so that you . . . appear to *mean* it, i.e. a life of poverty, but I do hope to go on with study, writing.[7]

He also hoped that monastic life would provide the discipline, prayer and communal support he needed for mental stability. He owed more to his Free Church background than has been generally acknowledged: for example, his evident pleasure whenever he stood against the tide; the high value he placed on preaching; his contempt for establishment Anglicanism; his defiant gesture in joining CR. He had a marked distaste for clerical marriage. He said that it was clerical marriage which had helped to make the Church of England so upper middle class.

Gore had founded CR in 1892 to be salt for society and a foretaste of the more disciplined and socially concerned community that he wanted the Church of England to be. Figgis also wanted it to be more intensive and less extensive. CR's life was small scale and intimate – there were only about fifteen brethren at Mirfield when Figgis arrived in 1907 plus two or three novices like Figgis. So it must have reminded Figgis of the intimate character of chapel life. From another angle it seemed to visitors like an Oxbridge High Table incongruously transplanted into the smoky West Riding. CR gave Figgis freedom to pursue his academic interests. Though CR had an episcopal Visitor, and brethren had to be licensed by the Bishop of Wakefield, it was an Order outside the parochial system, and so to the relief of most of the brethren, felt disestablished. Guaranteed by its Rule was that freedom which Acton had taught him to value: 'Nothing shall be finally required of any of the brethren which violates his conscience.' However, minor aspects of the life chafed, especially the constant interruption of the monastic Hours. Out for a walk with a guest he heard the bell for None. 'Let us be late for None,' remarked Figgis, 'but let us not be late for tea.'

Figgis was more fulfilled at Mirfield than he was anywhere else. But in one respect he was disappointed. He had joined CR believing that he would no longer be exploiting people. But he found that every piece of bread he ate and every train he travelled in were part of the economic system he thought he had renounced and left behind. Nor was he delivered from struggles about faith:

> To others faith is the bright serenity of unclouded vision; to me it is the angel of an agony, the boon of daily and hourly conflict.[8]

Five of the six founding members of CR had been members of the CSU. But now a more definite and boisterous type of Christian Socialism was developing in and around CR which identified itself more with the Labour movement and with a more definite socialist programme. In 1906 and 1907, Walter Frere, CR's Superior, and Paul Bull CR organized two conferences between church people and Labour at Mirfield. Keir Hardie was among those who spoke. Frere told the 1906 Conference that CR was 'communistic'. A number of those who attended the 1906 conference, including Frere and Bull, met a month later in Morecambe and created the Church Socialist League (CSL). From early days CR had been denounced by Protestants as romanists. Now they attacked as socialists as well.

In 1907 Figgis arrived at Mirfield at the height of the controversy. He was too detached or too independent to ally himself with either CSU or CSL or any political party. The progressivist view of history taught by many socialists was anathema to Figgis. During the Great War, with a good deal of satisfaction he predicted that the war would destroy the belief in inevitable and automatic progress, pull down the curtain on the Alexandrian age dominated by Westcott, reinstate the atonement as the central truth of Christianity in place of the incarnation and destroy 'the tepid weak tea of respectable choristers' Anglicanism'.[9]

However, his mental health suffered through a series of disasters. The corrected proofs of *Civilisation at the Cross Roads* went down with the *Titanic*. In 1915, on his way to Illinois to lecture on Nietzsche, his ship was tailed by submarines. Sailing again in 1918 to lecture in America, his ship was torpedoed. He escaped in an open boat, but his manuscript on Bossuet on which he had worked for years and other papers went down with the ship. He never recovered and was admitted to a mental hospital where he died in 1919, aged fifty-three.

Figgis throughout his life had a sensitive social conscience and was always something of a 'dissenter'. He grew to believe in a Catholic, corporate and sacramental faith, but he did not become a political agitator nor did he align himself with any political group. Above all he rejected that statism which characterized much socialism, Christian and secular, in favour of Guild Socialism and syndicalism. For Figgis the chief sin, particularly of his time, was avarice, mammon. He accused social reformers of evading that because they had ceased to believe in the Christian doctrine of sin. How many Christians (he asked) thought that they should live a less luxurious life than non-Christians? Yet we had to face the uncomfortable fact that the culture of the few is won through the meanness and avarice of the many. 'Why is civilisation to me so gracious a mistress and to others so hard a stepmother?'[10] He particularly disliked wealthy Christians who treated the church as their preserve, but 'like working men to look round our well-swept cathedrals with all the "nice" people living in the precincts'.[11] Because the unions expressed 'the principle of brotherhood', he regarded them as 'the most thoroughgoing Christian movement of the last century'.[12] Human beings were naturally 'associative' and only developed in society. Yet he believed in the conversion of individuals more than in legislation. 'Jesus came to alter men's wants. The real economic reformer is not the man who alters the laws, but he who changes the wants of a sufficiently large number of people to affect the markets.' 'Neither pure socialism nor absolute individualism finds warrant in the Gospel.'[13]

Figgis was a pioneer of pluralist thought in England. He came to believe that freedom was the goal of political action, that power could corrupt and that it should be dispersed in church as well as state. He therefore regarded the idea of a general will as dangerous. At a time when socialists, Christian and secular, and New Liberals were excitedly discovering the power of the state to better the human lot, Figgis rejected the concept of the sovereign or monist state and any tendency to deify it. Instead he believed it should be a community of communities which reflected both the variety and gregariousness of humanity. He advocated a dispersed authority for the church, as in conciliarism. 'Church authority is a communal fact in which every single member . . . has his part.' Like Gore (and the Free Church tradition) he argued for a disciplined church, even if it meant a smaller body. There was an unresolved conflict in the thought of Figgis and Gore between their desire for a church of the committed and their rejection of what Figgis called the tendency of Puritanism to make religion 'the privilege of the few'.[14]

Thus we have this remarkable spectacle of this Edwardian Anglican monk advocating a neutral state. The church should claim liberty to order its own affairs and to impose its own discipline. But disestablishment was peripheral. What mattered was the recognition that churches have power to develop and are not mere creatures of the state. Above all, Figgis passionately believed that 'Unless we can be the Church of the poor, we had far better cease to be a Church at all.'[15] It was his urgent desire to witness against mammon which took him to Mirfield. He also was a foe of squalor and inequality. The church based on baptism was 'a democracy . . . the commonwealth of God'.[16] In Christ, God shows himself not powerful and majestic but little and humble: 'God in his humiliation . . . changed the world more than all the armies of the emperors.'[17] His belief that power should be dispersed, coupled with his admiration for the rich variety of mediaeval society, led him to reject collectivism and be sympathetic to Guild Socialism. His anti-liberalism and his sense of apocalyptic set him over against much mainstream socialism which depicted history as an escalator leading humanity irresistibly through socialism into light and glory. His anti-liberalism was also evident in his rejection of what he termed 'the infallibility of the modern Western mind';[18] in his unequivocal repudiation of pacifism; in his fervent patriotism; in his expectation of imminent social catastrophe; in his rejection of the incarnationalism and immanentism of *Lux Mundi*. Gore went back to the Fathers, but Figgis looked to the Middle Ages. The atomism he so disliked derived, he thought, from the Reformation and Renaissance. On the other hand the liberal strand in him was evident in his beliefs that the sceptical mind has a role in the church and that the purpose of politics was the production of liberty.

It is regrettable that the least satisfactory aspect of his thinking – his nostalgia for the Middle Ages – should have fed the most adolescent side of Christian Socialism its ruralism, upper-class Arts and Crafts élitism, its unwillingness to get its hands dirty by working through existing political institutions, its lack of contact with working people. Second, we have noted the contradiction between advocating a church open to all, and proposing it should be a disciplined remnant. Third, he assumed that it was possible for Christians and non-Christians to agree on a common view of human society. Did he unconsciously take for granted natural ethics, or Christendom, both of which he explicitly rejected? Did he assume that the values of freedom, tolerance and democracy which upheld his pluralist state would be self-sustaining? But they are not. Was his neutral state thus an illusion? Yet Figgis rejected the idea of the common good. If Figgis had lived to see Stalin and Hitler, would he have maintained his position, which, despite all his talk of cataclysm, Armageddon and human sin, depended upon the continuance of a liberal Christian ethic? However, in 1994, Ian Markham in *Plurality and Christian Ethics* and David Nicholls in *The Pluralist State* both reconstructed a theological basis for pluralism. Nicholls was explicitly indebted to Figgis. Markham did not mention him.

The Guild Socialism to which Figgis pointed began in 1912 and was a creation, not of the workers, but of middle-class intellectuals, inspired by the anti-industrial tradition stemming from Carlyle, Ruskin and Morris. Like Morris they were hostile to the normal political processes. Figgis with his anti-collectivism and his concept of the state as a community of communities was a major inspiration to the Guild Socialists, including Maurice Reckitt and R. H. Tawney in his early days. Ironically for an anti-statist movement, it was through government subsidies that a few local guilds were established in 1920 for local authority housing. The lack of financial discipline created overmanning and other uneconomic features. A change in funding led to the winding up of the Building Guild in 1925. The whole concept, contends S. T. Glass, was unrealistic. Workers' control presupposed a degree of leadership and organization that the unions did not possess. The guilds threatened efficiency and therefore living standards.[19]

Guild Socialism was also influenced by the anti-collectivist writer, Hilaire Belloc, the Roman Catholic, who argued in *The Servile State* (1912) that because capitalism was unstable, the state would intervene and the workers would become slaves. He blamed capitalism on the Reformation. Instead of either capitalism or collectivism, Belloc and Chesterton proposed distributism which accepted the Guild Socialist method of production, but wanted the widest distribution of property. As Chesterton explained: '. . . a man felt happier, more dignified and more like the image of God, when the hat he is wearing is his own hat . . .' Some members of the Distributist League, founded in 1926 with Chesterton as President, believed that *Rerum Novarum* supported distributism. However, bitter disputes broke out as to whether the new society should sanction the use of machinery. Chesterton exulted when the Buckfast Benedictines built their Abbey Church with their own hands. Fr Vincent McNabb, an enthusiastic distributist, arrived at one meeting clad entirely in

home-spun garments. Such élitist games gave Christian
Socialism a bad name. The rich enjoyed buying hand-produced
artefacts, but what the poor wanted was a plentiful supply
of goods at prices they could afford. Belloc's critique of state
power strongly influenced English Roman Catholicism against
collectivism.[20]

By 1913–14 a considerable group in the Church Socialist
League, including Reckitt, Penty, Widdrington, Bull and
Tawney, had become advocates of Guild Socialism. A. J. Penty is
regarded as its originator. He was an Anglican mediaevalist, a
disciple of Ruskin and Morris. His book *The Restoration of the
Gild System* (1906) proposed a return to hand-produced goods
and agriculture. When people were satisfied in their work, society
was healthy. Both Reckitt and Widdrington were opposed to the
Labour Party because of its Fabianism and collectivism. By 1919,
Reckitt believed that Guild Socialism would satisfy the craftsmen
of the Morris school, avoid Belloc's servile state, answer Penty's
fears of industrialism and include elements of French syndicalism, American industrial unionism and Marxist socialism. On the
other hand there were some in the CSL who wished for affiliation
to the Labour Party. Widdrington wanted CSL to develop a
'Christian sociology', a Christian doctrine of society.[21] 'Christian
sociology' became a key concept in conferences between 1919 and
1921 led by Widdrington and Reckitt. At these conferences *The
Return of Christendom* (1922) was planned. Thus the Christendom
Group emerged. It worked through the annual Anglo-Catholic
Summer Schools of Sociology, established in 1925 in response to
Bishop Weston's challenge at the 1923 Anglo-Catholic Congress
to find Jesus in the slum as well as in the tabernacle. They lasted
for thirty years and despite their title were open to all denomin-
ations. The participants were mainly middle class, unlike those at
the summer schools of the [Roman] Catholic Social Guild
(formed 1909), the majority of whom were workers. The split
within the CSL resulted in the creation of the Anglo-Catholic
League of the Kingdom of God (1923) which avoided any references to common ownership or socialism and the Society of

Socialist Christians (1923) which was inter-denominational and affiliated to the Labour Party. Egerton Swann in 1922 defined the three pillars of a Catholic sociology: distributed property, the just price and a guild system. In 1931 V. A. Demant, who became the leading thinker of the Christendom Group and later Professor of Moral and Pastoral Theology at Oxford, offered a more theoretical definition of Christian sociology:

> A Christian Sociology recognizes that there are objective social relationships which are to be judged better or worse from a doctrinal Christian standpoint . . . the Church historically and actually has something to say about the nature of government, the liberty of the person, economic justice and the right distribution of property . . . The key-word of this sociological question for the Christian is *justitia*, which transcends questions of personal attitudes and connotes a 'rightness' in political, economic and other social *relationships themselves* for the Christian faith to proclaim.[22]

The Group became the most influential body of social thinkers in the Church of England between roughly 1920 and 1950. Reckitt influenced the COPEC report in the direction of Guild Socialism. The Group dominated the Malvern Conference. A major report for the Church Assembly on Anglican social attitudes, *The National Church and the Social Order* (1956), was written by Philip Mairet, a long-standing member of the Group.[23]

The Return of Christendom was the first attempt at what Reckitt termed '"autochthonous" sociology, growing from its own Christian roots'. Gore wrote a cautious preface. The contributors had the awesome experience of reading their essays to him one by one before publication. His introduction criticized them for not making clear what kind of economic and industrial reconstruction they proposed. Reckitt asserted that the ills of society arose from the 'decay of the great mediaeval standards of vocation and fraternity', so 'nothing remained to preserve the purpose of society as the glorification of God'. Though we could not go back to the Middle Ages, we could go forward with their ideas. Penty's polemic against industrialism argued that the ideal of the Middle Ages was not the pursuit of riches but the seeking of the kingdom and so were 'not perplexed by the problems of riches and poverty as it perplexes us today'. Agriculture and craftsmanship must replace trade and commerce in public esteem. Workers should be protected by a 'Just and Fixed Price under a system of Guilds covering the whole of society'.[24] The flight of the Group towards mediaevalism is also illustrated by Ruth Kenyon's *Syllabus for Study Circles on Catholicism and Industry* (1928) prepared for that year's Anglo-Catholic Summer School of Sociology. 'In the days of Christendom the Mass was the centre round which the whole of life revolved.' She then quoted a fellow Labour Party and Christendom Group member, Sir Henry Slesser, Solicitor General in the 1924 Labour Government: 'it cannot be denied that *the loss of control over the world* (my italics) which has rendered the modern church so impotent to cope with our increasing individual and social demoralization has definitely dated from the decay of belief in the reality of that adorable mystery.' The Syllabus ends:

> If the Catholic Faith can again *dominate civilisation* [my italics], in what kind of ways will it change the industrial system? If one day the world's workers by hand and by brain send their representatives to a great Mass of Christ the Carpenter in St Peter's at Rome, from what kind of industrial organisations could those workers fitly come?[25]

After the Malvern Conference, members of the Group were mortified when they were told their contributions were not understood. So they published another symposium, *Prospect for Christendom* (1945). The contributors included Charles Smyth and T. S. Eliot, both high Tories. The Group had moved far from socialism. The subtitle 'Essays in Catholic Social Reconstruction' suggested that it was a contribution to post-war life. But it characteristically sailed above actual concrete issues of

1945, such as the bankruptcy of the nation, the Beveridge Report, the 1944 Education Act, how to avoid a return to unemployment, church reform. Instead the same static theme of Natural Order reappears. Reckitt distanced the essayists from those who join 'parties and movements'. Ordinary people hardly appear. When they do, they are handled gingerly with tweezers, as in this passage by Mairet:

> An employer of industrial labour, of long experience and good insight into the minds of workers, tells the present writer that, in his opinion, the dislike of the average man for machine-minding – or shall we say his inability to like it – is so complete that, if it is not cured, it will bring the civilisation of technics to a breakdown.

Human beings, contended Patrick McLaughlin, were suffering a nemesis for their disobedience – soil erosion and famine; the dislocation of relationships – though this is much less pronounced in rural areas which are 'peaceful and harmonious' while urban life 'by its violation of natural laws and rhythms, issues inevitably in competition and strife'. Tom Heron, a Managing Director, idealistically likened work to marriage – it must rest upon 'the basis of mutual attraction and intellectual consent'. Kenyon criticized the profit motive and compared the motivation of factory workers and servicemen, forgetting that servicemen were conscripts and not necessarily filled with altruism. Widdrington's paid what was for a member of the Group an unusually warm tribute to the early Labour movement. Perhaps he remembered his first wife, Enid Stacy. He worried about the Group's rejection of normal political processes:

> Our detachment has carried with it dangers: the danger of becoming academic, and of forgetting that reform is not to be wrought by religious preaching at a long-distance telephone far from the places where things are done. The re-establishment of contacts with the workers must never be absent from our minds . . . [26]

The inauthenticity of the Group is summed up in the character of Maurice Reckitt, its convenor. His father had inherited the firm which made Reckitt's Blue. His mother was happy to enjoy her husband's wealth, but so disliked commerce that she forbade the company to advertise its product in St Leonard's-on-Sea where she lived. Maurice, brought up by her in a precious form of Anglo-Catholicism, was uninterested in the workers. It was the intellectuals who influenced him – G. D. H. Cole, Penty, Chesterton, Belloc, A. R. Orage, Figgis and C. H. Douglas, the creator of the theory of Social Credit. He stayed clear of politicians, and treated all economists as rogues. His father's wealth made it unnecessary for him to have a job. He attended endless meetings interspersed with ballroom dancing and champion croquet. It was typical of his solipsist world that though he enjoyed foreign travel, he refused to learn a word of another language. When he and a friend were discussing 'peasants' – a type of person Reckitt had never met – the friend retorted: 'The trouble with you, Maurice, is that you always look on life through the steam-heated windows of a wagon-lit.' Yet this was the man who thought he knew how to reconstruct British society.[27]

Nevertheless, members of the Group realized earlier than most people the ecological dangers created by pollution, recognized the dangers of centralism and were sceptical about nationalization. Demant believed that capitalism was in decline because economic criteria were given precedence over all others. But socialism was part of the problem, not the solution. The state could never be the source of healing for society. In a rapidly changing society, the Group did not seek for God in change but in a freeze-framed, transcendent and self-selected Catholicism. As Denys Munby charged, they made little attempt to understand how the world functioned. He was a disciple until Preston told him to study economics. John Macmurray, reviewing *The Prospect for Christendom* wrote:

A theology which finds its first principles in an authoritative revelation is committed to a pattern of personal life which is eternally right, and which must be independent of the changes in the functional ordering of human relations brought about by technological advances . . . These writers . . . do not see that a dogmatic theology must frustrate their effort to supply a Christian sociology.

Valerie Pitt at the end of the 1950s lamented to Reckitt that the Group never tackled real situations to see how its principles might work out. It is tragic that a group which was out of contact with working people and political parties, was mesmerized by simple 'solutions' like Social Credit and the rejection of modernity and lacked economic competence should have held sway so long. As Ian Markham remarks: 'Nostalgia for Christendom is understandable, but deeply damaging.'[28]

The formidably erudite John Milbank stands within the tradition of the Group, but stated in *Theology* (September 1988) that he rejected their two-tier model of nature and supernature and their sacralization of power. But he admired their readiness to question certain assumptions, such as absolute state sovereignty. Elsewhere he has written about intermediate groups in the spirit of Figgis and about industry in the spirit of Ruskin. 'The pathos of modern theology is its false humility,' he began *Theology and Social Theory* (1990). 'Once, there was no "secular" . . . Instead there was the single community of Christendom, with its dual aspects of *sacerdotium* and *regnum*.' It ends with a vision of theology as once again queen of sciences.[29] Malcolm Brown commented in *Crucible* (October 1996): 'Its weakness seems to be principally that its relation of Christian ethics to wider society is essentially aggressive – because Christianity is the best way to understand reality. This does not sound promising in a multicultural and non-consensual world.' The impenetrability and privacy of Milbank's language is strange for someone offering political, that is, public theology. Ironically it appears to confirm the post-modernist claim that all truth is private.

What is Roman Catholicism's contribution to the search for community? *The Common Good* (1996), a study prepared by the

Roman Catholic bishops of England and Wales, represented two
new departures. For the first time the bishops were collectively
making a considered political stand. Up to the 1970s they were
studiously a-political, determined to prove themselves loyal
subjects. It is not surprising therefore that, of the three major
Christian traditions in England, it was Roman Catholicism which
gave the most uncritical support to the two World Wars. Second,
the bishops paid warm tribute to the social thought and action of
other Christians including both Kingsley and Temple (§5). Both
Wales, A Moral Society (1996) and *Unemployment and the Future
of Work* (1997) were prepared by ecumenical groups with
Roman Catholic participation. Yet until recently Roman Catholic
social thinking has been formulated in separation from that of
other churches and had been expressed mainly through papal
encyclicals. What do these say about society and community?

Though there are differences between the encyclicals since
Rerum Novarum (1891), ingenious efforts are made to produce a
seamless continuity to enhance respect for the *magisterium*.
Preston discerned 'a movement to the Left'. But this oversimplifies.[30] The complex system of checks and balances within
encyclicals and their opaque style make them capable of being
interpreted quite differently by different groups. So *Rerum
Novarum* was called the 'Workers Charter' because it recognized
trade unions and denounced exploitation of the workers, but it
also declared 'private ownership must be preserved inviolate' and
rejected common ownership (§23). *Centesimus Annus* (1991)
balanced a condemnation of unbridled capitalism with criticism
of the welfare state for leading to 'a loss of human energies and an
inordinate increase of public agencies' (§48). The rejection of
individualism by *Quadragesimo Anno* (1931) and its commend-
ation of the corporate state were seized upon by both fascists and
socialists as supportive of their views. Yet Temple praised it and
Rerum Novarum for presenting society as a community of communities.[31] *Quadragesimo Anno* declared that moderate socialism
was now closer to Christian teachings and took many forms. Yet
it continued the papal caricature of socialism: '"Religious

Socialism", "Christian Socialism" are expressions implying a contradiction in terms. No one can be at the same time a sincere Catholic and a true Socialist' (§III.2b). (But, the ingenious say it all depends by what is meant by 'Socialism'.) In 1991 John Paul II in *Centesimus Annus* denounced socialism as totally suppressive of individuals (§13). Milbank believes the papacy has resisted both socialism and feminism because they challenge patriarchal authority.[32] Interpreting papal teaching is complex because the Roman Catholic Church is always unwilling to admit it has changed its mind. 'What happened before 1891 under Pius IX, and before that, seems to have been banished to a lumber room . . .'[33] Religious freedom, repudiated by the *Syllabus of Errors* (1864) was commended by Vatican II. In 1956, Pius XII rejected conscientious objection, but Vatican II and the recent *Catechism* (2311) sanctioned it. Far from being always 'on the side of the workers' as apologists assert, Roman teachings were used in support of Fascism, which so attracted upper-class English Roman Catholics between the wars. Even during the war, Cardinal Hinsley kept a photograph of General Franco on his desk. *Quadragesimo Anno*'s idea of subsidiarity was used to justify Mussolini's state in which capital and labour joined in self-governing groups under the Fascist party. Yet there have been elements of continuity:

> . . . Leo's reaction against capitalist ideology [in *Rerum Novarum*] which was content to treat labour as a thing, as inert a factor of production as land and capital . . . was a valid insight. It has meant that papal teaching has never accepted the philosophy of capitalism.

Stanley Hauerwas sees Leo and his friend Marx as 'fundamentally conservative radicals challenging . . . the development of industrial capitalism which . . . was destroying any form of community . . .'[34]

Nevertheless the bishops in *The Common Good* felt that they had to explain that when popes condemned socialism, they did not of course mean the Labour Party, but only continental versions. They also hastened to add that papal condemnations of 'unlimited free-market, or laissez-faire, capitalism' did not 'apply indiscriminately to the Conservative Party' (§56).

In recent years Roman Catholic social teaching has become better known, partly through ecumenical cooperation, partly through the debates about the European Union (influenced by Roman Catholics like Jacques Delors), partly as a result of the Roman response to the New Right. In 1996 Archbishop Carey and other Anglican bishops praised their Roman Catholic colleagues for reasserting the concept of the 'common good' in their report.[35]

What elements in Roman Catholic teaching have attracted Christian Socialists?

First, the concept of the common good has attracted the Left. This originated with Aquinas, but is rooted in beliefs about community in the Old Testament, in Romans 13 and in Aristotle's teaching that life is complete only in the *polis*. The term has become familiar in the Church of England through the 1980 eucharistic liturgy; the promotion of the common good is commended in the 'Duties of Church Membership' (1996). *The Common Good* states:

> The common good stands in opposition to the good of rulers or of a ruling (or any other) class. It implies that every individual, no matter how high or low, has a duty to share in promoting the welfare of the community as well as a right to benefit from that welfare . . . The Catholic doctrine of the common good is incompatible with unlimited, free-market, or laissez-faire, capitalism which insists that the distribution of wealth must occur entirely according to the dictates of market forces (§70, §76).

Lord Plant, the Anglican political philosopher in the 1995 Gore Lecture 'Theology and the Common Good' (given prior to the report) stated that the free market was 'a kind of institutional embodiment of the subjectivity of value and individual preference'. But 'we cannot make do without collective moral notions and the market cannot be regarded as a morally free zone'.[36] Tawney regarded belief in the common good, or common weal, as a distinguishing mark of the socialist. John Atherton, once an Anglican socialist, now argues that there cannot be a common good without a shared value system. In any case the concept was too static, too restrictive of choice. The market 'rules out of court once and for all the pursuit of a distinctively Christian society'. In reply, Preston agreed that post-modernism increased scepticism about a common good, but contended that social values could not be left to market forces, but need fostering, not least by the churches. The concept must allow for development and for conflict, because some sentimentally believe that if everyone cooperated the common good would be realized. The 'concept of the common good is fundamental to Christian social theology . . . there should be no question of abandoning it'.[37]

Second, Roman Catholic teaching has attracted Christian Socialists by its criticisms of unrestricted competition, the elevation of profit as a chief motive and the idolatry of the market.

> . . . the proper ordering of economic affairs cannot be left to free competition alone. From this source have proceeded in the past all the errors of the 'Individualistic' school (*Quadragesimo Anno* §II.5).

> A business cannot be considered only as a 'society of capital goods'; it is also a 'society of persons' . . . (*Centesimus Annus* §43).

> . . . economic freedom is only one element of human freedom. When it becomes autonomous, when man is seen more as a producer or consumer of goods than as a subject who produces and consumes in order to live, then economic freedom loses its necessary relationship to the human person and ends up by alienating and oppressing him (*Centesimus Annus* §39).

Socialists who have rejected collectivism but retain a faith in cooperative enterprises or copartnership can feel supported by the doctrine of subsidiarity: 'a community of a higher order should not interfere in the internal life of a community of a lower order, depriving the latter of its functions . . .' (*Centesimus Annus* §48).

Third, papal teaching about social justice attracts socialists – the just wage, the modification of the teaching on the inviolability of private property (in *Populorum Progressio* 1967), the call for a fairer share of wealth within and between nations.[38] *Populorum Progressio* quoted St Ambrose:

> You are not making a gift of your possessions to the poor person. You are handing over to him what is his. For what has been given in common for the use of all, you have arrogated to yourself (§23).

Laborem Exercens (1981) went further than previous teaching in asserting workers' rights: the right to property was subordinated to the right to common use (§14); labour had priority over capital (that is, labour is the efficient cause, capital the mere instrument) (§12); joint ownership of industries should be considered (§14); unions were necessary to protect workers (§20); the right to work was fundamental (§4); strikes were legitimate as a last resort (§20).[39] Roman Catholic teaching has also become more sensitive to 'structures of sin' – environments which predispose people to evil (*Sollicitudo Rei Socialis* 1987 §36). John Paul memorably defined his teaching as 'the need for conversion to one's neighbour, at the level of community as well as the individual' (quoted in *The Common Good* §48).

The opaque Vaticanese in which Roman Catholic social teaching is given, its magisterial tone and its supposed authorship by one man all limit its appeal and accessibility. However, some perceive changes towards a more inductive approach and a greater readiness to listen to others.[40] Roman Catholic teaching on subsidiarity and the common good would be more convincing if the papacy and Vatican themselves put it into practice by devolving power and by listening to the laity. Preston also points out that

. . . there is the usual assumption in papal documents, and often in those from other Churches, that the Church stands in an independent principled position apart from the causes and struggles which divide humanity. There is no recognition that it has a keen nose for its own self-interest as an institution . . .

Elsewhere he also justifiably laments the lack of 'a radical eschatological paradox' in church pronouncements, though this is 'the most distinct strain in Jesus' teaching'. Because the church finds this difficult, it domesticates it.[41]

There is little evidence of dialogue between the Vatican and those who find papal social teaching unacceptable, though *The Common Good* (§4) broke new ground by inviting dialogue with those who found its teaching 'unsatisfactory'. Lord Rees Mogg, a right-wing Roman Catholic, fiercely condemned *Rerum Novarum* for leading to the disastrous corporatism of fascist Spain and Italy and of the European Union. He dismissed *The Common Good* as 'a serious error of episcopal judgment'. Paul Brett, when Director of Social Responsibility in the Chelmsford diocese, feelingly described how a group of Roman Catholic businessmen struggled with *Laborem Exercens*, and were torn between their respect for papal authority and their conviction that to follow it would spell financial ruin.[42]

We now turn to what at first sight might seem the very different world of Scottish Presbyterianism. Yet as we shall see, by the Second World War it had unwittingly converged with aspects of papal social teaching. What kind of community and society did it hope for in the first half of this century?

During the First World War, the assemblies of the Church of Scotland and the United Free Church discussed the Church of England's National Mission. But many Presbyterians disliked its call for corporate repentance. They had become pietistic and individualistic. So when a United Free Church Report of 1917 criticized economic individualism and seemed to favour Christian Socialism, prominent figures were outraged. Tragically, during the 1920s, both Presbyterian churches lost interest in post-war reconstruction.[43] By contrast, significant elements in the Church of England were (as we saw earlier) playing a more than ever active role in social affairs. Many Presbyterians hoped that the new national church created in 1929 would establish a Christian commonwealth in Scotland. John White, the first Moderator, a Tory paternalist, believed that the church should not criticize the state, but relieve poverty and unemployment through charity. The dark side to the push for a Christian commonwealth was an ugly campaign in the 1920s promoted by the General Assembly of the Church of Scotland against Roman Catholic Irish immigrants. In the 1930s some Presbyterian church leaders praised aspects of Nazism. But by the mid-1930s, dissenting voices emerged – including social campaigners like George MacLeod, ministering among the poor, who felt betrayed by the church's failure to support social justice. The leadership was quite prepared to ask the government for legislation against Irish immigration, but said it was not competent to comment on unemployment or the means test.

However, a group of social thinkers including John Baillie, Joseph Oldham and MacLeod, felt impelled by the Oxford Conference and the ecumenical movement to struggle for a new social order and a church transcending nationalism. In 1940, Baillie, who had worked with Niebuhr in New York, became convenor of a Commission to interpret the significance of the war. It rejected the so-called political neutrality of the previous leadership. Reacting against pietism, Baillie had been drawn to Christian Socialism. So the church turned away from the ideal of a Christian commonwealth of parish communities to work out the Christian morality for a pluralist society and a welfare state.

The Commission concluded that this was best done through middle axioms, but unlike Temple it believed that the church as a corporate body should lay down definite policy guidelines.

Oldham believed passionately that the true understanding of Christian faith came only to those who had felt 'the full pressure of the forces that dominate modern society'. Therefore the experiential pole of the middle axiom was as vital as the theological one. The Commission favoured 'an economy controlled for the common good'. Nevertheless public ownership or control was not an end in itself. A collectivist economy was not necessarily more humane than an unregulated one. But the Commission supported measures to reduce extreme inequalities, wanted full educational opportunities for all and a living wage. The work of the Commission fashioned 'a subversive Christian memory of resistance to an idolatrous pre-war status quo in a racist church and means-tested society'. Its vision of a new society was strikingly similar to that of Temple and other Christian Socialists and reflected the shift in the national mood towards a more egalitarian society.[44]

So far in this chapter we have been concerned with theories about community. We conclude with some examples of attempts by Christian Socialists to create community.

Eric Gill (1882–1940) was a prophet and artist craftsman in the tradition of Carlyle, Ruskin and Morris. He both loved and sharply challenged the Catholic tradition. His father was a dissenting minister who later became an Anglican priest, and fathered a large family, whom he called by Victorian names including Maurice, Kingsley and Carlyle. They lived on high ideals and little money. Eric Gill spent much of life looking for the ideal family – what Speaight, one of his biographers, called the 'unanimous society' – yet he could never understand why people were so different from himself.[45] Paradoxically, he thrived on conflict and highly risky relationships. Throughout his life he tried to create what he called 'the cell of good living in the chaos of our world' in order to reintegrate 'bed and board, the small farm and the workshop, the home and the school, earth and heaven'.[46] In 1913 he became a Roman Catholic but remained a dissenter – indeed at that date to convert was an act of dissent. He was convinced of the ugliness of industrialism and the dignity of working with one's hands and regarded himself as a socialist. In 1912, while still an Anglican, he listened attentively to Gore and Chesterton speaking on the social obligations of Christianity, probably at a CSU meeting.

In adult life he moved restlessly from place to place as the focal figure in a succession of art and crafts groups, in search of the perfect community. Often he could not settle, and simply used each place as a base for expeditions. Yet there were times when, despite the sexually anarchic life he led, he realized the integration for which he longed in the context of the daily discipline and worship of the Dominican Third Order to which he belonged. So one visitor, unaware of the intricate sexual relationships and personal conflicts beneath the surface, compared the Gill household with Holbein's picture of St Thomas More and his household. He moved from Fabian socialism to Guild Socialism and distributism. All his three communities were rural retreats from urban living, though he loved small compact cities like Chichester, and regularly visited London.

He, Fr Vincent McNabb, the Dominican, and others believed at the end of the First World War that capitalism was about to collapse. Gill thought that the economic changes which resulted from the Reformation had fractured spirituality. His first community at Ditchling was constituted as the Guild of St Joseph and St Dominic, 'a religious fraternity for those who make things with their hands'. The factory system was inconsistent with Christianity because it robbed the workmen of responsibility. His war memorial for Leeds University depicted Leeds merchants and others who had grown rich through the war being driven out of the temple by Christ. His later pacifism, based on the belief that war grew out of greed, his communism, his support for the Spanish Republicans and his art celebrating the erotic all brought him into conflict with the church. He craved authority, but also needed to defy it. He used to say, 'Thank God, the milk will spill: how could I drink it otherwise?'[47] There was an increasingly wide gap between the public *persona* of the devout Roman Catholic and the private reality. He violently attacked birth control but used contraception in his various affairs. He argued that the only cure for unemployment was the abolition of machinery, but bought a car.

An early champion of the liturgical movement, then hardly known among English Roman Catholics, he believed a central altar was needed to express the common life and was the religious equivalent of common ownership and workers' control. Having served in the First World War, he decided to be a conscientious objector in the Second World War, despite being shaken by Nazi wickedness – he never had much sense of evil. Appropriately enough, this dissenting Catholic was buried in a cemetery next to a Baptist chapel.

Two of his most important legacies were his attempts to develop a religious concept of work and to unite eroticism with Christianity. 'It All Goes Together' was the title of one of his essays; it did not, in practice, for most of his life, but he hoped it would in heaven. He desired to be remembered as a workman – hence his gravestone inscription PRAY FOR ME/ERIC GILL/STONE CARVER. But in the final analysis, despite the attractive aspects of his vision and art, he ran away into a make-believe mediaeval world which had nothing to say to working-class people.

The Presbyterian minister George MacLeod (1895–1991) might seem to have little in common with Gill, but they recognizably belonged to the same generation and shared some similar aspirations.[48] Both came from ecclesiastical families. Gill's grandfather and great-uncle had been Congregationalist missionaries, two of his brothers were Anglican missionaries, a sister was an Anglican nun. All, in their different ways, wanted to change the world. MacLeod's dynasty included six Moderators. MacLeod, unlike Gill, was brought up in comfort. The family dressed for dinner. There was a written menu. George MacLeod remained a Victorian gentleman for the rest of his life. He went to Winchester, was confirmed and imbibed a good deal of Anglicanism. At the time, he reacted to the war with conventional patriotism, became an officer and won the MC. Gill by contrast was exempt until September 1918 when he became a lowly driver for the RAF, because he was busy sculpting the Stations of the Cross for Westminster Cathedral. MacLeod was learning about the great gulf between the world of the men and that of the officers. In 1922 he met Tubby Clayton, the former Anglican chaplain who became his example and mentor. The ideals of Toc H which Clayton had founded in 1919 were to influence Macleod's community. Toc H sought to perpetuate in the postwar world that spirit of comradeship between the classes which (it was said) had characterized the trenches.

As a young minister at St Giles', Edinburgh, MacLeod was confronted by the poverty around. He discovered that the poor were alienated from the church. At St Cuthbert's his liturgical innovations showed Anglican influence. Like Gill he was drawn to Catholicism, though he defined it differently. In 1933, at Govan Parish Church, Glasgow, he was about to break down with overwork, but deliverance came from an unexpected quarter – a Russian Orthodox Easter service in Jerusalem. For the first time he discovered worship and the communal nature of the church. For him conventional pietistic and individualistic Presbyterianism was dead. He returned to tell the bewildered people of Govan that a new society must be born. But before 'how to share' (politics) there had to be the 'will to share' (religion). He proclaimed a return to Knox's Primitive Catholic Church with daily worship, liturgical prayer and frequent communion. He believed that there was a Scottish and Celtic basis for this newly-found Catholicism. Traditional Presbyterians were outraged. Like Gill he moved towards pacifism. Both became myth-makers. Unlike Gill, MacLeod was puritanical about sex and married very late.

MacLeod dated the idea of Iona from a meeting between him, a well-heeled minister and a destitute man, bitter about the hypocrisy of the church. To MacLeod the fact that the rebuilt Abbey was surrounded by community buildings in ruins was a parable of what was wrong with society and the church. He planned to revitalize the Church of Scotland by a brotherhood (wholly male) in which the newly-ordained would serve for the first two or three years of ministry. But first they had to learn what community meant through working together, restoring the community buildings and creating communal and liturgical worship, then almost unknown in Presbyterianism. After that they had to be prepared to minister in teams in difficult areas.

Paradoxically, this new venture by a pacifist received its first substantial donation from an arms manufacturer. Paradoxically, too, MacLeod's military bearing and his commanding manner marked him out as a member of the officer class. He wrote to his initial recruits like a CO to tell them what uniform to wear and what clothes to bring. The day began with a naked swim in the freezing sea. He wanted a society which cherished both the collective and the individual. Critics called the Iona venture 'half-way towards Rome, and half-way towards Moscow'. As a pacifist, MacLeod was banned from the BBC in wartime. After the war, the man who inherited the baronetcy in 1944 wore his old Wykehamist tie and MC with pride and enjoyed welcoming the Royal Family, campaigned with increasing passion against nuclear weapons. He pictured the Holy Spirit as a wild goose, and promoted Presbyterianism as democratic Christianity, but he ran the Community as an autocrat. By the 1950s there were 140 full members and thousands of supporters and his style was becoming less and less acceptable. This Victorian gentleman had little understanding of the sexual and theological revolutions of the 1960s. His socialism was not an ideology, but a gut reaction against injustice and inequality. It was not until 1969 that, despite his opposition, women were allowed to join the Iona Community. In 1967 he resigned as leader and accepted a peerage. The community found it difficult to believe either piece of news.

Unlike Gill's community, Iona has continued and prospered. People come from all over the world for the day or to stay. The Community's administrative centre is in Glasgow, not Iona. But it was to Iona not Glasgow to which 200,000 people travelled in 1997, many of them ironically seeking a romantic, otherworldly version of Celtic Christianity which the Community specifically rejects. In 1996 it had 200 members. They live in many different parts of the world. The Community believes that its first task is 'the building of community in a world marked by division, injustice and isolation'. Its members keep a rule about prayer, the use of time and money, meeting together and work for peace and justice. The rule includes a specific commitment against nuclear weapons.[49] Though not a specifically Christian Socialist community, it arose out of that tradition and continues it. The growth of a strong Labour tradition in recent years in Scotland and the widespread and spirited Scottish resistance to Thatcherism both owe something to the Presbyterian rejection of hierarchy and the Scottish sense of community which Iona draws upon and nourishes. Scottish Labour politicians, including the late John Smith, have come for consultations to Iona.

Yet Iona is still suspect to elements within Presbyterianism (both within and outside the Church of Scotland) for being Romish, Anglophile and socialist. What began as a training scheme for young ministers is now a renewal movement for the whole church; what began as a male, clerical group is now largely lay and includes women. What began as Presbyterian now includes Roman Catholics, Anglicans and Protestants. At the centre of the cloister, rebuilt to facilitate community, is a sculpture representing Mary emerging from a vast heart held up in the beak of a dove and received by a lamb. The sculptor was a Jew. This sculpture focusses the incarnationalism of the Iona tradition, but its readiness to interpret this in inclusive, not exclusive terms. Its erection in 1958 was offensive to some Presbyterians. It had been given by a descendent of Robert Owen, the creator of the New Lanark Community, so that tradition too is now included in Iona. 'Matter matters' MacLeod would say, and often told the story of the boy who threw a stone at a stained glass window depicting the incarnation. It took out the 'e' in 'Highest' so it now read 'Glory to God in the High St'. Yet MacLeod also knew, not least from experiences on Iona, that another realm is intertwined with this, and that this world, though God's, could be very evil.

We now look briefly at four Anglican Religious Orders affected by Christian Socialism.

In March 1892, before the Community of the Resurrection was founded in July, Gore gave the fullest exposition he ever provided of his understanding of the Religious Life. That he gave it in the course of a paper on the vocation of the CSU to a meeting of the CSU reveals how much Gore believed that such communities should be paradigms for society, heralds of social righteousness:

> We should do again what was done in the early monastic movement . . . We should draw together to centres, both in town and country, where men can frankly start afresh and live openly the common life of the first Christians . . . a life of combined labour, according to different gifts, on a strongly developed background of prayer and meditation, and with real community of goods . . .

The church, Gore concluded, had spent too much energy trying to get people to church. Now was the time for the church 'to put social morality, Christian living, in the forefront of its efforts'.[50] In its early years, most of CR were identified with the CSU. Later some brethren, including Frere, second Superior, helped to create the CSL. But after the First World War, most brethren were politically quiescent in England. However CR's extensive work in South Africa and Rhodesia directly or implicitly challenged racism. This challenge was focussed in the 1950s by the overtly political activities of Fr Trevor Huddleston, CR's Provincial in South Africa, an ardent Christian Socialist. A son of the Raj, his social conscience had been stirred by visits to the mission in Camberwell run by Lancing, his public school. He and other brethren had deepened their socialism by attending the Anglo-Catholic Summer Schools of Sociology and by contacts with radical figures such as Fr Basil Jellicoe, the priest and housing pioneer of Somers Town. However, Anglo-Catholicism, which included a tradition of opposition to racial and class divisions, by its sacerdotalism erected a new division in the Body of Christ – that between priests and lay people. So it was several years before CR admitted lay brethren and then for a long time treated them as second class. Despite its Christian Socialist reputation, CR in its early and middle years was too public school and Oxbridge to attract many members from working-class backgrounds.[51]

The Franciscan-type Society of the Divine Compassion was founded in 1894 by a Christian Socialist, the Hon James Adderley, who had been greatly influenced by Gore and Scott Holland. He learned about working-class conditions from living at Oxford House, Bethnal Green, of which he became Head 1884–85, and from the union leader Ben Tillett. Adderley's concept of socialism was corporateness, so after attending Edward VII's Coronation he wrote: 'This is Socialism at last' because he had experienced 'the power and glow of a united nation'. To him the war demonstrated what was possible 'in a united (that is, a socialist) nation'. He supported the formation of the ILP. The initial inspiration of the SDC was not from St Francis but from St Vincent de Paul whom he regarded as a social reformer. As the SDC developed, its members sought to relate St Francis to the twentieth century. The urgent need now was not to beg with the beggars but to work with the workers and to ensure they had work to do. The brothers, based in the East End at Plaistow, ran a printing press and watchmaking business. Their aim was 'to share and sanctify the experiences of the poor, to hallow commercial life and to recognize the dignity of labour'. Fr William devoted himself to the dockers and he and other clergy in 1906 led a group of communicants in a march of 10,000 unemployed men to Hyde Park. They bore banners declaring 'In the name of Christ we claim that all men should have the right to live' and 'God and the Church teach that all should work. We ask for work for those who want it.' The SDC merged with the Society of St Francis in 1952.[52]

Adderley also played a leading part in founding in 1898 a Franciscan sisterhood, the Society of the Incarnation of the Eternal Son. It was led by Mother Gertrude, a member of the CSU, later a keen supporter of the Labour Party and a Liberal

Catholic. The community was committed to the practical expression of the gospel and the study of social questions, and cared for poor boys from workhouses and attempted to share the poverty of those around. The community lasted until 1964. Unlike many other Victorian women's communities then it was not divided into choir and lay sisters, essentially a class distinction. In the All Saints Community, Oxford, when it was proposed in 1925 that lay sisters should also sit in choir, a choir sister described it as 'simply a concession to Socialism'.[53]

The Society of St Paul was founded in Calcutta in 1889 by Fr Charles Hopkins. He had previously been asked to resign as port chaplain in Rangoon after organizing seamen into an embryo trade union. In 1893 he became local president of the National Sailors and Fireman's Union and placed the Brotherhood he had created at its disposal, to the alarm of local church and civil authorities. Eventually the community settled in Alton, Hampshire, from where in blue pilot suit, pectoral cross and peaked cap he sallied forth in 1911 addressing mass meetings of striking sailors and firemen and marched in processions. In 1917 he helped to establish the Naval Maritime Board, a conciliatory body for the mercantile marine. He died in 1922. Over the years the Society evolved into the present Benedictine Order.[54]

Finally, we shall consider three Christian socialist priests who worked to create community in their parishes. Like Gore they believed that the church should be a eucharistic community ready to stand against the status quo, despite the fact that regular communion was not part of working-class Christianity. But they also wanted the church to be a source of community for all who lived in the parish. These two understandings of the church as both social critic and as social cement were not easily reconcilable.

Conrad Noel (1869–1942), vicar of Thaxted, Essex, from 1910 to 1942, was the son of a poet and grandson of an earl.[55] He learned his socialism from the Fathers of the Church while studying for the priesthood at Chichester Theological College, and developed his Arts and Crafts English Catholicism under the influence of Percy Dearmer of the CSU, when Noel was a curate to him at St Mary's, Primrose Hill. Noel was presented to Thaxted by the Countess of Warwick, a former mistress of Edward VII. She had become an ardent socialist, but annoyed the SDF by chartering a special train to take her home from its conference in 1905. She employed 150 staff on her estate and enjoyed an annual income of £30,000 (£1.5m in today's terms). Noel relished her luxurious hospitality when writing his radical *Life of Jesus*. To Thaxted Noel brought much needed drama, colour and fun. He drew Gustav Holst to live in the village and to make music there, he revived Morris Dancing and gave the congregation (especially women) a hitherto unknown degree of participation in the liturgy. Milbank comments: 'The joy of Thaxted was a wise joy. The liturgy and the music and the dancing were as essential to Christian socialism as work amongst the poor . . .'[56] Noel wrote: 'We preach the Christ Who through all His life stressed the value of the common meal, the bread and wine joyously shared among His people, the Mass as the prelude to the New World Order in which all would be justly produced and equally distributed.'[57] Noel called Christ the 'Divine Outlaw', but he believed in expressing Christianity through the medium of the upper-class Arts and Crafts movement. Like many aesthetic socialists he was a mediaevalist, a ruralist and hated industrialism. (Gill fiercely criticized working-class Roman Catholicism for its deplorable taste. On the other hand, Fr Raymond Raynes, CR, who had worked among the poor of the Johannesburg townships, argued that the use of the artistic in religion could alienate ordinary people who were more at ease with the vulgar and homely.) Noel created a remarkably beautiful church and liturgy at Thaxted and a community which attracted as many from outside as inside the parish. But did it attract the farm workers?

Noel's Catholic Crusade (1918) – he broke away from the CSL in 1916 – had at its height less than two hundred members and no political influence. He knew little or nothing about economics, had no coherent understanding of authority (for all his talk of community he was an autocratic individualist) and was only happy as the religious and political rebel free from responsibility. As J. R. Orens pointed out, his millenarianism was 'a political disaster' which undermined the Crusade's credibility and fostered his egocentricity. His 'wishful thinking blinded him to the nightmarish character of the Soviet state'. He had 'the old-fashioned Tory's unhealthy disdain for commerce and contempt for the middle classes'.[58] Thaxted, however, owed more to Maurice, Ruskin, Morris and Dearmer than to Marx. Marx bored him. Thaxted, like Gill's communities, was a holiday from urban Britain. Nor was the nation going to look for spiritual and political guidance to Noel's two favourite saints – John Ball, the fourteenth-century rebel priest, and Noel's highly romanticized version of Thomas Becket.

Two priests influenced by Noel attempted to create (unlike him) an urban Christian Socialism.

The first was John Groser (1890–1966).[59] After war-time service as a chaplain, he became angry in the 1920s when hopes of a new social order were crushed. He believed that the workers felt let down by the church during and after the General Strike. He joined the Catholic Crusade and spent nearly all his ministry in the East End. In the 1920s he was in conflict with the diocesan authorities because of his radicalism. In the General Strike he was beaten by the police. In 1939 he helped to organize rent strikes in Stepney. In the Second World War, when food was short, he smashed open a government food store and fed the hungry. Like Noel he was an exponent of Arts and Crafts. When he was unemployed in 1928–29 he helped to make ends meet with weaving. He taught his parishioners folk songs and country dancing. He encouraged the women and girls of the parish to wear bright headscarves and to get rid of lace curtains and aspidistras. In his parish church he created an open sanctuary with a nave altar to enable more corporate worship and decorated it with fabrics woven by himself. The debt to Morris and the kinship with Gill is obvious. As Master of St Katharine's, Stepney, 1948–62, a settlement and conference centre, he delighted in creating a common life, serving the area and drawing others, including ordinands, to share his religious and social vision. Unlike Noel he believed in consultation. But he considered society to be in a state of war and believed that he should align himself with the victims. He left Noel's Catholic Crusade after he was told to support the Communist not the Labour candidate in the 1930 by-election. He joined the Society of Socialist Christians, which was, unlike the Crusade, inclusive, a good mix of lay and ordained from various churches and which kept its feet on the ground through affiliation with the Labour Party. Groser knew where he was when he was fighting the battles of the 1920s and 1930s. He lost his bearings when in the 1950s the now more affluent workers chose not ethical socialism but consumerism. In 1949 he played the Archbishop in the film version of Eliot's *Murder in the Cathedral*. For Groser, as for Noel, Becket symbolized the need for the church to be prepared to stand against the state.

Alan Ecclestone (1904–92) ministered in industrial parishes in Cumbria and Sheffield.[60] In 1948, disillusioned with Labour, he became an ardent and uncritical member of the Communist Party. He came to Marxism through Morris, the Catholic Crusade and John Macmurray. For Ecclestone, as for Noel and Groser, the heart of his faith was expressed in the eucharist, a paradigm of what society should be. 'Discovering Community' is the title of one of the chapters in his biography. One of the most important ways in which he pursued this was through the weekly Parish Meeting which acted as a forum for all the parishioners. It had as its basic agenda, 'What does it mean to be the church?' This question in his view always had a political dimension. The small self-determining group was not only essential for the life of the church, but for democratic society. The church, he believed, should be a network of revolutionary groups at the heart of society. A German refugee pastor told him that it was the lack of community in the German church which made it easy prey for Hitler. Ecclestone, like other Christian Socialists who were orthodox Christians, described community in trinitarian language. When he left one parish, a parishioner said he had learned that 'The worst of us can be of use'.

Unlike Noel and a lot of other Anglican Catholic Socialists, Ecclestone was not a mediaevalist, nor a nostalgic ruralist. Unlike them, he appreciated the religious and political contribution of the Nonconformist tradition. Like Tawney he was passionately committed to his part-time work as a WEA tutor. One of his favourite quotations was from the Spanish philosopher Miguel de Unamuno, who described his mission as 'to make all men live the life of inquietude and passionate desire, to shatter the faith of men here, there and everywhere . . . for the sake of faith in faith itself'. Ecclestone himself wrote: 'You will need an eye for the vision, and to see beyond what obscures.' Both quotations sum up the impact of this intense, disturbing and inspiring priest. We shall consider him further in the next chapter.

7

Dissenters

Despite all its talk of fellowship and community, the Christian Left has often been rent by divisions. So far we have mainly concentrated upon the mainstream: Holland, Gore, the CSU, Temple, Tawney, the war-time consensus and papal social teaching. But Nonconformity, religious and political, is fissiparous. Many Christian Socialists were Anglo-Catholics or Nonconformists, and therefore religious dissenters, or like MacLeod and Gill were at odds with their own churches. The kaleidoscopic character of the Christian Socialist societies has been well described by P. d'A Jones and Chris Bryant, so it is unnecessary to repeat their catalogue. Christian Socialism, like Labour, has been gravely weakened by division, political immaturity and incompetence.

This chapter describes some of those Christian Socialists who have rejected the liberal reformist type of socialism in favour of more radical alternatives. Some of those we discussed in the last chapter, like Groser, Noel and Gill, could also be classed as 'dissenters' but perhaps their primary concern was for creating community. Elsewhere, I have distinguished between creative and uncreative dissenters. It is easy for groups within churches and political parties to be 'uncreative dissenters – that is people who criticize those in power, but have no experience of exercising power, and often have neither the wish nor the ability to do so. Their natural *attrait* is opposition.' By contrast those who try to exercise 'creative dissent' – different from both the conformist and the uncreative dissenter – try to be true to 'the subversive character of the biblical message' but know 'at first hand what it means to exercise authority and power, what compromises and patient negotiations are necessary to produce change and where the levers of power are situated and how best to use them.' I regard Bishop George Bell as the paradigm of creative dissent in the twentieth century.[1]

The political achievements of Arthur Henderson and Peter Lee illustrate the capacity of the Free Church tradition to exercise a remarkably creative influence on public figures. But aspects of the careers of Margaret Thatcher, Tony Benn and Michael Foot demonstrate its capacity also to have a baleful influence on politics. Both Benn and Foot come from well-known Nonconformist families. Like Margaret Thatcher, Benn's father enjoyed the Nonconformist hymn:

> Dare to be a Daniel,
> Dare to stand alone . . .

Tony Benn has felt most at ease standing alone, but his dissent has often been uncreative and wilful. Mrs Thatcher saw herself as a crusader surrounded by enemies. So, even as Prime Minister, she remained Leader of the Opposition. Michael Foot tells how he was brought up to believe that outside the stockade of Liberalism and Nonconformity were massed the forces of darkness which must be fought to the death.[2] When after many years of enjoyable opposition to his own party, as well as to every other, he attained power as Minister, then as Leader, he had no idea how to handle it.

Some on the Left have spoken eloquently about the brotherhood of all in the one world, but then devised a socialism which could only be practised in a nationalist siege economy. They often shared other delusions: that the workers were always right and always victims; that self-seeking would be cured by structural change; that state benefits were always merited and beneficial; that fundamentally, the Soviet system was morally superior because it was not based upon profit.

Of course there is a place in the dialectic for those who, like Jeremiah and Jesus, stand for the community by standing alone against it. But it is a vocation of great peril. The urge to stand apart can be as much a reflection of temperament as is the urge to identify with the mainstream. Some on the Left have always been tempted to place purity of ideology or theology above the need to exercise power from within the system. Those who accept cabinet posts (or bishoprics) are assumed by the classic dissenter to have abandoned their principles. Some dissenters have little theology of the state, and are, in effect, benevolent anarchists, sustained by an optimistic estimate of human nature. They believe that the qualities and ethics of individual relationships can be translated simply into the large-scale relationships of societies, corporations, nations. Reinhold Niebuhr has been accused of expecting too little from groups. But he was bracingly realistic about the human condition and therefore dismissive of utopianism: 'society is in a perpetual state of war . . . the dream of perpetual peace and brotherhood for human society is one which will never be fully realized'. He was always warning against what has been termed 'the new dawnism', one of the banes of modern politics.[3]

First we shall consider those who have dissented from the mainstream of Christian Socialism as Marxists. Many Christian Socialists, like others on the Left, hailed the Russian Revolution (and particularly the early stages) as an exhilarating event. So Gore, who in 1909 had protested against the repression of constitutional reform in Russia, heralded the March revolution (which overthrew the Tsar and established a provisional government) with 'extraordinary satisfaction'. George Lansbury's *Daily Herald* organized a meeting at the Albert Hall on 31 March to celebrate the events. Socialist clergy, representatives of the arts and academic life, filled the seats behind the platform, while 12,000 crammed the Hall and 5,000 had to be turned away. Lansbury was chairman and speakers included Maude Royden, the Anglican feminist. Clara Butt led the audience in singing a hymn which concluded:

Through the thick darkness Thy kingdom is hastening;
Thou wilt give peace in Thy time, O Lord.[4]

The Left believed that history was an irresistible march from
tyranny to justice, from feudalism to democracy, from hierarchy
to equality. Therefore they had an in-built bias towards the
Soviet system and many (at least at first) followed the Webbs and
Shaw in seeing it as a new civilization, a beacon beckoning the rest
of the world onwards. Charles Raven, Regius Professor of
Divinity at Cambridge, an Anglican modernist priest, pacifist,
socialist, wrote in 1935 that the Soviet system had 'falsified the
predictions of its critics, and has shown a remarkable power
not only to establish a new type of social order, but to inspire its
people with a zest for life'. Joseph Needham, the Cambridge
scientist and polymath, an Anglican Lay Reader and closely
associated with Thaxted, said of Marxism: 'The phoenix of the
Kingdom is rising from the ashes of the Church's failure.'
However, Tawney was not seduced. He did not feel, like many
intellectuals on the Left, alienated from Western society. He did
not think that Stalinism provided an acceptable solution to social
problems. His Christianity provided a doctrine of humanity
which was antagonistic to Marxism.[5]

It is said that Marx was no more a Marxist than Luther was a
Lutheran; that Christianity has also failed to live up to its ideals;
that like Christianity, Marxism is pluralist; that Marx was not
more antagonistic to religion than Kierkegaard. Marx's greatest
value is that, like Freud, he disconcertingly exposed the fact
that things are not what they seem to be on the surface; that
underneath our apparently benevolent actions and unconditioned
theological statements are unsuspected economic and class
motivations. Over against an atomistic view of society which
exaggerated the degree of human freedom, he produced an over-
simple, if necessary corrective: 'It is not the consciousness of men
that determines their existence, but, on the contrary, their social
existence determines their consciousness.'[6] Marx, like the biblical
tradition, condemned the worship of goods and money. Nicholas

Lash in his detailed and sympathetic discussion of Marx nevertheless ultimately came to the conclusion that the concept of
Christian Marxism is incoherent. One reason is that Marxism is
optimistic:

> . . . it is the characteristic weakness of both optimism (the voice
> of comedy) and of despair that, forgetful of the fact that the
> story has not ended, they suppose the future to be 'closed'. In
> other words, both optimism and despair take it upon them-
> selves to provide the unfinished narrative with the ending
> which it has not yet, in fact achieved . . . I have suggested that
> hope consists in the refusal to succumb to either of the twin
> temptations of optimism and despair. Perhaps we could say
> that hope is inherently unstable, precarious . . . optimism, with
> its sights set on the far horizon, is only too often destructive
> of that very freedom whose eventual fulfilment it so con-
> fidently announces . . . Despair surrenders the future;
> optimism sacrifices the present. The precariousness of hope
> arises from its refusal to tolerate either of these destructive
> 'renunciations'.[7]

Dialogue between Christians and Marxists uncovered a shared
biblical heritage, a similar commitment to both the importance of
history and to an eschatological dimension. But can Marx's vision
of the eschaton achieved in history through revolution by the
proletariat be compared with the eschaton as the goal beyond
history brought about by God?

The best known Christian Marxist in the middle part of this
century was Hewlett Johnson (1874–1966), Dean of Canterbury
1931–63.[8] He was well known partly because he was a flamboyant
personality, partly because of the office he occupied (abroad he
was often confused with the Archbishop of Canterbury). The son
of a prosperous Manchester industrialist, he qualified as both
a civil and mechanical engineer. For three and a half years
he worked on the shop floor of an engineering works. There
he was introduced to socialism by two workmates. After reading

theology he was ordained in 1905 to a parish in Altrincham in which, he was horrified to discover, there were two churches, one for the rich, the other for the poor. When later he became vicar, he ran holiday camps for the poor and was beginning to wage war with the Council about their insanitary housing conditions when war broke out. Meanwhile he had learned about Christian Socialism from Donaldson and Noel. In June 1917 he chaired a meeting in Manchester addressed by Bertrand Russell to congratulate the Russian people on their revolution. Appointed Dean of Manchester in 1924, he campaigned for clean air and better housing. He later asserted that because he was appointed by Ramsay MacDonald he had a special responsibility to preach socialism – an oddly Erastian argument. In fact he probably owed his appointment to Temple, whom he regarded as a mere social reformer. Johnson's engineering training gave him a scientific approach to social questions. So he welcomed the car as cleaner than horses whose manure created disease; he preferred electricity to coal because it was cleaner. E. W. Barnes, Bishop of Birmingham and a mathematician, was partly also attracted to socialism because of its promise to plan and distribute resources rationally.[9]

When in 1931 Johnson moved to be Dean of Canterbury, he missed the industrial and commercial world of the North and looked elsewhere for stimulation. This he found in fact-finding tours of China (five months), Russia (three months) and Spain. His book *The Socialist Sixth of the World* (1939) appeared just when Russia had invaded Finland (which he condemned). But it became extremely popular when Russia joined the Allies and even Mrs Churchill was ready to launch the Aid to Russia Fund in 1941 and to visit Russia and Stalin. Johnson explained:

. . . this book . . . attempts to explain in simple non-technical terms a great experiment in a new order of society . . . based on clearly defined principles which are thoroughly understood and gladly accepted . . . co-operation replaces competitive chaos and a Plan succeeds the riot of disorder . . . The community rather than the self-seeking individual stands in the centre of the picture . . . The elimination of the profit-seeking motive makes room for the higher motive of service. The rational organisation of production and distribution of wealth welcomes science as an ally and transfers the emphasis from scarcity to abundance.[10]

Such sentiments, so clearly indebted to Tawney and the Christian Socialist tradition, convinced readers that Russia embodied what most people wanted for post-war Britain. No wonder the book sold well.

It was his visit to Spain in 1937 which woke in him a hatred of Fascism and led him to greater sympathy for the Communist cause. His visit to Russia that year convinced him that Marxism worked and that its results were Christian, whereas the Western economic order was both 'flagrantly unChristian and palpably unscientific'.[11] As an engineer, rationalist and modernist he had been initially fascinated by Mussolini's great railway stations of marble and steel. His proposal to fit an internal porch of plate glass and chromium at Canterbury Cathedral was not approved.

Attitudes to Russia changed dramatically after Hitler's invasion of 1941, and Johnson, through Temple's support, was granted extra petrol coupons to enable him to travel round the country to promote a sympathetic picture of Russia. In 1939 he had praised Stalin as 'a giant among pygmies'. In 1945 he met him and found him 'a kindly geniality'. When the Cold War changed attitudes again, Johnson's continued support of Communism brought him ridicule and hatred, especially when he supported Chinese allegations that the Americans had used germ warfare in the Korean war. Other Communists deserted over Krushchev's speech at the 20th Congress or over the invasion of Hungary, but Johnson's faith remained unshaken. His romantic hyperbole effortlessly soared over disagreeable facts into a cloud of utopian rhetoric. In 1956, the year of the invasion of Hungary, Johnson published sermons about Christianity and Communism which were as naive about the New Testament as about

Communism. The feeding of the 5000 'anticipates Communism'. Jesus cared for universal brotherhood; so does Communism. Jesus like Lenin had faith in the common people. Jesus was rejected by the upper classes. Lenin was 'beset by the armies of nine nations'. Jesus rejected racial barriers; so does Stalin. 'The clash between the egoistic and altruistic instincts has gone' in Russia, he claimed.[12]

As an engineer he was more interested in results than theories, though Edward Norman claims he was 'perceptive' in his handling of Marxist theory and that 'his contribution to removing misunderstandings between Marxism and Christianity was considerable'.[13] His sense of social responsibility, derived from an upper-class and evangelical upbringing, led him to believe that Jesus had identified himself with the depressed classes. Yet he owned shares in the family firm, inherited money from his first wife, held assets in Canada beyond the reach of the taxman and owned several houses. Gollancz charged him with vanity and arrogance. Groser regarded him as 'a Communist stooge who does harm to the cause'. Hastings observes that there was 'a certain intrinsic silliness in the preaching of social revolution by a gaitered cleric from the comfort of a cathedral close'.[14]

Hewlett Johnson never actually joined the Communist Party. Alan Ecclestone (1904–92) did – in 1948.[15] For twenty-one years he and his wife faithfully attended weekly branch meetings which, after a time, were held in the vicarage. Unlike Johnson, Ecclestone devoted himself to ordinary people for nearly forty years in a succession of obscure northern industrial parishes. He was not much known until during his retirement he produced *Yes to God* (1975) which won the Collins Religious Book Prize. Johnson was sometimes away from Canterbury for months on end. Ecclestone served his people with Benedictine-like stability. Johnson was a large man, an unctuous actor with a touch of Dickens' Mr Chadband. Ecclestone was intense, like a tightly-wound spring.

For Ecclestone, a parish outing would never be just fun. It had to be an an educational project which was prepared for months beforehand, with literary and historical studies of the area to be visited. A parish visit to the theatre was preceded by careful study of the play text. As a boy he had won a scholarship to the Newcastle-under-Lyme High School, but his parents had to struggle to find the money for uniform and books, so he worked desperately hard, terrified to fail. 'The sense of being driven remained with him throughout his life, and was partly responsible for the urgency and seriousness which marked everything he did.'[16] His mother transmitted the earnestness of her Nonconformist background. His great-grandfather had been imprisoned as a Chartist. Gentle with his parishioners, he could be withering towards clergy who did not share his intense convictions. To some he seemed a steely Commissar. He bitterly reproached the English, because they did not react with a Kierkegaardian either/or to life and faith. They would never make revolutionaries. A revolution, he wrote, 'means being prepared to be troubled in spirit till the heart is broken, being ready to come broken in heart to the place where the temporal and the eternal meet'. He quoted Péguy: 'To pray that a whole people be spared from falling among the dead souls, the dead peoples, the dead nations'. He urged his readers to ponder the words: 'Try to conceive their intensity, feel their burden of anguish . . .' On the 50th anniversary of the Russian Revolution he celebrated the Soviet Union as 'a great achievement of the human spirit'.[17]

He believed that Marxism would enable Catholic Christianity to achieve a world society. Socialism was about using all resources to bring fulfilment to life. The Party reminded him ruefully of the Church of England – more concerned about doctrine than action or thinking. He stayed on in the Party over Hungary and Czechoslovakia, but seems to have withdrawn towards the end of his life.[18] He used to say that just as Christians stayed in the church, despite its record of persecution and anti-semitism, so it was possible to stay on in the Party, despite it having behaved badly and being trapped in dogma. It was his passion for peace which had drawn him into the Party and he became deeply involved in the Peace Congresses. He was chairman of the

Sheffield Peace Committee. Attlee and Bishop Bell denounced
the Second World Peace Conference held in Sheffield in 1950.
Beginning in 1962 he stood unsuccessfully five times as a
Communist for Sheffield City Council. In 1965 he preached at his
old College, St Catharine's, Cambridge, when I was chaplain. At
High Table I asked him whether he was now a City Councillor.
He told me that he wasn't. The former Master, an old military
man, hearing this, leaned over and commented, 'So glad, padre,
that you don't meddle in politics. Great mistake for padres to
meddle in politics.' Alan smiled wanly, but said nothing.

Stanley Evans (1912–65) trained at Mirfield, which produced a
steady trickle of politically active priests, including John Groser
in England and Ambrose Reeves in South Africa.[19] He served
four London curacies in eleven years and from 1947–52 was in
the wilderness without any church appointment. His left-wing
views did him no good with church authorties, especially his support in 1953 for the Rosenbergs, the Americans executed in 1953
for spying in Russia. When, in 1955, he was instituted to his first
living – Holy Trinity, Dalston – he centred it upon the Parish
Eucharist and Parish Meeting, like Ecclestone. From 1959–61 his
curate was Paul Oestreicher. In origin German-Jewish, he had
been Niemöller's assistant in Germany before ordination, and
became a key figure in East-West relationships, in left wing
groups and CND.

Evans had once denounced Mervyn Stockwood as a Fascist for
criticizing the Soviet Union. In 1960, Stockwood, now Bishop of
Southwark, appointed him Chancellor of the Cathedral and the
first Principal of the Southwark Ordination Course. This, the
first non-residential ordination course in the Church of England,
attempted to build bridges between church and the industrial
world, and to break away from the Oxbridge style of training for
the priesthood.

From the 1940s Evans was a ubiquitous figure in the English
Left; he chaired the British Soviet Friendship Society in
the 1940s, built relationships with the Eastern bloc and was the
moving figure behind the Council of Clergy and Ministers for

Common Ownership which had sprung from the Malvern
Conference. Its chairman had been Bishop Blunt of Bradford, but
he resigned in 1947 because of its uncritical support of the USSR
and was succeeded by Hewlett Johnson. As early as the 1950s,
Evans grasped how crucial was the issue of race. He readily used
progressivist phrases like 'the forward march of man'. The real
division between Christians was between those who believed in
the coming of the kingdom of God on earth and those who did
not.[20]

Evans does not seem to have been a member of the Communist
Party, but he covered the Mindzenty trial for the *Daily Worker*.
He paid a warm tribute to Stalin at a memorial service in 1953.
After the revelations at the 20th Congress his eyes were opened,
and he confessed in 1956 that he had been 'grievously wrong'
about aspects of life in the East:

> however admirable may be the economic and the moral basis of
> a social system – and the Soviet idea of ownership is both eco-
> nomically and morally sound – there is no limit to the mistakes,
> the follies and the crimes which can be perpetrated within it.

In 1962 in a Tawney Lecture on equality, he lamented that at
Labour Party conferences the hotels where the various delegates
stayed indicated their place within the hierarchy and that in
Russia

> with that singleness of purpose which was one of the out-
> standing characteristics of Stalinism, the results of which some
> of us should have noted sooner than we did, the whole concept
> of equality was cast aside as a 'left deviation' and a whole caste
> of VIPs was produced and equality went overboard . . . [21]

Roman Catholics made little direct contribution to Christian
Socialism until the 1960s and 1970s, largely because of the con-
tinuing suspicion of socialism engendered by papal encyclicals.
But John XXIII in *Pacem in Terris* (1963) and the Second Vatican

Council encouraged Roman Catholics to have a less embattled
attitude to the world, including the Communist countries. In
December 1958 a group of young radical Roman Catholics began
meeting under Dominican auspices. One result was that from
1964 a magazine called *Slant* appeared, committed to 'socialist
revolution, not just as one aspect of Christian engagement . . . but
as the central perspective within which the revolutionary message
of the gospel can find articulation in our time'.[22] *Slant* criticized
the papal social encyclicals for failing to tackle the evils created by
capitalism.[23]

The most influential product of the Slant group was *The New
Left Church* (1966) by Terry Eagleton, the result of an interaction
between Leavisite cultural concerns and Catholicism and
Marxism. To show how fragmented English society was,
Eagleton paraded Carlyle, Ruskin, Dickens, Morris, Leavis and
Raymond Williams. Intense and pretentious, the book reads like
an undergraduate essay. He argued that Christian vulnerability
was essential: 'Lawrence understood this – how, to possess new
life, you have to venture into the unknown, you have to lay yourself open to be wounded, as Connie Chatterley does.' There follows a very Lawrentian and male-centred description of sexual
intercourse. Eagleton claimed that the immanent Christ was central to Christian Socialism: 'Whenever two or three are gathered
together, in a pub or discussion group or works committee, Christ
is the ground of their communication, the living principle of their
community.' The book began with a call to 'intensity', to live as
'potential martyrs', to be ruthless, all illustrated with references
to Golding, Greene and Eliot. But it ended more tentatively.
'The Christian has to make some sort of commitment . . .' But to
what? To radicalism 'prepared to use almost any kind of weapon
to bring about justice' or to liberal reformism? The Christian
society 'already exists in the liturgical community'.[24]

Adrian Hastings christened them 'intellectual Beatles' who like
the Distributists were 'almost entirely theoretical in approach;
and 'made no attempt to inter-act with any real centre of power'.
Nor did *Slant* have any roots among the workers. The last issue

of *Slant* appeared in 1970. That year Eagleton declared: 'The priest is best understood as a revolutionary leader on the Leninist model.' As Hastings remarks, much more important and more effective were CAFOD founded in 1961 and the Catholic Institute for International Relations established in 1965.[25]

Until only a few years ago, the Eastern bloc seemed immutable. In 1980 John Kent thought it likely that political Marxism was going to predominate globally in thirty years time. Irene Brennan in 1983 pointed to the fact that a third of the human race was under Marxist rule as a sign of its dynamism.[26] In 1990, Alan Booth, former Director of Christian Aid, wrote about the significance of the collapse of the Berlin Wall and of the Eastern European regimes in 1989 and the end of Communist rule in Russia in 1991.

So much has the general world view of the last hundred years been coloured and influenced by Karl Marx's understanding of history that only now are we beginning to realize that we have come to the end of a whole age. Lots of people who find that prospect daunting will try to persuade themselves that what has failed is an aberration called Stalinism, that Marxism refreshed by *perestroika* can make a new start . . . But in reality it is the very foundations of the Marxist analysis that have given way. The belief that human rationality could uncover the inner con-tradictions of our economic and social systems, and replace them with an alternative that would release for all humankind the potential harvest of modern science and productive processes was a heady dream that supplied the dynamics of the communist revolutions . . . In 1989 it had become manifestly a nonsense, when queues for basic necessities were endemic throughout Eastern Europe . . .

But Booth contended that the 'illusions of Marxism' have pene-trated deeply into human consciousness – so, for example, Jacques Delors asserted that to fail to accept European federalism would be 'missing the tide of history' as though we could foretell its direction. The 'key issue is that the death of Marxism leaves an enormous hole in Europe's understanding of itself. In falling it has brought down with it much of the structures of thought to which we had grown accustomed since the time of the French Revolution.'[27] By 1998, John Gray was arguing that the collapse of Communism had enabled the creation of a truly global capitalism and the retreat of social democracy and managed capitalism. The world was now experiencing a more volatile and predatory type of capitalism which created instability and unemployment, thus giving Marx's analysis of capitalism a new lease of life.[28]

It is important to remember those fellow-travelling intellectuals who did so much to soften attitudes to Communism, like the Webbs, Shaw and even Kingsley Martin. In 1889 Webb wrote that 'the perfect and fitting development of each individual is not necessarily the utmost and highest cultivation of his own personality, but the filling . . . of his humble function in the great social machine'.[29] John Torode indicts them:

> These, remember, were the people who in pre-War years claimed that Stalin's famine, which killed several million peasants as an act of policy during forced collectivisation, was a natural disaster. They reported that the purge trials of the late Thirties had been impeccably conducted . . . Part of the intense emotional appeal that communism retained to an astonishingly recent period can be explained if one accepts it as a millennial cult disguised as the ultimate scientific philosophy . . . Quasi-religious certainty in such a context provides a vehicle for guilt as well as a licence for dishonesty and inhumanity on a grand scale. Marxism combined elements of Predestination with the spirit of the Inquisition.[30]

It was not simply the poverty of the people of Eastern Europe revealed in 1989 which shook the Left. It was also the degradation of all life through pollution from ancient and inefficient industrial plants. Yet apologists had often argued that though the people in Communist countries were poorer, because industry was for service, not profit, it cared for workers and environment. Then came Chernobyl. Nor will Orlando Figes in *A People's Tragedy, the Russian Revolution 1891–1924* (1997) allow us to explain it away by treating the Russians as victims of first the Tsars, then incompetent politicians, then Lenin and Stalin. It was the Russian people (Figes contends) who fervently created anti-Jewish pogroms, committed atrocities, enthusiastically participated in the Red Terror and during the famine of the 1930s even ate their own children.

The collapse of Communism has also undermined the claims of liberation theology, though the term includes a wide spectrum of attitudes. Archbishop Tutu has been described as an advocate of liberation theology, but he draws more on Moses and Jesus than on Marx. It has been said that Marxism enables abstractions like salvation and love to be made concrete; that religion provides the poetry which stimulates the imagination in ways beyond Marxism.[31] Preston writes:

> This assertion that Marxism is the science of society, unearthing general laws of social change, seems always to be assumed as obvious and not argued. It has in fact to be seriously questioned. In practice the liberation theologians take what they want in a very broad way from Marxism to give them confidence in action with the poor, often partially demythologizing it.

Preston concludes:

> In detail I do not think liberation theology can be of much help to us. What is important about it is that in its analysis it not only stresses commitment to the poor, but it raises critical questions about the church itself . . . how far is the church herself part of the structures of oppression?

He praises liberation theology for inspiring basic communities.[32]

The implosion of Communist Societies and the espousal of the market economies by social democratic parties suggest that there will be no simple return to planning and nationalization. On the other hand, human beings, not least those exposed to the visionary qualities of Christianity, are unlikely to give up dreaming of a more equal, fairer, less acquisitive and more cooperative type of society. David McLellan offers the two Marxist insights: that there can be no common good when a minority own the levers of society and operate them to their own advantage; that human material progress has been made through the 'largely unrecorded and invisible labour of individual men and women'.[33]

We turn to some of those 'dissenters' among Christian Socialists who are not Marxists.

Until recently, Donald Soper (1903–) has been the best known Methodist and possibly the best known Christian in Britain.[34] By the 1970s he had become a legend, like Bernard Shaw or Malcolm Muggeridge, a character, a rebel of the kind the British enjoy domesticating and neutralizing.

Since 1927, first at Tower Hill, then at Speakers' Corner, he has fielded a quarter of a million questions in his weekly dialogues with the crowd, and he continued this into his nineties, despite severe arthritis. Since the 1930s he has readily commented in a pithy style to the media on almost any subject. 'The man talks in quotes' exclaimed a delighted journalist. Soper's style was shaped by the needs of the platform and the pulpit, in that order. He revels in controversy, and gives an almost obsessive attention to the media – an example of what Michael Ramsey called the tyranny of the contemporary. He criticized the Duke of Edinburgh for playing polo on Sundays, campaigned against prison conditions, advocated voluntary euthanasia, vegetarianism, and teetotalism, marched against war, nuclear weapons and anti-semitism. He has been a restless matador, always on the look-out for a bull. The twentieth-century figure he most resembles is George MacLeod.

Sometimes his throw-away remarks have been foolish, as when he justifiably aroused the wrath of the Anglican Tory Lord

Hailsham in 1955 for saying that Conservatism had 'no philosophy of life as is demanded by Christianity' and that socialism
was 'the political framework of the Gospel of Jesus'. In 1957 he
welcomed a more understanding attitude to homosexuality, but
added that 'a disarmed world would be a world in which homosexuality would die out'. He also stated that the holocaust was
'the result of going to save the Jews . . . if you employ violence
. . . you may in fact increase it'. No wonder Ulrich Simon, the
German Jewish refugee, many of whose relations died in the
camps, found Soper's account of the world totally incomprehensible. After a visit to Russia in 1954 with a Christian group, Soper
said that he had not discovered a Christian dissatisfied with the
regime, and that labour camps were little different from any other
prisons.[35]

On the frontier, in the open air, he discovered that people were
not interested in the authors he had studied at theological college.
Surveying the first few years of his open-air ministry, he concluded that half the questions were about the disparity between
the life of Jesus and the style and concerns of the church, its blessing of battleships, its wealth and failure to tackle social problems
like poverty and unemployment. Yet his audience would be
hardly representative of the population and would include a high
proportion of axe-grinders and the disgruntled. Were they
genuine accusations or excuses and alibis passed down the generations? Soper continued to condemn those prominent features of
working-class life – drink and gambling. He even refused sherry
trifle and ticked his staff off when they went to a pub for their
lunch. Despite his readiness to censure anything from Picasso to
the Beatles, he came over as one who enjoyed life.

Increasingly he drew upon an inner devotional discipline,
drawn from Catholic tradition; his natty bow ties were replaced
by a cassock, he came to value silence, retreats, the Good Friday
Three Hours Devotion and even the rosary. The eucharist is
central for Soper, but its significance is more transcendent than
political: 'When I stretch out my hands to receive the bread and
when I lift up the cup to my lips I testify to the life which goes

beyond the world of sense and time; that world where alone is peace and justice and love.'[36] All that would be of little interest to the general public who judge Soper by his fruits. Soper quotes a favourite text of Christian Socialists: 'He that doeth the will, shall know of the Gospel.' The word he proclaimed became flesh in the admirable variety of social welfare schemes at his West London Mission – prison work, hostels, clothing and meals for the needy. One Christmas morning Soper gave breakfast to 1000 children. The Mission had been founded in 1887 by Hugh Price Hughes, the Methodist Christian Socialist, as a direct response to *The Bitter Cry of Outcast London*. All this was admirable social work in the Victorian tradition, but hardly reform, let alone revolution. Working people responded to his pastoral warmth and Cockney humour, but his efforts to encourage them to be regular worshippers were largely unsuccessful.

The leading figures in the Labour Party to whom he has been closest have largely been those like Foot and Benn, who are most fulfilled in opposition. Soper was an ardent Bevanite. He said in 1965:

> The foundation of my Socialist belief is that I regard Socialism as the economic and political expression, in time, of what I believe to be the Kingdom of God . . . I am very well aware that there is much more in Christianity than in Socialism. But for me, Socialism is the extension of the teaching of our Lord . . . For me, Clause 4 expresses, within the framework of a contemporary economic situation, what I believe to be the ultimate principle that emerges from our Lord's teaching, that this world ought to be conceived as a home, the goods of the world ought to be set on a family table . . . and what they need should not be provided for them according to their ability to pay for it, but because it belongs to them.[37]

Soper distrusted Gaitskell, Healey and Kinnock but was close to Wilson, who with his wife came from Congregationalist stock. He is deeply concerned that New Labour is 'canoodling with

capitalism'. 'A Labour Party which is not Socialist is a contradiction in terms, and more or less a waste of time.' He continues to
believe in 'the practicability of the Kingdom of God on earth'.[38]

He was brought up in a conventional Nonconformist home in
the aftermath of Boer war jingoism and the hyper-patriotism of
the First World War, but several experiences in the 1920s altered
his outlook: he was a delegate to COPEC; a visit to a factory converted him to socialism; he sided with the strikers in the General
Strike; as a young pastor he encountered real poverty; at his first
Tower Hill meeting he was floored when he was asked about
Marx, so he went away and studied him. He does not appear to
have been influenced by Carlyle, Ruskin and Morris. Tawney's
Religion and the Rise of Capitalism had a tremendous effect on
him. Tawney's rejection of the acquisitive society appealed to
Soper: 'Enlightened self-interest, theologically, is only a bap-
tismal word for selfishness . . . people's lives consisteth not in the
abundance of the things that they possess . . .'[39]

Though increasingly Catholic in forms of devotion, theologically he has remained a Liberal Protestant. He is highly
selective about the Bible – he has little time for much of the Old
Testament; the Song of Songs is 'wholly irrelevant' to Christ;
Jesus is central; he hardly mentions St Paul or Revelation.
Essentially a man of the Enlightenment, he trusts 'in the power of
reason to discover truth by enquiry, dedication and testing. For
him the world is basically a reasonable place.'[40] Many of his political misjudgments (and his absolutist pacifism) have arisen out of
an optimistic view of human nature and a progressivist view of
history. He believes that the kingdom of God can be secured by
political action. From 1964 he was a Labour Alderman (if rebel-
lious). His acceptance in 1965 of a peerage disappointed purists.
In 1960, he played an important role in the creation of the inter-
denominational Christian Socialist Movement (CSM) out of the
Socialist Christian League and the Society of Socialist Clergy and
Ministers. He became its first chairman. Anglo-Catholics were
suspicious of Soper because of his puritanism. Tawney was on
the platform at the launch and John Groser, Stanley Evans and

Tom Driberg spoke. In the 1960s and 1970s, public ownership was central for CSM. It affiliated to the Labour Party in 1986 to influence it from within. Its members voted to change Clause 4 in 1995.[41]

Soper has always been at ease with the establishment. He sent his children to public schools, has lived in Hampstead Garden Suburb for most of his ministry, enjoys the House of Lords and when the Queen asked him to bring his wellingtons to Sandringham, he happily obliged. A columnist wrote perceptively in 1992:

> There is in Soper's life so much of an England that is lost or half-forgotten. Joseph Rank's Methodist Central Halls, outdoor meetings, pacifism, ethical socialism, passionate discussion of issues, working men's missions, and a belief in the perfectibility of men in society.[42]

He remains, as one might expect, entirely untouched by the psychotherapeutic revolution. Is he one of those figures which society needs, 'who bear for it its hopes and aspirations which in its better moments it yearns to accept, whilst remaining ambivalent about the consequences of their implementation'?[43] Does Soper by bestowing divine blessings upon ideological factionalism and optimistic utopianism, share responsibility for keeping the Labour Party anachronistic and on the margins for so long? Maybe he will be remembered not as a politician but as a winning, courageous and vibrant personality?

John Vincent (1929–) Director of the Sheffield Urban Theology Unit 1969–97, also a Methodist minister, was in his early days much influenced by Soper.[44] Vincent also focusses on Christ of the Synoptic Gospels (for Vincent especially St Mark) to the exclusion of much of the rest of the Bible and tradition. He is also eucharistic. Though less identified with the Labour Party than Soper, like him he stands within an older tradition of Christian Socialism. Like Soper he is an ardent peace campaigner, but unlike Soper not a dogmatic pacifist. Like Soper and MacLeod,

Vincent coins memorable aphorisms. Unlike Soper, he is a New Testament scholar. He has lived in an inner city community for much of his ministry, whereas Soper separated where he lived from where he ministered.

The models for Vincent's Urban Theology Unit, his 'Seminary in the Street', included Bonhoeffer's Finkenwalde Seminary, the early Dissenting Academies, the South American Liberation Theologians' Institutes, the Chicago Urban Training Centre. Founded in 1969, it seeks to create an urban Christian discipleship through a community of study, committed to inner city Sheffield, and works to empower the poor. The Sheffield and other ashrams which have sprung from the Theology Unit have been influenced by the East Harlem Protestant Parish, the Iona Community Houses and Anglo-Catholic settlements and inner-city priests. The whole project has had general connections with Christian Socialism, defined broadly as a search for paradigm communities. Vincent in *Alternative Church* (1976) surveyed new forms of Christian community ranging from the Northern Irish Corrymeela Community to Ivor Smith-Cameron's House Church in Clapham.

Vincent is regarded as Britain's leading urban theologian. He has long concentrated on St Mark's Gospel and contends that discipleship rather than beliefs is the essence of faith. This austere Gospel written for a community facing persecution and martyrdom has a strong eschatolgical thrust. This produces a radical type of discipleship attractive to Vincent as a prophetic personality. 'You will be hated by all' (13.13). But the New Testament church discovered that eschatology had its limitations. It flashes like lightning across a dark scene, illuminating it more dramatically than the street lights, but their more humdrum light persists and goes on being needed, long after the lightning has passed. New Testament writers after St Mark had to modify his concept of Christian discipleship because history persisted and there was much ordinary life to be negotiated. Robert Carroll in *When Prophecy Failed* (1979) showed how the Old Testament prophetic tradition ran into the sand because of its defects. Wisdom literature (neglected by Christians) offered an alternative which focussed on how to cope with today rather than with the eschaton.

Vincent concluded early in his ministry: 'I need to find a place where Gospel things might happen.' Urban theology is 'boundary theology'. It takes context seriously. One of Vincent's aphorisms is, 'Where you are is who you are'. Theology is a reflection on action. It begins with events not ideas. This has led Vincent into political action, particularly about peace and urban society. His thesis is that the poor understand Mark because what matters to them is *praxis*. He starts not with crucifixion-resurrection, but incarnation – hence his move to inner-city Sheffield. Therefore to struggling local churches he asks, 'What have you got going there? How can we protect it and let it grow?' Vincent has been likened to John the Baptist. Certainly he can be scathing about both church and society and is capable of making others angry too, as when he told some Cambridge undergraduates that a privileged place like Cambridge militated against discipleship. Does he want the poor who have 'bettered themselves' to return to inner-city poverty? To quote the title of the book by Richard Harries, Bishop of Oxford, 'Is there a Gospel for the rich?'[45]

Alan Billings is an Anglican priest and former Labour Deputy Leader of Sheffield City Council, member of the *Faith in the City* Commission, who has now renounced socialism. He criticizes Vincent for not engaging with the critique of socialism developed by the Right, nor with the implicit abandonment by New Labour of egalitarian socialism. Billings assaults traditional left-wing convictions on a broad front: inequality is both inevitable and necessary; poverty is not usually the result of injustice; when poverty is understood as injustice, 'self-improvement is not attempted and charity and philanthropy are treated with contempt'. He gives the example of a group of Hispanic Pentecostalists in Brooklyn, who through the gospel were given individual worth and spiritual power. 'Victims became agents.' Far from Christianity needing to be secularized (as was thought in the 1960s and 1970s) it is 'at its most powerful when it is at its most religious'.[46]

John Vincent by contrast gets his congregations to sing this hymn to the tune of the 'Red Flag':

> His Kingdom makes our hopes arise;
> All shall be free, and good, and wise,
> All will their heavenly fullness bear,
> All will have riches, all will share.

Vincent writes of Jesus the politician whose project was the inauguration of the kingdom: 'it exists where and when certain things happen' such as healing and repentance, hidden within secular events. The gospel offers 'radical humanization (removal of hierarchies), reversals (elevation of "little ones") and radical community'. The Jubilee tradition (Lev. 25.8–13) provides a way to embody the kingdom. Jesus 'turns his back upon the middle class from which he comes and becomes a friend of outcasts and sinners' but politically sits on the fence. He creates a community of disciples who take the 'Journey Downwards' to stand beside the poor. Vincent envisages reproducing this today in surprisingly traditional forms reminiscent of Toynbee, Hall and Gore. He proposes the creation of 'some twenty-first-century garden villages, Port Sunlights, Moravian settlements and Villages in the City'.[47] Vincent's passionate advocacy on behalf of a group of inner-city ministers was crucial in the creation of the Methodist 'Mission Alongside the Poor' formed in 1983, two years before *Faith in the City* appeared.

Can a settlement in the inner city of largely middle-class professionals, most with secure incomes, really constitute a 'Journey Downwards'? The adoption of the term 'ashram' for the associated communities does not suggest a deep identification with working-class culture. The UTU does not seek much interaction with other strands of the Christian social tradition. Is what Vincent calls its 'liberation style methodology', picturing society engaged in warfare between rich and poor, with the middle classes playing a particularly culpable role, mere assertion or based on scrupulous social analysis? Sometimes Vincent removes variety and ambiguity from God and the Bible in the interests of platform rhetoric:

> ... all theology begins because of the situation of the poor ... a rediscovered Bible discovers a God who is not in favour of the powers, who all the time through scripture is at war either with the kings, or the priests, or the authorities, and who then appears in Jesus Christ, who futiley rides on his donkey down into Jerusalem representing the Galilean uprising of the peasants.[48]

Vincent's partial version of Jesus, based largely on his reading of St Mark, implicitly dismisses the further reflection of the church about Jesus in the New Testament and beyond. It also suppresses the wide circle of Jesus' social relationships and the fact that he seemed more concerned with inner motivation than social class.

But perhaps it is enough (and more than enough) that even in retirement Vincent goes on ministering, thinking and provoking in the inner city, looking for the signs of the kingdom, now here and now there, for as he rightly says, it is not possble to *establish* either a liberated state or the kingdom of God.[49]

Kenneth Leech (1939–), the most widely read of contemporary Anglican social thinkers, has worked as a priest for over thirty years almost entirely in London and mostly among those on the margins.[50] He first lived in the East End as a student in 1958. Since 1991 he has been community theologian at St Botolph's, Aldgate, financed in part by the Christendom Trust. This is a multi-racial and multi-faith area in which he is engaged with problems of drug abuse, sexual exploitation, racialism and the homeless. 'In this context' (he writes) 'I have both tried to reflect within, and in co-operation with, the small faith community called church, and to struggle towards a public discourse which is nourished by, but not restricted to the Christian tradition.'[51] But he also has a wide-ranging ministry across the country and in the States.

The earliest article by him I have come across (1965) broached

some of the themes which have recurred since: biblical eschatology and apocalyptic as offering a revolutionary understanding
of history; the corporate nature of salvation; his passion to
re-awaken a social conscience among Anglo-Catholics; the
celebration of heroes of the social movement – Maurice,
Headlam, Noel; the need to take Marxism seriously. In 1974 he
made an impassioned attack on Anglo-Catholicism for offering an
individualistic gospel and for making the liturgy an end in itself;
on the church for accepting 'the conventional wisdom of the new
capitalism' and its inequality. 'Kidnap the theologians' he cried;
transfer them to places of engagement. 'Kidnap the Bishops' who
are identified with a small segment of the population, removed
from urban life. He offered 'Contemplation and Resistance' –
a characteristic combination – for which spiritual direction to
deepen the spiritual life was essential. He pleaded with the
Catholic movement to become 'an effective counter-society' with
'cells of holy discontent' in which the 'powers of the age to come'
were already operative.[52]

In 1976 he attempted to make what he now grants was a too
simple link between theology and political beliefs. As Maurice
Wiles insisted in response, there was no evidence that Enoch
Powell was a monophysite (as Leech implied) or that the Arians
oppressed the poor. 'You can't settle your Christology first and
then deduct appropriate attitudes from it. The position is far
more complex.' Another strand in Leech's thought was revealed
when he agreed with the liberation theologian Segundo that
Christianity was 'essentially minoritarian'.[53] Meanwhile Leech
had become well known through *Soul Friend* (1977), a rich study
in spiritual direction which again linked it with political action:

No spiritual direction can be seen as adequate in Christian
terms unless it is preparing men and women for the struggle of
love against spiritual wickedness in the structures of the fallen
world and in the depths of the heart . . . In such contemplative
spirituality lie the resources for resistance to injustice.

In *The Social God* (1981) he insisted: 'The doctrine of the Trinity is essentially the assertion of the social nature of God.'[54]

Leech's cameos of his mentors and heroes reveal who he admires and where he belongs – they are all priests, all male (though his support for women priests alienated traditionalist Anglo-Catholics), little known, mostly on the frontiers of the church. He does not write about those who exercise power in church or society, say, Temple, Lansbury or Cripps. There are resemblances between Leech and Headlam, founder of the GSM, both more at home on the frontiers of the church; both wary of political and ecclesiastical establishments; both supportive of homosexuals; both Liberal Catholics; both sacramental and liturgical. In 1974 Leech floated the idea of a support group for Anglican Catholic clergy, mostly in the East End, who were also disturbed by the decadence and pietism of Anglo-Catholicism.[55] The Jubilee Group (Lev. 25) resulted, and he became its leader, though he does not accept that title.

The early manifesto of 1975 drafted by Rowan Williams (now Bishop of Monmouth) and John Saward was described by a founding member as a 'rant' and included the apocalyptic statement: 'Now that we are in the death-throes of late capitalism . . .' It now (1997) describes itself as 'a network of socialist Christians' (not 'Christian Socialists'). From the first it has had an anarchic style, and has been a network not an organization, with no membership. People are not removed from the mailing list if they cease to pay their subscription. Any document can be copied – nothing is copyright. It has no organizer as such. The result is that from early on, 'Jubilee' meant Leech, because he was the one member who wrote well-known books on political spirituality, whereas Jubilee symposia are mostly published privately or obscurely. A recent statement from the Group speaks of 'an important anarchist tradition within the network'. Leech wrote in 1994 about the Jubilee Group: 'It is messy, chaotic, not an organization, more a way of life, a tendency, a direction, a loose framework through which left-wing Catholics in the Anglican tradition can think through issues, can support one another and can help to forward ideas.'[56] In practice this means that the Group depends on Leech to carry it. Its anarchism reduces its effectiveness and cohesion and diminishes one's confidence in its political judgment and skills. (The GSM had similar problems and weaknesses.)[57] Leech wrote in a 1997 newsletter about 'a complaint which constantly crops up that people feel only in touch with Jubilee in a haphazard way, and often do not receive discussion papers or receive notices of meetings [until] too late'.

The Group's need to be in opposition, even if this means opposing the opposition, was illustrated in a revealing incident in January 1997. Tony Blair, then Leader of the Opposition, visited the East London Group. The *New Statesman* for 24 January described the members of the Group as 'eating out of his hand'. Leech expressed his annoyance in the issue of 31 January because (as one would expect) everyone who spoke disagreed with Blair but were united in thinking that by their own definition, Blair was not a socialist, and told him so.

Leech's analysis in 1988 of *Faith in the City* reveals his thinking. On the one hand he praised it as 'thorough and well-researched' and 'of abiding significance . . . marked by a sensitivity and an ability to listen which is refreshing', and for exposing the poverty and despair in society. But he said it had criticized the church's middle-class character without any suggestions for remedying it. It said nothing about racism as 'a structural reality in church and nation' and paid little attention to class conflict. It assumed most people shared Christian principles and failed to produce a theology of society. Today 'the powers that be are beyond the range of rational and moral criticism, beyond shame . . . this calls for a prophetic rather than a reformist response'. The church must be constantly disengaging itself from the values of the age. Because the report did not realize this, it failed to be 'a witness to the transforming power of the Kingdom of God'.[58]

Leech's most recent book, *The Sky is Red* (1997), has a characteristically apocalyptic title. He confesses he is now 'unclear' about many things, but his voice retains its urgency. A striking chapter 'Despair and Desolation' is headed with a text from Isaiah 8.23: 'For is not everything dark as night for a country in distress.' He argues that there has been a massive increase in hopelessness in Britain in recent years. He reflects on how much worse the drug problem is now than when he gave his (unheeded) warnings thirty years ago. Yet many Christians do not understand, because they have never faced despair. A desert spirituality of aloneness and stillness is essential if those who share others' despair are not to be destroyed by it. From this book it would seem that his understanding of socialism has become opaque. He rejects 'statism' and contends that nationalization has 'nothing particularly to do with socialism' which 'by its very nature implies the abolition of private ownership of capital', yet claims that 'markets are not intrinsically inimical to socialism'. He laments the abandonment of socialism by the Labour Party but then says that it has 'never been a socialist party'.[59] He shows little evidence of having assimilated the significance of the collapse of the command economies of eastern Europe or the globalization of information, capital and labour. The Group has never entered into a real dialogue with the New Christian Right, as though enemies must be kept at arms' length. However, Kate Soper of the Group has written:

> . . . we should be prepared to look very closely at how far the notion of 'authentic socialism' has depended for its political innocence on the reality of a history which has always denied it the test of implementation . . . it is not the market economy which is responsible for the difficulties of reconciling liberty and equality, democracy and efficiency, cultural pluralism and social cohesion, national self-determination and international cooperation. Capitalism is one bad solution or irresponsible evasion of these problems, but the problems have to do with the intransigence of social reality itself, and cannot be wished away by demonising an existing order.[60]

But the last word should go to Leech:

I want to insist against the pragmatists and reformers that the

Utopian vision, the dreaming of dreams, is a necessary part of politics . . . 'practical' men and women who ridicule it are on dangerous ground and risk destroying that which gives their own work any real rootedness and foundation.[61]

By the sudden death of David Nicholls (1936–96) the Church of England lost a memorable priest, the academic world lost an original political scientist and those of us who knew him lost a remarkable friend. After academic and chaplaincy posts in London, Trinidad and Oxford, for the last eighteen years he had been vicar of the largely working-class parish of Littlemore, near Oxford.[62] His PhD thesis (1962) was about Figgis, the pluralist whom we discussed in the last chapter. Nicholls reworked his thesis into *The Pluralist State* (1975). When it appeared there was little interest in pluralism because there was agreement across the political spectrum that the state should continue to play a dominant role in social and economic life. The book's critique of statism, which had seemed so irrelevant in 1975, by the second edition in 1994 was at the top of the political agenda. There had been a revolt against the state as owner or agent, accompanied paradoxically by the centralization of power through the strangling of intermediate levels of government. Meanwhile communist countries had developed a huge bureaucracy and exercised ruthless power. When this collapsed, the Left began to rediscover Guild Socialism and cooperative and syndicalist forms of society. The concept of subsidiarity became familiar through debates about the European Union. The churches, he believed, had adopted statism as part of their 'left-of-centre liberalism'. It was not the role of government to seek a common good, but to enable groups to realize their own goods. 'Pluralism does not require consensus.'[63]

At times he seemed to favour the benevolent anarchism associated with the Jubilee Group of which he was a member. Large organized groups in church or state made him feel claustrophobic. By contrast he was devoted to his parish and church, to the hospital and school. He called himself a socialist but was wary of the term because of its statist overtones. He advocated 'social-ism from below'. He had learned from Acton and Figgis that centralized power nourishes original sin. He did not consider that devolution and anarchism can produce factionalism from which people seek to be delivered by 'strong government', as happened in 1979.

He was strongly critical of the political outworking of the Liberal Catholicism of the *Lux Mundi* tradition with its proposed Christianization of the state. He disliked Holland's optimism about progress and human nature, his image of the state as home and his belief that the paternal role of the state was a reminder of the care of the heavenly Father.[64] He criticized Temple for his moralism, optimism and social conservatism, accused him of having almost no historical sense and of advocating consensual politics based on the chimera of the common good. The all-benevolent God became a model for the paternal welfare state.[65] 'The God of British Christianity in the twentieth century is a God of conciliation and of peace at any price, who never takes sides.' He questioned the use of the social model of the Trinity to promote a community without conflict. Not all conflicts were destructive. 'Conflicting claims and counter-claims may provide a healthy dynamism, a stimulus to progress and the elimination of specific evils.'[66]

He considered that it was impossible to move straight from scripture to political assertions. Scripture was socially con-ditioned as were those who quoted it. 'With much of its income deriving from investments and property managed by the Church Commissioners, its officials enjoying a comfortable standard of living and a degree of job security unknown among most fellow citizens, the general endorsement given by the Church of England to the current political system is not surprising.'[67] He was suspicious of 'aid' and 'the service of others' which too often created dependence. He reiterated New Testament warnings against riches. The aim of social policy should not be the raising of the lifestyle of the poor to that of the rich, but the reducing of the lifestyle of the rich so that they might have a chance of entering the kingdom. But he distrusted talk of indentification with the poor by those who in the last resort could withdraw to their families or monasteries.[68]

He used his acute sense of humour to prick the bubbles of the pompous. When the two Archbishops in 1975 launched their calamitous 'Call to the Nation' he wrote verses which began:

> Said Primate Coggan to Primate Blanch,
>   'I seem to sense an avalanche
> At any rate, a serious drift.'
>   'You're right. The country needs a lift
> On our toboggan',
> Said Primate Blanch to Primate Coggan.[69]

When Nicholls' bishop, Richard Harries, a social ethicist, wrote a pamphlet on business ethics with the chairman of United Biscuits in 1993, Nicholls wrote a hilarious but barbed Open Letter to him ('Of Bishops and Biscuits or How the Cookie Crumbles'). It mocked the bias and vacuity of such aspirations as 'the necessity of underpinning and suffusing the whole of our commercial life with clear moral principles'. He used the name of a macaw acquired in Trinidad, 'William Paley, Archdeacon Emeritus', as a *nom de plume* for letters to the press and for his reports about the Haiti elections for *The Daily Telegraph*. Paley was listed in the Oxford Diocesan Directory as a non-stipendiary curate of Littlemore. Nicholls' laughter put down the mighty from their seat. But as with Leech (who preached at his funeral requiem) it was easier to discern what he was against than what practical alternative programme he proposed.

Dissent takes other forms. Bob Holman was Professor of Social Administration in the University of Bath. During the 1960s he became disillusioned with the church because it lacked social concern and with the Labour Party because of its factionalism and the wealth and careerism of some of its leaders. Re-reading the Bible he rediscovered Christianity as a religion for the oppressed.

He then began to learn about the life of Lansbury. This showed him how a Christian could live as a socialist. Holman left his post in 1976 and for a decade worked with a Church of England Children's Society community project. For the last ten years he has been employed by the residents of a Glasgow estate where 70% of children come from families with low incomes. Unlike most Christian Socialists he is an ardent Evangelical, attends a Salvation Army citadel, runs a Covenanters' Group single-handed, but also has links with Iona. He has described how as a professor he had academic standing, good salary and house and travelled extensively:

> Yet, in a strange way, these freedoms had constrained me so that I was distanced from those in social need and from God. I think it is fair to say that I had become imprisoned by sin . . . In moving into a different sphere of life, I found a closeness to other humans . . . above all the knowledge of being in obedience to God.

He was outraged to read of the London Docklands Development Corporation spending £100,000 on a party when so many people around him were trapped in poverty. He prefers to work for a neighbourhood group rooted in the locality than for national charities based in London whose officials are paid high salaries.[70]

Mary Beasley, a member of the Jubilee Group, grew up in a fox-hunting fraternity. A wheelchair user, she now lives in inner-city Birmingham working from a former brothel in an apostolate among the homeless, alcoholics and drug addicts and trying to make the church more aware of their needs. A national network grew out of her work, 'Mission to the Margins', helped by Kenneth Leech. Why, she asks, are those on the margins such a threat – is it because they make 'a constructive critique of society' and challenge our dependence on status and possessions? Is this why any talk of equality is frightening? Mary is part of what Leech calls 'the Christian rebel tradition'. She believes that 'the ministry of Jesus was an expression of power coming from the margins', for on the margins we encounter God and our illusions are strippped away.[71]

Ann Morrisy, ministry advisor to the London diocese, also draws on insights from liberation theology (without revealing any particular political affiliation) to provide a framework for community ministries. It may be that 'the secure are likely to receive most from an encounter with the poor and marginalized . . . it is the poor and dispossessed who preach the Gospel, in its fullest sense, to the rich and powerful'. They 'are likely to be the first to recognize the radical, "upside-down" nature of the Kingdom of God'.[72]

Another form of dissent with Christian Socialist roots creates community groups, which either for pragmatic reasons or out of despair with established politics, by-pass the normal system. TELCO ('The East London Communities Association') is actively supported by the churches, mosques, temples and other groups. It tackles questions of social justice, unemployment, housing, health funding, relationships with the wealthy employers of Canary Wharf. It questions local MPs and councillors and quizzes potential candidates. The first of such groups began in Bristol in 1990. Since then they have spread to many urban areas.

The Bradford Faith in the City Forum has produced a moving record with the imaginative title *Powerful Whispers* of how the various churches stimulated two years' debate by the people of Bradford.[73] Four public hearings were organized by the churches, at which ordinary people spoke to, and were heard by, those who make decisions for the Bradford Metropolitan District. As one of the report's authors, Elaine Appelbee, wrote in *Crucible* (April 1997): 'perhaps the Magnificat could be read as raising up the lowly and bringing down the mighty to a point where they can speak directly to one another'. Could this be what is meant by 'socialism from below'?

8

Politicians

The majority of the Christian Socialists we have discussed so far have been clergy. Most of them have not been involved in front-line politics. In this chapter we shall look at Christian Socialist politicians, all but two of them lay, a few now largely forgotten, most well known. They are not simply socialists who have been church attenders, but Christians who have attempted to articulate the theological basis for their convictions. Their passion for the improvement of society was derived not from economics or sociology but from Christian imperatives.

We begin with three local councillors. It is important to remember that English (as distinct from Welsh or Scottish) Anglican priests are legally unable to stand for Parliament. However a number of priests have been elected as councillors.

One of the most unusual and most powerful of Anglican socialist priest-councillors was John Wilcockson (1872–1969), whose achievements have been unearthed and skilfully presented by Christopher Ford.[1] He not only came from a poor working-class background, but as a priest remained working class. He was also unusual in being an Evangelical as well as a socialist. Evangelicals then were traditionally Tories. In 1921 Wilcockson listed those who had influenced him – Maurice, Kingsley, Lansbury, Gore, Temple, C. W. Stubbs (Bishop of Truro) and E. L. Hicks (Bishop of Lincoln). His list shows that by then there was a distinct Anglican social tradition to which appeal could be made. None were Evangelicals.

Brought up in great poverty, he became a clerk and raised

himself through evening classes. He then became a stipendiary Reader (lay preacher and pastor) in north Manchester. His rector, a Tory, aided by the wealthy, built a new school, created a parish room, recreation field and working men's club. In the 1890s he was in charge of the Ragged School and Church Mission. The Bishop of Manchester, James Moorhouse, who chaired the Lambeth Conference Committee which in 1888 looked favourably on socialism, founded a theological college in Manchester in 1890 for working-class ordinands. Wilcockson went to train there in 1897 and was ordained by Moorhouse in 1900. As a curate to another Tory vicar he helped to create recreation facilities for the workers and actively supported the Church Army's work among the homeless and unemployed, including rural colonies where the workless were taught to farm before emigrating. Wilcockson's own history of self-improvement and his moralism made him a natural supporter of the COS distinction, adopted by the Church Army, between the deserving and undeserving poor. He had no time for those who refused work. During this time he was probably being influenced by the Manchester branch of the Christian Social Union, chaired successively by A. T. Lyttelton (contributor to *Lux Mundi*, brother-in-law to E. S. Talbot) and by Hicks (then in Salford).

In 1915 he went to his first living in Farnworth, near Bolton, and stayed there for the rest of his active ministry until the age of seventy-one in 1943. In 1916, two very different experiences changed his life. First, in the summer he was horrified to see swarms of flies around the middens of the houses. He was devastated when the landlords ignored his call to improve the sanitation. Hitherto he had believed that it was possible to appeal successfully to the consciences of the well-off. Second, he learned from Christian Socialists like Temple, Scott Holland and Lansbury during the National Mission that autumn that social sin must be taken as seriously as personal sin.[2] The discovery of social sin in his own parish; the welcome he felt for the early stages of the Russian Revolution; the way in which Ramsay MacDonald linked socialism with Christ and the Gospels: all led him to preach in 1917–18 a series of evening sermons about socialism, mostly to manual workers. He quoted the bishops' sympathy for socialism at the 1888 Lambeth Conference. Christianity was a social religion. Morality must deal with questions like 'our vicious competitive system', not just sexual issues. By 1918 he had joined the Labour Party, because it was 'an ethical society, and was striving to give the workers life more abundantly'. He also needed a political force behind him in order to transform the town. Soon he was preaching a politicized faith following 'in the footsteps of the Socialist Jesus – despised, rejected and crucified by the Tories of His Day'. To his critics he quoted the Archbishop's Fifth Committee (whose members had included such Christian Socialists as Tawney, Gore, Bell and Lansbury).3 In 1919 he was elected to the Council where he campaigned for better sanitation, housing and education, more open spaces and municipal and state ownership. His support for striking railwaymen in 1919 – he held a special service for them – showed he was moving to the Left. Clergy who supported capitalism he described as 'enemies of the Cross of Christ'. He became the most dominant figure on the Council and secured major improvements in the quality of life of the town.

But significant rifts began to develop between him and the Labour Party by the late 1920s. Wilcockson believed that the party was forsaking its Christian roots. Whereas he strongly supported church schools, the party favoured secular education. He was saddened that despite his and other clergy's support for Labour so few workers and Labour activists attended church. The crunch came in 1933 over the Council's permission for Sunday cinemas. He believed this would commercialize Sunday and deprive workers of a rest day. He resigned from the party after fourteen years as Leader of the Labour group. Henceforth he stood as an Independent, though his socialist faith was undimmed. Ironically in 1937 his efforts to attract more worshippers included Sunday evening film services. Here was someone who had given his life for working people and had remained within the Victorian expression of its culture, but resented it when they moved beyond his aspirations for them and rejected the moral leadership of the church. It is significant that in his parish he was unable to create lay leadership. His style had been autocratic and top-down from his early days as a priest in Tory paternalist parishes and he continued this style later as a politician and social reformer.

Charles Jenkinson (1887–1949)[4] was another Anglican priest, councillor and housing reformer, but a bigger man than Wilcockson, more intelligent, less partisan. He also was brought up in great poverty. As a young man he worked as a book-keeper and helped J. E. Watts-Ditchfield, vicar of St James-the-less, Bethnal Green, an Evangelical with a social conscience. Early on, Jenkinson showed his fighting spirit by campaigning against pew rents and by arranging a Church Socialist League mission whose speakers included Ramsay MacDonald and Conrad Noel. This drew Jenkinson and Noel together. Jenkinson became Noel's lay secretary and disciple.

During the war he served as a pacifist in the Royal Army Medical Corps. In 1919 he went up to Cambridge to read law and then prepared for ordination at the modernist college Ripon Hall, Oxford. He was ordained in 1923. He was now a Liberal Catholic with (like Noel) a touch of modernism. Maurice was one of his favourite authors. He was a singular personality. He disliked wearing a clerical collar but was happy in a cassock. He outraged Anglo-Catholics by his use of the liberal *Songs of Praise*, his support for the ordination of women, and evening communion; but dismayed Evangelicals by his use of incense.

He never confused socialism with Christianity, or with its fallible instrument, the Labour Party. He was a socialist because he believed that all were equal in Christ and that the state should promote justice as well as maintain order. By contrast with Wilcockson's cheap jibes against opponents, after the General Strike he paid tribute to Baldwin's courtesy. After his curacy, he asked for the hardest parish in the country and was sent to Holbeck, Leeds, in 1927. Unlike Wilcockson he had an almost mystical reverence for the church.

Leeds, he discovered, had some of the worst housing in the country, with 72,000 back-to-back houses, densely packed, 27,000 of which had outside closets shared between houses. Thirty per cent of the population lived in houses unfit for habitation. In the worst areas there was a high incidence of tuberculosis and infant mortality. One woman came to the vicarage in tears because of the rats. But if she left a night light for her baby, its warmth caused bugs to fall from the ceiling all over the cot. In 1930 Jenkinson was elected as a Labour councillor and flooded Leeds with 20,000 copies of a speech advocating massive slum clearance. The bishops had for some time campaigned nationally about housing, led by Cyril Garbett, then Bishop of Southwark. Labour's 1930 Housing Act fulfilled some of the bishops' hopes. The Leeds Clergy Chapter and Archbishop Temple of York gave strong backing to Jenkinson's campaign. In 1933 Jenkinson became chairman of the Housing Committee of Leeds City Council and, working closely with the City Architect R. H. Livett, proposed the largest scheme of slum clearance outside London. This provoked bitter opposition not only from landlords but also from some tenants who clung to their old haunts where everyone lived very close together. Jenkinson was tough, unsentimental and at times dictatorial. He knew what was best for the people and that consultation would delay the process, by which time Labour might be out of power again. He even demolished his own parish and led his parishioners to the windy heights of Belle Isle, where the widely-spaced houses seemed to them calculated to prevent the creation of community. By the outbreak of war, 20,000 new houses had been built. Against some Labour opposition, he adopted a system of means-tested rents, so each family was given the appropriate size of house whatever their income. The poorest paid only rates. He was not surprised or fooled by those who made false claims. At one meeting a man complained that undesirable people were being sent to live near him. Jenkinson responded: 'Who the devil is any man to say "my fellow man is not to live where I live"?' He explained Christian equality: 'I, as a priest of the Catholic Church, am bound to admit to the Family of God, with the same baptismal service, the child of a prince, of a prostitute or of a drunkard.' Likewise he drew lessons from the other major sacrament: 'How can we . . . protest at the Eucharist that we are in love . . . with our neighbours, and then tolerate such conditions for children and neighbours as exist in Leeds?'[5]

Throughout his twenty and more years in Leeds, he was rooted in parish life and the daily eucharist. In the parish he could be as autocratic as he was in the city. Like Gore he refused to preach a soft faith without challenge or tears. He was something of a baptismal rigorist and refused to allow fringers to have music at their weddings. He accepted that England was becoming a pluralist society and unlike Wilcockson refused to campaign against Sunday cinemas. In 1947 he became Leader of the Labour Party in Leeds and in 1948 Chairman of the Stevenage New Town Development Corporation, but still continued his priestly ministry in Leeds. He was characteristically planning to paint the ceiling of his lofty church just before he died: he believed strongly in the importance of simple manual work.

Peter Lee (1864–1935)[6] exercised notable leadership in local government in Durham and represents a characteristic contribution of Nonconformity of that time to Christian Socialism. Lee's grandfather had been a gypsy and Lee had the look of a handsome Romany. His father was a miner; his mother, a chapelgoer, broadened family life by reading aloud Dickens, Scott, Bunyan and the Bible. Peter Lee started part-time work at the age of nine in a mill. At sixteen he was hewing coal. He took an increasingly important role in union affairs. He married, embraced Primitive Methodism, gave up drink and fighting, improved his education, became a popular lay preacher and local councillor. Called out one night to pray with a dying woman, he was shocked by the stench of the open sewers nearby. He vowed he would work as a councillor to secure proper sanitation for the area and a water tap in every house. He nourished his young men's class at the chapel on the Bible, Ruskin, Bunyan and the lives of the great. In 1919 he became first Labour chairman of the Durham County Council.

In 1932 he was chosen as President of the Miners Federation of Great Britain. Though a moderate, he had no illusions about the need for conflict. 'War as a rule is a hard and cruel way of settling disputes but there are times when injustice, poverty and hardship are worse to bear than to fight in endeavouring to remove those evils.'[7] For forty years he preached in the chapels of County Durham. For him there was no division between personal and corporate salvation. He preached that we are all members of one another with the duty to give service as well as rights. He loathed idleness whether it was produced by wealth or unemployment. The new town of Peterlee founded in 1947 was named after him.

George Lansbury (1859–1940) was born of working-class parents, both of whom took to drink. This was why he was a life-long abstainer.[8] After a semi-nomadic life – his father worked on railway construction – the family settled in East London. The vicar of Whitechapel, J. F. Kitto, who prepared George for confirmation, was the first of a series of East End priests who deeply influenced him. Through participating in various church groups, he learned leadership and public speaking. He discovered St Francis, and felt a call to the simple life. Later on he developed connections with two groups of Anglican friars – the Franciscans in Dorset and the Society of the Divine Compassion in Plaistow – and Fr Andrew SDC (a socialist) became his confessor. He lamented that because he had married, worked for capitalists and been a capitalist, he had been forced to compromise, but realized that even as a friar he would have been dependent on the capitalist system.[9]

Early on he came to believe that neither the Tories nor the Liberals had anything to offer to the workers. His first political work was as a Poplar Guardian. With financial help from an American businessman he secured land for farm colonies for the unemployed. He became a member of the Poor Law Commission and signed its Minority Report. In 1910 he was elected as MP for Bow. During the First World War, his Christian internationalism led him to join the ecumenical pacifist group the Fellowship of Reconciliation, to support Conscientious Objectors and to oppose conscription. After the war his uncritical accounts of his visits to Russia and his support of strikes probably accounted for his exclusion from the 1924 Government. As Commissioner of Works in the second Labour government he promoted recreation. He believed that 'all our faculties of mind and body' should be used 'for the glory of God'. Catapulted into the leadership of the Party by the defection of MacDonald, he managed to keep the Party together and promoted the talents of Attlee and Cripps. But he had too much of the dove and not enough of the serpent and was therefore not equipped to reconstruct the Party after 1931. A rabbinic story tells how for twenty-four hours the Evil Inclination was locked up. But during that time no one married, no one conceived, no one built a house. That is to say, good and evil impulses are inextricably and uncomfortably linked. He resigned as Leader in 1935 after the Labour Party Conference at which Ernest Bevin savaged him for his refusal, as a pacifist, to support measures against Italy which was about to invade Ethiopia.

A. J. P. Taylor called him 'the most lovable figure in modern politics'.[10] Holman's biography pays tribute to Lansbury as the Christ-like figure who delivered him from disillusionment with both church and Party. It is easy to understand why children crowded round chanting 'Good old George'. Lansbury did not simply talk about socialism, he embodied it by his readiness to forego material security and personal advancement. His commitment to the poor led him to live in the East End for over seventy years and to be a Poplar councillor for much of that time. This taught him the meaning of a cooperative community:

> Whatever future there may be for me, my most cherished memories will be of the long, long years of work and pleasure, agitation and propaganda, carried on in company with these countless numbers of people, most of whom possess no money, no property, but who do possess the greatest of God's gifts to man, the spirit of comradeship and loyalty to each other . . .

People were free to knock at the door at any time. As he told Fr Groser:

I would sooner be here in the Bow Road where the unemployed can put a brick through my window when they disagree
with my actions than be in some other place far away where
they can only write me a letter. It's good for me, and it's better
for them.

Holman claims that he died 'almost penniless'. In fact he left an
estate of £1,695 gross (say £40,000 now), £916 net (£21,500).[11]

It is strange that, though he accepted the need for industrial
conflict and supported the militant wing of the suffragettes, he
denounced the use of force in international affairs and was so
naively trusting of the dictators. He thought the major cause of
war was inequality and that socialism would cure it. In September
1938 in the middle of the Munich crisis, in a message to Benes, he
compared the Czechs' sacrifice to that of Christ, and counselled
him to accept the German terms: 'Friendship to aggression, without limit, is the way of Christ.' Like other pacifists he assumed
that the lifestyle of Christ could be simply transferred into international relationships. The crucifixion of Czechoslovakia did not
redeem Hitler. Lansbury shared the inverted patriotism of the
Left and therefore hesitated to criticize the dictators because of
what the British had done in Ireland and India.[12]

Lansbury's socialism grew out of his faith. He was a Christian
before he was a socialist. All people and both sexes were equal
before God. He accepted those of other religions or none – God's
empowering was available beyond the boundaries of Christianity.
He went away from the church for about ten years before the
First World War. Lang, then Bishop of Stepney, befriended him
and drew him back. His son said: 'His happiest days were those
which followed his return.' In the 1920s he withdrew again for a
short period because the church was not radical enough, but
Fr Groser, himself in conflict with the church authorities for his
political views, brought him back. He never went to church
'merely to hear the preacher' but to enter into communion with
God.[13] He was another socialist for whom the eucharist created a
paradigm community:

Kneeling with others at the altar of the sacrament will and can bring no real peace unless those who so kneel spend their lives as brothers and sisters, and this is quite impossible within a system of life which depends on the ability of the children of God to dispute, quarrel and fight for their daily bread.[14]

Years as a Poplar councillor convinced him that there were resources of leadership among the people of the East End. He was a romantic who readily quoted *Unto This Last* and waxed eloquent about 'journeying to the Promised Land', and was naturally attracted to the face-to-face social work offered by Mary Hughes (daughter of Thomas Hughes) at the 'Dew Drop Inn'. But he was bitter about the motives of those who lived at Toynbee Hall and then became MPs or civil servants, as though the sophisticated, the technocrat and the powerful had no place in socialism.[15]

Arthur Henderson (1863–1935) was a pivotal figure in the transition from a party of protest to a party of power.[16] He did much to create the alliance with the unions, he had a major hand in forming the constituency structures and the 1918 Constitution with its famous Clause 4 on common ownership and finally became one of Britain's more notable Foreign Secretaries 1929–31. His nickname, 'Uncle Arthur', indicated that his were a safe and respectable pair of hands. Beatrice Webb said of him:

He had no intellectual distinction; no subtlety, wit or personal charm. Nevertheless he was an outstanding personality, because of his essential goodness, absence of vanity and egotism, faithfulness to causes and comrades, and a certain bigness, alike of soul and person, which made him continuously impressive in all the circles he frequented.[17]

Born in Glasgow in poverty, in his teens he discovered the regenerative power of chapel life. A religious conversion led him to become a Sunday school teacher at a Wesleyan chapel, a leader of a young peoples' group, a visitor to the sick and needy and later a lay preacher. He also became a life-long abstainer from drink, gambling and smoking. Apprenticed to the iron industry, he soon became a union branch secretary. His Methodism inclined him always to moderation and appropriately he became the first secretary of the North-Eastern Conciliation Board in 1894. He was elected to the Newcastle City Council as a Liberal, an advocate of municipal socialism and a critic of the Poor Law. In 1903 he was elected as a Labour Representation Committee and union MP. Later he became one of Labour's leading supporters of the First World War. From 1915–17 he was in the Cabinet. Characteristically during the General Strike he tried to mediate and proposed a Parliament of Industry. Henderson was sympathetic to co-partnership which Lansbury and others regarded as impossible because of the inherent strife caused by capitalism.

Henderson was a keen participant in the Wesleyan Methodist Union for Social Service, largely founded by S. E. Keeble, a socialist Methodist minister, in 1906. Henderson told a Brotherhood meeting in 1908: 'No longer were they satisfied with seeking to lead the individual to patient resignation . . . The doctrine of contentment had given way to one of divine discontent.' Yet he always argued that without individual regeneration social reform would fail. When he said that 'the workers had more to fear from the evils of drink and gambling than from capitalism' some union members were furious. He replied that he wanted to liberate them from both the capitalist and the brewer.[18]

Henderson said in 1929 that the Labour movement 'received much of its driving force and inspiration from radical nonconformity', and that the bulk of Labour MPs 'had graduated into their wider sphere of activity via the Sunday School, the Bible class, the temperance society or the pulpit'. But how many retained an active membership as adults, when as corporate bodies the Free Churches kept their distance from Labour?[19] Yet late Victorian and Edwardian socialism easily slipped into using evangelical language. Individuals were exhorted to 'turn' to socialism just as sinners were to 'turn to Christ'. Converts were told 'a change of heart' was necessary as well as a change in society. Terms like 'apostle', 'evangelist', 'gospel', 'new life', 'salvation' were taken over.[20] But after the General Strike some Labour supporters withdrew from the chapels in which Liberals still predominated. Also in the 1920s some Free Church people were turning to Conservatism, fearful of Bolshevism and won over by Baldwin's charm and Free Church ancestry. The National Government, with its promise of an end to divisions and strife was attractive to many church and chapelgoers. It was the Conservatives now who had the most Unitarian MPs, while the Quakers, also liberal theologically, were moving to Labour. The chapels now played much less part in the formation of future Labour politicians. The WEA and extra-mural groups took on that role. The puritan ethics of the chapels were now less appealing to society and to Labour.[21]

As we saw in chapter 2, women made a considerable contribution to Christian Socialism, but hardly any became well known. However, in 1928 Margaret Bondfield (1873–1953) became the first woman Cabinet minister.[22] She was brought up as a Congregationalist in religion and a radical in politics. She began as a pupil teacher at the age of thirteen, then worked as a shop assistant. At first a member of the SDF, her Christian faith led her to reject class war and she became a Fabian and very active in her union. She attended the King's Weigh House chapel, but left when a deacon rebuked her for attending a union meeting one Sunday instead of church. He told her to choose between them. She did not attend church for twenty years as a result, but returned to King's Weigh House chapel during the ministry of Dr W. E. Orchard, a pacifist and socialist, and he greatly deepened her faith and spirituality.

She worked with Gertrude Tuckwell and the Dilkes in the Womens' Trade Union League. Unlike some on the Left she supported the contributory principle in National Insurance because it helped people 'to realize the seriousness and responsibility of citizenship'. As Minister of Labour in the second Labour government, she was exceedingly unpopular because of her economic conservatism and failure to reduce unemployment: 'like all her senior colleagues in the 1929 Labour Government, her intellectual equipment for the political and economic problems . . . was wholly inadequate'.[23] She stayed with the party when MacDonald formed the National Government, but failed to get re-elected in 1931.

John Wheatley (1869–1930) was the most successful Minister in the 1924 government and the first Roman Catholic to come to prominence in the Party.[24] He grew up in poverty and went down the pit at the age of twelve. After the 1906 General Election he wrote to the *Glasgow Observer* claiming 'The Catholic Church has always leaned more to socialism or collectivism and equality, than to individualism and inequality. It has always been the church of the poor, and all the historical attacks on it have emanated from the rich. Its Divine Founder on every occasion condemned the accumulation of wealth.'[25] This curious version of history was to become common among Roman Catholics of the Left. Wheatley had been influenced by *Rerum Novarum* and an Italian book on Catholic socialism. He formed a Catholic Socialist Society in 1906 and joined the ILP in 1907, claiming its socialism differed from that condemned by the pope. But for the next few years he faced bitter hostility from his clergy which came to a climax in 1912 when, attending church, both he and socialism were denounced from the pulpit. Angry parishioners burned his effigy in front of his house, singing 'Faith of our Fathers'. He was elected to the Glasgow Corporation in 1912. During the war he became convinced that an increase of state power was inevitable. He combined radical with constitutional activities, on the one hand opposing the war and conscription and leading a rent strike in 1915, on the other hand convening a committee to relieve unemployment by public works. He was elected to Parliament in 1922 and he and the ten new Labour MPs, the focus of so many hopes, were seen off to London by a crowd singing metrical psalms.

Though a vociferous rebel in the Commons on behalf of the poor, he had become a successful businessman and lived in a mansion. He became Minister of Health in 1924 and his Housing

Act, providing for an expansion of public housing, was one of the few achievements of the government. In Farnworth, Wilcockson immediately took advantage of it and drew up a scheme for 330 new houses. Wheatley faced a challenge to his faith when a delegation of libertarian socialists, including H. G. Wells, asked that welfare centres should be allowed to give contraceptive advice, but he escaped the dilemma by arguing that only parliament could sanction such a change. When the government fell, he was able to campaign again for 'socialist' policies and led the opposition to many of the policies of the 1929 government. He believed that poverty was created by under-consumption and that therefore purchasing power should be increased. When he died he left over £16,000 (nearly half a million in today's terms) a substantial mansion and a controlling interest in his printing and newspaper business. Sheridan Gilley describes him as a paradox: 'the rotund, self-made businessman . . . the clerical bogy-man and devout Roman Catholic; the pragmatic statesman of the Housing Act . . . and the rebel who was to be suspended by Parliament . . .' But Wheatley demonstrated for the first time 'the significant contribution that Roman Catholic MPs could make to the life of both the Labour Party and the nation'.[26]

This was an important break-through, for the Roman Catholic leadership until the 1960s was keen to combat socialism and to promote a purely Roman Catholic vision of society.[27] Working-class Roman Catholics who were solidly Labour had nothing in common politically with the world of *Brideshead Revisited* and upper-class Roman Catholics with their right-wing, even Fascist, sympathies. This huge political division reinforced the determination of the hierarchy to remain a-political. Though members of Religious Orders, like the Jesuit Fr Plater and the Dominican Fr Vincent McNabb, played a significant role in developing a Roman Catholic social conscience, the bishops remained non-committal. But 1918 was a watershed. More Roman Catholics got the vote. The decline of the Liberals and the signing of the Anglo-Irish Treaty opened the way for Roman Catholics to support Labour. However, the Party Constitution of 1918 for the first time committed it to collectivism. Cardinal Bourne's Pastoral Letter of 1918 showed some sympathy with the workers' revolt against capitalism. By then, thinking Roman Catholics who were not of the Right were agreed on a more equal distribution of property, the centrality of the family, the just wage, and were suspicious of state power and collectivism. The Catholic Social Guild (1909) propagated official social teaching, but its membership was small (3,910 in 1939) and eschewed political action. (By 1967 when it was disbanded, its membership had fallen to 1805.) Encyclicals condemned socialism. But were the Labour Party and the unions socialist? In 1919 the Bishop of Salford declared that Roman Catholics should not belong to the party. Other bishops temporized. However, in 1924–25 Cardinal Bourne declared that Labour was not strictly socialist and was no threat to religion. This conclusion was inevitable as many Roman Catholics now were members. On its part, the party had softened towards church schools and was less dominated by teetotalism. Unlike Roman Catholics on the continent, Romans here did not create separate unions in accordance with *Rerum Novarum*. Nevertheless, there were sporadic outbursts of friction between Roman Catholicism and Labour over the Spanish Civil War, birth control and Popular Front activities. Yet, despite the fact that by 1949 some 80% of Roman Catholics voted Labour, 'the number of individual Roman Catholics in Britain who put their heads above the parapet to argue for Catholic socialism between the 1920s and the 1960s was tiny'.[28]

Clement Attlee (1883–1967) epitomized the Anglican paternalist tradition expressed through the public school and Oxbridge settlements.[29] His father, a Gladstonian Liberal, was a successful solicitor: he left £70,000 (over three million in today's terms). Clement's parents were devout Anglicans who taught their children a strong sense of social responsibility. Family prayers with the servants began each day at 7.30 a.m. The children knew the Gospels and Acts by heart. Only Clement had difficulty with the Anglican ambience and was bored in church. His sister became a missionary, one brother became a priest, another retired early to devote himself to charity work, another was a Christian Socialist schoolmaster. After governesses (one of whom had looked after Winston Churchill), Attlee went to prep school and Haileybury which had been founded to prepare men for serving the Empire. He was confirmed there but was already an agnostic. Yet five of his closest Oxford friends became priests and he declared that religion had been the primary source for British socialism apart from Owen.[30] Interviewed by Kenneth Harris two years before he died, Attlee said it was his inherited social conscience which had taken him into politics. Unlike his family, he was 'one of those people who are incapable of religious experience . . . Believe in the ethics of Christianity. Can't believe in the mumbo-jumbo.'

Harris: 'Would you say you are an agnostic?' Attlee: 'I don't know.'[31]

At Oxford he was an 'ultra-Tory'. In 1905 while working in his father's firm, an event changed his life. His brother Lawrence took him to a boys' club that Haileybury had established in Limehouse. Despite its motto 'Sursum Corda' and the fact that it was staffed largely by old Christian Haileyburians, it was entirely secular, a kind of OTC for the poor, a junior section of the Territorials. Following the family tradition of Christian service to the less fortunate, Attlee started to go each week to help. All wore uniform and he enjoyed the drilling and marching. He was quite ready to expel slackers. In 1907 he became resident manager and he lived there for seven years. In the process he got to know Stepney people and realized for the first time how the poor lived – the casual labour, the slum landlords, the sweating. He began to examine the whole economic system. It was not enough for the rich to help the poor. They must get off the people's backs. In later years he often told the story of a barefoot girl who caught up with him in the street and asked where he was going. He told her he was going home to tea. 'Oh', the girl responded. 'I am going home to see if there is any tea.' To him that was the stark contrast between the security of the comfortable and the insecurity of the poor.[32] Encouraged by his favourite brother and mentor, Tom, a

Christian Socialist, he read Carlyle, Ruskin and Morris. *Unto This Last* made him a socialist. His favourite passage from all these books was Morris's statement, 'Fellowship is heaven, and lack of fellowship is hell.' He joined the ILP in 1908 and tried to convert trade unionists to socialism.

In 1909 he became full-time secretary at Toynbee Hall, but stayed only a year as it was insufficiently radical. He became a tutor at the LSE but was always ready to serve the local people, as when he helped to feed dockers' children during the 1911 Strike. When war came, he showed himself a traditional patriot and defying the anti-war sentiments of the ILP, volunteered, was commissioned and fought in Gallipoli. In 1922 he married and moved from the East End where he had lived since 1907. Though he was an alien, he had won the people's hearts by his selflessness. He was Mayor of Stepney 1919–20 and became MP for Limehouse in 1922. He was known in the 1920s and 30s as 'Major Attlee'. He never revolted against his background or pretended he was working class. He cherished many traditional Victorian values and wanted to share them with the workers. He sent all his children to fee-paying schools.

Attlee 'had a high regard for custom, tradition and ceremony'. When he visited Republican troops in the Spanish trenches he wore a three-piece suit and homburg. This Anglican agnostic and upper-class Major with the clipped, laconic voice, who had lived in the East End for many years without thought of reward, the epitome of Victorian values, satisfied the Party's wish to appear decent, respectable and trustworthy. Even Richard Crossman thought him a near saint. Yet he could be ruthless and held together a Cabinet of powerful and quarrelsome colleagues. Two stories illustrate both his traditionalism and his modesty. Sir John Russell, later Ambassador to Spain, in 1945 was a junior official in Whitehall. He received a summons to Number Ten. He expected to discuss some matter of state. The Prime Minister asked him whether he was the son of a Russell he had known at Haileybury. 'Yes', said Russell. Attlee replied, 'I was his fag. He was very nice to me. Remember me to him.' As Russell left he added 'The name's Attlee'. When he was dying he told his daughter, 'I've just remembered the names of every boy in my form at Haileybury.'[33]

Someone who as Prime Minister still tapped out his speeches with two fingers on his old portable typewriter could not understand the more individualist and consumerist society which developed in the 1950s. Working people, to whom he had tried to pass on the values of the Bible, Ruskin, Carlyle and Morris, celebrated the end of rationing and wanted a little affluence. His socialism had been a response to Edwardian poverty. But he represents a tradition of ethical socialism, of Christian selflessness and *noblesse oblige* which has contributed more to Labour than has often been recognized. The concluding sentence in his Pooterish autobiography of 1954 quoted the Catechism and declared: 'I have been a very happy and fortunate man in having lived so long in the greatest country in the world, in having a happy family life and in having been given the opportunity of serving in a state of life to which I had never expected to be called.'[34]

Sir Stafford Cripps (1889–1952) was 'a political figure whom it is near-impossible to describe for a generation that did not know him. Indeed he was a puzzle, a man of paradox, to those who did.'[35] Cripps's father was a wealthy and devout lawyer who became Vicar General of the York and Canterbury Provinces in turn and the first chairman of the House of Laity in the Church Assembly. Though a Tory MP he was given a peerage by Asquith and as Lord Parmoor joined the 1924 Labour government. Party allegiances were less important than principles to both father and son. Cripps's mother, Beatrice Webb's sister, had worked with Barnett of Toynbee Hall and so was an earnest practical Christian. She died when Cripps was four. The children, she instructed, were to be brought up simply and as 'undogmatic and unsectarian Christians'.[36] Cripps's life was a surprising mixture of ancient and modern and took unexpected turns. At Winchester the headmaster, H. M. Burge, taught him a socially-concerned Christianity. He turned down a scholarship to New College Oxford (his father's old college) to study chemistry at the newly-established University College London. Unfit for war service, he drove an ambulance in France until he was recruited to manage the largest munitions factory in Britain. After the war, now married to a rich heiress, he became a successful lawyer and bought a manor house, but also sought to serve the post-war world through the ecumenical movement.

Then his life took another sudden turn. Through some legal work about municipal housing, he encountered poverty for the first time. So when MacDonald asked him to join the government as Solicitor General in 1931, he agreed and won a by-election. But a few months later in the General Election, the Labour Party was reduced to forty-six seats and he suddenly found himself with Attlee helping Lansbury run the Party. Naive, self-opinionated and a political greenhorn, he alarmed leadership and electorate alike by advocating a revolutionary policy which seemed to threaten the monarchy, promise a General Strike and a temporary dictatorship. His pursuit of a United Front with Communists led to his expulsion in 1939. Yet when Attlee had become Leader of the Opposition in 1935, it was a donation from Cripps which made it financially possible for him to continue until a salary was agreed.

In 1940 Churchill appointed Cripps, still an Independent, to be Ambassador to Moscow where he did much to forge the Grand Alliance. When he returned, a poll declared him to be the most popular politician after Churchill and Eden. His religion revived and he formed a close relationship with Temple as both strove to prepare the church for its post-war role. 'Is Cripps the new Wesley?' asked the *Daily Herald* after Cripps had joined Temple and Garbett in the Albert Hall in September 1942 to launch the series of meetings on post-war reconstruction. In *Towards Christian Democracy* (1945) he expounded the typical lay Anglicanism of the period – suspicious, like his mother, of 'ritual', 'dogma' and 'creeds'.

Christianity was fundamentally 'simple'. 'If Christ was, in fact, divine, then there can be no argument as to whether His teachings were the best . . . He has given us the final and divinely

authoritative moral code . . .' Religion, he reiterated, was about
this world not the next. He did not, like Temple and other
Christian Socialists, draw social implications from the sacraments. He criticized the church for failing to convince people
between the wars that ecumenism could overcome national divisions. He looked forward to a society based on equality, service,
care for the poor. Public ownership would remove tensions
between employers and employed and replace acquisitiveness
with service. A community was likely to be more Christ-like than
individuals. So Christ's kingdom would be established on earth.

During the war, Cripps also became close to Bishop Bell, to
Mervyn Stockwood, his vicar in Bristol for which he was MP,
and to John Collins, a prophetic RAF chaplain who in 1946
created Christian Action which did notable work, not least in
aiding the victims of apartheid. In 1945 he made a remarkably
overt Christian election broadcast: 'Let those of us who boast the
proud title of Christian follow the precepts of our great Teacher,
and make ourselves the selfless guardians of our neighbours . . .'[37]
(He did not ask what the 'neighours' would think of being
assigned to 'selfless guardians'.) It was his Christian convictions,
combined with an austere personal regime, adopted for health
reasons, which made him a persuasive advocate of national
self-sacrifice as Britain struggled to emerge from the war. His
moralist reputation was one of the greatest assets of the government, though his handling of devaluation clouded it somewhat.
'There, but for the grace of God, goes God', Churchill is supposed to have remarked. Attlee described him as a 'political
goose', yet appointed him to high offices. For many Christians,
during and after the war, Cripps embodied lay Christianity.
Preachers quoted his remarkable statement to the Commons as
Minister of Economic Affairs on 23 October 1947:

> I wish that today our country could refresh its heart and mind
> with a deep draught of that Christian faith which has come
> down to us over 2000 years and has over those centuries
> inspired the peoples of Europe of fresh efforts and new hopes.

Before he announced his resignation in 1950 due to ill health, he stayed overnight with Stockwood. He asked for an early call: 'I want my last engagement in Bristol to be at the Communion Table.' Though admirable, he was at times unappealing. It is surprising now to discover that Victor Gollancz, who was not uncritical of him, ranked Cripps with Schweitzer 'as one of the two great Christians-in-action that the the last half century has produced'.[38]

The life of Frank Pakenham, Lord Longford (1903–) follows a pattern which seems familiar – the story of a sensitive, Christian and wealthy peer who discovers poverty and becomes a socialist. But as an Irish eccentric and maverick there is much unexpectedness about his life. A member of an ancient Anglo-Irish family, he was brought up as an Irish Anglican with a strong sense of *noblesse oblige*. But he went further and identified himself with the Irish against the British. When he joined the Labour Party in 1936 he announced: 'I am a socialist because I am a Christian.'[39] His admiration for the Irish Roman Catholic contribution to republicanism and his desire to identify with Irish working-class religion were among the factors which led him to become a Roman Catholic in 1940. When later he developed an interest in Roman social theology, his faith replaced socialism as the central influence on his life. No doubt he also branched out beyond politics because he was not a particularly adept politician. Early on he developed a concern for prisoners. When one prisoner was released, with a characteristic mixture of naiveté and generosity, he invited him and his family to his home and produced a celebratory bottle of Liebfraumilch and tall glasses to the bafflement of the visitors.

Pakenham's Roman Catholicism seemed odd to a Party which identified it with Fascism and believed that history was moving from religion to rationalism. Nor was his socialism acceptable to many Roman Catholics of his own social level. During the war Roman Catholics became increasingly worried about state control of education and health. In 1944, the Bishop of Leeds accused the mild R. A. Butler, the Minister of Education, of sleeping 'with a copy of *Mein Kampf* under his pillow'.[40] Pakenham had been one of Beveridge's aides, yet his mentor Fr d'Arcy was cool about the Report. On the Sunday after publication, his parish priest, like many Roman clergy, denounced it. Roman Catholics were concerned that the increasing power of the state would be used to inculcate a moral outlook unacceptable to themselves. From the nineteenth century onwards, they had taken advantage of the British liberal state to create an anti-liberal ghetto regime which enforced obedience. This carefully protected ghetto was now threatened as the bombing dispersed parishioners, improved educational opportunity enabled more Roman Catholics to go into higher education and the state became more collectivist. So Douglas Woodruff, editor of *The Tablet*, quoted Belloc on the 'servile state' and advised Roman Catholics to vote Conservative in 1945. Total opposition to the welfare state persisted in certain Roman Catholic quarters until the 1960s. In 1991 *Centesimus Annus* reiterated traditional objections. The task of the state, according to the doctrine of subsidiarity, was to co-ordinate local and neighbourly welfare work, not to create huge bureaucracies which deprive local groups and individuals of their responsibilities: 'needs are best understood and satisfied by people who are closest to them and who act as neighbours to those in need' (§48). Not suprisingly, therefore, when Pakenham's children attended their (fee-paying) Roman Catholic schools, they were taught a good deal about the evils of socialism.

It was as Minister for the British Zone of Germany 1947–48, responsible for some twenty million people, that he enjoyed his finest hour in politics. He was criticized as naively pro-German, but he was supported by Bishop Bell, a fierce opponent of the post-war policy of ostracizing and punishing Germany. He arrived in Berlin in November 1947, and courageously announced to the Germans: 'I am a believer in Christianity, both as regards justice and mercy. In this job I shall attempt to apply Christian principles . . .'[41]

In 1981, despite by now being more concerned with his work in prisons and other similar concerns than with politics, and despite Labour's lurch to the left under Michael Foot, he explained why he was not joining the SDP but staying with Labour:

> The Labour Party with all its faults stands . . . for a belief that all men and women are of equal significance in the sight of God . . . 'When thou givest a feast, thou shalt call the poor, the maimed, the lame and the blind and then thou shalt be blessed.'[42]

It seems a long time since those two years when John Smith (1938–1994) held the leadership of the Labour Party. He, Hugh Gaitskell and Neil Kinnock to some extent were modernizers, but none of them planned the wholesale transformation which Tony Blair has achieved. The Labour Party now seems like the Roman Catholic Church after the Second Vatican Council, so changed that older supporters say that it is not the party they joined. But the reformers claim that the old values have remained the same; it is only the form in which they are expressed which has altered. The political commentator, Andrew Marr, then of *The Independent*, himself a Scot, wrote (13 May 1994) that the London based political classes had never quite understood John Smith. He had grown up in communities in the west of Scotland. His experience of those villages where all sorts of children rubbed shoulders in the same playground symbolized what he wanted Britain to become.[43] After his first heart attack he decided to climb all 277 of the 3000' Scottish mountains. It was not only an enjoyable challenge. He also found a touch of the divine in the wild landscapes. Gerard Manley Hopkins' poem 'Inversnaid', celebrating weeds and wildness, was read at his memorial service in Westminster Abbey. Smith was deeply influenced by the absence of hierarchy in the Presbyterian tradition to which he belonged, by its deep seriousness and by the Iona Community, whose leader was a close friend. His urgent desire to reform the Lords had a Presbyterian edge to it. Hammering the table, he told Andrew Marr that the bishops in their rochets and the Lord Chancellor in his wig and stockings looked like men 'in women's clothing. We're just not having that sort of thing' (*The Independent*, 28 June 1997). Flummery and privilege, like poverty and injustice, roused his anger.

It was Smith's 1993 Tawney lecture which made the public aware of the revival of Christian Socialism.[44] His advisers are said to have warned him against referring to his faith lest he be accused of sanctimoniousness. Even though there was only one reference to God, the *Daily Telegraph's* headline was 'Sanctimonious Smith' and *Tribune* warned 'Labour must not abandon secularism'.[45] In the lecture he paid tribute to Tawney's ethical socialism. No Christian should claim that Christians must be socialists, but politics 'ought to be a moral activity and we should never feel inhibited in stressing the moral basis of our approach'. He celebrated Temple at length and praised him for recognizing the role of self-interest but also that human beings had capacities and achievements which could never be derived from self-interest. People live in communities and individuals are best fulfilled in fellowship. He pleaded for devolution and a renewal of local government.

Nowadays, some in the Labour Party look back to Smith as representing values and attitudes which they feel have been eclipsed. They praise him because he was not dominated by the demands of the media, for the honestly redistributionist character of his 1992 draft budget, because he was close to the unions and proclaimed a more traditional and egalitarian socialism than Tony Blair.

Britain was surprised by the depth of feeling his death aroused. The Iona Community were amazed by the number of people who came to pay their respects at his grave near the Abbey. Many stood by it in tears. Until the 1997 General Election, Labour was weak in England but strong in Scotland. The Scottish rejection of Thatcherism was particularly vehement. The Scots felt that a policy alien to their tradition was being imposed upon them by the English against their will. Through the 1980s and 1990s, the Scottish influence on Christian Socialism, particularly as mediated through Iona, was strong.

Between Gaitskell and Smith, most of Labour's leading figures were self-confessed rationalists. Labour lost touch with its Christian roots. Harold Wilson's Nonconformist allegiance was too shallow to provide any theological sustenance. The advent of John Smith coincided with, and encouraged, a resurgence of Christian Socialism. Between the 1950s and Thatcherism, many Christian Socialists concentrated on campaigning against war, nuclear weapons and apartheid. Bishops criticized aspects of government policy from Suez to Rhodesia, from racial discrimination to Premium Bonds, but basically the churches trusted the intentions of the various governments, all of which upheld the war-time consensus on the welfare state and full employment. This was symbolized by Edward Heath's preface for the new edition of Temple's *Christianity and Social Order* in 1976. But the upholders of the consensus had grown complacent, believing its validity was self-evident. When the confident and ruthless forces of Thatcherism swept across their ill-defended positions, their obsolete equipment proved no match for the ferocious weaponry of the New Right. The incompetence and divided state of the Labour Opposition after 1979 created a political vacuum. For some years the most trenchant criticisms of Thatcherism were voiced by bishops like Runcie, Sheppard and Jenkins. They defended the consensus derived from the Temple tradition which in the Thatcher years suddenly looked radical. The church leaders' new role gave them a higher political profile than at any time this century, but also divided them from many in their congregations who welcomed the punitive moralism of the New Right.[46]

Of the ecclesiastical critics, the most rumbustious and theological was David Jenkins, Bishop of Durham from 1984–94. He had previously worked out his political theology at the World Council of Churches and then at the William Temple Foundation, Manchester. When he became bishop, his interventions in the miners' strike, his outrage at growing poverty, his attacks on idolatry of the market, led many to think of him as a socialist. 'The government, whatever it says, seems in action to be determined to defeat the miners and thus treat workers as not part of "us". They also seem to be indifferent to poverty and powerlessness.' He certainly admired the Marxist critique, even if he rejected some of its conclusions. But he confessed that if he had lived in a socialist society he would probably have attacked the idolatry of the state. He did not believe that politics could 'bring in the Kingdom of God' and he supported 'pragmatic, consensus politics'. In the 1980s what counted to the poor was that someone in authority shared their anger.[47]

Three factors helped church leaders in their new function. First, Mrs Thatcher herself moved the debate on to a theological plane by presenting her policies, helped by Brian Griffiths, an Anglican Evangelical, in the language of nineteenth-century Christian Political Economy.[48] The debates about economic and social policy echoed those in the Victorian period. In 1988 Mrs Thatcher expounded the political implications of her evangelical individualism to the General Assembly of the Church of Scotland. (The General Synod of the Church of England did not extend a parallel invitation to her.)

Second, the churches had learned a good deal about radical social theology from their world-wide networks. This was typified by *Bias to the Poor* (1983) by David Sheppard, Bishop of Liverpool. He is probably one of the last in a long line of Anglican bishops who have looked to the state as the prime solvent of social problems. He played a leading part on Archbishop Runcie's Commission which produced *Faith in the City* (1985). It had been appointed as a result of a letter to *The Times* (27 May 1981) from Canon Eric James, a long-standing Christian Socialist, which pressed for such an enquiry. The Church Urban Fund, one result of the Report, has raised enough from the dioceses and elsewhere to award £29 million by 1998 to over 1300 inner-city projects. The Press conducted a campaign of unprecedented ferocity against Runcie for his opposition to the spirit and policies of Thatcherism.[49]

Third, the appointment of Basil Hume as Archbishop of Westminster in 1976 ended a long tradition of political detachment by English Roman Catholic leaders. He tellingly voiced his distress, often in consort with other church leaders, about what he regarded as the damage inflicted by government policies. As part of the theological response to Thatcherism, Roman Catholic social teaching emerged from the shadows, and as we saw in chapter 6, aspects of it proved attractive to Christian Socialists. Nevertheless papal social teaching tends only to be known by a small minority of politically and socially aware Roman Catholic activists, usually of the Left. In 1993 the then Conservative Minister, Ann Widdecombe, converted to Rome over the ordination of women and what she regarded as the politicization of the Church of England. In 1994 she scathingly dismissed Archbishop Carey's Easter sermon as 'a party political broadcast' because he had deplored the widening gulf between rich and poor. The next day, Ian Louden, secretary of the Catholic Institute of International Relations, rounded on her for displaying 'a worrying ignorance. What exactly have the new wave of Anglicans joining the Roman Catholic Church been taught about the Church's social teaching, the "option for the poor" and its relation to the Gospel message? . . . What she is not entitled to do is to imply that the Anglican Church differs from the Roman Catholic Church in believing that work for social justice is a constitutive dimension of preaching the Gospel' (*The Independent*, 4/5 April 1994)

After years of friction between Downing Street and Lambeth, it was a memorable moment when on 9 September 1997, George Carey became the first Archbishop of Canterbury, and probably the first religious leader, ever to address the TUC Congress. He was able to claim past membership of NALGO and the ETU. He declared that much of the work of unions was 'the advancement of Christian Kingdom values'. He contended that the churches had been in the forefront of challenges to 'monetarism' and 'one eyed individualism', quoted the Roman Catholic Report *The Common Good* on workers' rights and Tawney's celebration of the revolutionary character of the *Magnificat* at the end of *The Acquisitive Society*: 'A society which is fortunate enough to possess so revolutionary a basis, a society whose Founder was executed as the enemy of law and order, need not seek to soften the materialism of principalities and powers with mild doses of piety administered in an apologetic whisper.' Delegates gave him a standing ovation, applauded his references to Bishop Sheppard and welcomed the churches' report *Unemployment and the Future of Work* (1997) which Sheppard had chaired.[50]

The actual Christian Socialist Movement (CSM) was launched on an ecumenical basis in 1960 at a meeting chaired by Donald Soper. CSM remained a left-wing group of about five hundred members, largely Bevanite, then Bennite, but in the 1980s grew considerably, affiliated to the Labour Party in 1986 and agreed to the change in Clause 4 in 1995. Nevertheless, it retains among its aims 'the common ownership and democratic control of the productive resources of the earth'. In 1998 it claimed four thousand members, including about forty MPs and five members of the Cabinet. It remains to be seen whether it will develop political and theological teeth and like the CSU encourage its members to engage in social action. In addition to Smith and Blair, a number of leading figures made known their Christian allegiance, including Gordon Brown, Jack Straw, Paul Boateng, David Clark, Frank Field, John Battle, Chris Smith, Michael Meacher and Brenda Dean. Though the *Dictionary of Labour Biography* reveals more Anglican participation in the Labour movement than is generally recognized, Anglicans have not played a major role in it. It is therefore striking that currently three offices of particular moral influence, that of Prime Minister, Home Secretary and Minister for Welfare Reform, are occupied by Anglicans. Both Blair and Straw were confirmed when adults, Blair as an undergraduate, Straw as recently as 1989. Not all those mentioned above are members of CSM. Some dislike the term 'Christian Socialist', believing that it divides Christians, and prefer the term 'socialist Christian'.[51]

Frank Field (1942–) was appointed by Tony Blair to be Minister for Welfare Reform in 1997. Unusually for a Minister of State, he was made a member of the Privy Council, a sign of the crucial nature of his role. Brought up in a churchgoing, working-class family, he won a scholarship to a grammar school and

studied politics and economics at Hull. He exemplifies those
virtues of self-help and hard work he commends to the nation. He
began to be known to the general public after becoming Director
of the Child Poverty Action Group in 1969 and the founder of the
Low Pay Unit in 1974. He started to question Labour's welfare
policies. As an MP from 1979 he demonstrated his independent
mind by advocating the sale of council houses even before Mrs
Thatcher and by advising the public to vote tactically. A deeply
committed Anglican, he is a Vice-President of The Prayer Book
Society (a sign of his traditionalist faith). He founded and is
President of 'Broken Rites' for divorced clergy wives (a sign of his
traditionalist morality). He admires those who like Margaret
Thatcher, Tony Blair and Bishop Bell stand up and argue their
case against fierce opposition, as he did when attempts were made
to de-select him. Conversely he criticizes Davidson and Temple
for temporizing. It is not easy to reconcile his desire for the
church to be more subject to parliamentary control with his
support for devolved authority in the state, or with his advocacy
for citizens to take more responsibility for their lives. He wants
the church to be ready to stand prophetically against the state, as
Bell did. Yet he criticizes the church for recovering the eucharist
as its main service, just when English people reject the common
dining table in favour of individual consumption of convenience
foods, as though the church should always reflect the national
outlook and never elevate it. Yet he also urges the church to
stand against the modernizing tide by using more widely the
Prayer Book and Authorized Version because they are so rich and
evocative. He supports the establishment because it provides (he
believes) a Christian moral framework for the nation, to which the
government could appeal as it educates the nation in the moral
implications of welfare reform. He rejects the argument that were
the church to take ultimate responsibility for its own affairs
('stakeholder religion'?) it would be more adult and could be more
prophetic. He praised *Faith in the City* for prompting the nation
to seek an alternative to Thatcherism, but criticized it for lacking
a theological basis; for not realizing that (for example) a move of

the church's headquarters from Westminster to an inner-city location would demonstrate that the church was really committed to inner-city areas; for not considering what Tawney called 'the problem of riches' alongside 'the problem of poverty'; for not explaining how its proposals would be financed.[52]

Four aspects of Field's proposals for welfare reform reveal salient features of his socialist Christianity.

First, he proposes a new balance between the individual and the state. In 1981 he complained: 'The debate in the Labour Party at the present time is dominated by those whose overwhelming emphasis is on changing the structure of society, while leaving unmentioned the crucial importance of individuals changing their attitudes, beliefs and above all their actions.'[53] The concept of 'stakeholder', popularized by Will Hutton in *The State We're In* (1995) and by Tony Blair is a key idea for Field. The citizen should cease to be a passive recipient and gain ownership in a new National Insurance scheme controlled by contributors. He quoted approvingly Lord Plant's dictum:

> Moral reformers are essentially bottom-up reformers. Values can only be effective in politics when they are widely shared and the task of the moral reformer is to take the long view and try to transform the values by which people live and the direction that he wants to see. The mechanical reformer is a top-down reformer . . . [54]

Field often refers admiringly to the welfare role of Friendly Societies and unions in the nineteenth century. They combined self-help and mutual support, rewards for good behaviour and sanctions against dishonesty. Thus they inculcated those virtues of self-improvement, work, thrift and honesty which he admires. He thinks that it was 'in the replacement of those self-governing guilds and societies by top-down state provision that much of today's welfare ills are to be found'.[55] Faith in the omnipotence and omniscience of the state (partly a legacy of war-time), implicit in the top-down approach, has severely declined. He distinguishes between the government, which is only one body in the state, and the whole state or community which comprises all the groups which make up society.

> Once the individual and the state are seen to have different parts to play in a joint endeavour the conflict [between state and individual] ceases. The individual makes choices, the state makes it possible for the individual to make those choices within a fair and efficient framework, whilst recognising that there will always be some groups of people who will not be able to take that responsibility for themselves.

> The multiplicity of other organizations, with sovereignty over different parts of our lives, provide the fertile soil of a truly free society.[56]

Here Field comes close to Figgis's concept of the state as a community of communities, but unlike Figgis he believes in a common good. Beveridge, Field claims, cut the link between welfare and self-improvement and that should be restored. Welfare is not about providing the poor and disadvantaged with benefits, but about helping them wherever possible to liberate themselves from their poverty, as council house sales liberated them from 'the serfdom' of 'autocratic local authorities'.[57]

Second, Field is representative of the wider revival of ethical socialism associated with the Tawney tradition and recently with Norman Dennis, A. H. Halsey, Alan Deacon and others. Dennis, a Fellow of Newcastle University and a Labour Party member, in a recent study of poverty, denounced the 'no fault' theory of human behaviour, and the secular, liberal moral climate which had taken over not only large areas of the party, but also the church and society. Crime was not caused by poverty (he argued) but by the decline of the family and by feckless young men who fathered, then abandoned, their children. Before the 1960s, he claimed, at the centre of Labour ideology was 'the aspiration that the values of the virtuous working-class family (solidarity, self-sacrifice, fidelity, the primacy of the family's common good) should be spread to all areas of society'.[58] Halsey maintains that 'the decline of the nuclear family is not merely at the root of many social evils but is the cancer in the lungs of the modern left'.[59] Melanie Phillips praises Field for attempting 'to re-site welfare within its original framework of moral judgments' which had been swept away by 'a Marxist world-view which represented individuals as the helpless tools of economic circumstances beyond their control'.[60] Field believes that 'Single parenthood is the major cause of family poverty', bluntly advocates cutting 'the supply route to single parenthood' by changes in the pattern of welfare and education to identify and help the low achievers most likely to become single young mothers. Similarly, 'the supply routes to young unskilled unemployable males need to be cut'.[61] One of his major themes is that the welfare system is not morally neutral: 'a major consequence of welfare is now the cultivation of idleness, fecklessness and dishonesty'. Its rules 'block the very process we should be aiming to achieve – maximizing a person's natural instincts to leave the welfare roll'.[62] One of welfare's roles is to teach values 'to reward and to punish. The distribution of welfare is one of the great teaching forces open to advanced societies.'[63] These rewards and punishments would be self-selected when claimants agreed or disagreed with the conditions attached to the benefit.

He has been accused of using the language of the Charity Organization Society and of implying that poverty is the result of defects in character. He denies this and criticizes the Left's argument that poverty is created by the system. We need a fresh emphasis upon personal responsibility.[64] Like Tawney, Field maintains that all human projects must take into account the Christian belief that human beings are fallen but are capable of being redeemed. Thus he remarks, echoing Niebuhr, 'all political strategies end in failure'. Therefore we should not construct a Whig interpretation of welfare history, as though at some point it had reached, or could reach, a perfect equilibrium.[65] He accuses Richard Titmuss, whose ideas on welfare dominated the post-war period, of overestimating human altruism and of underestimating human sinfulness, a 'dangerous' and 'futile' legacy.[66] Instead of appealing to altruism, Field advocates 'a brotherhood underpinned by self-interest'. Hence the idea of stakeholder welfare. Hence the need to convince the better-off that it is in their interest to help the less fortunate, which is a form of loving your neighbour as yourself. Following Niebuhr and Temple, he argues that love can usually operate only in small groups, but that in larger groups justice is the appropriate moral aim. The common good is central to Field's thinking. He paraphrases the Catechism's definition of a sacrament: 'the inward meaning of equality is given an outward expression in welfare's incorporation'.[67]

Third, his proposals take into account the huge changes in society and welfare since the war. Post-war, two-thirds of people drawing benefits were retired. Now over two-thirds of welfare expenditure is on people of working age – the unemployed, single parents, the disabled. Since 1979 one-third of all manufacturing jobs have been destroyed, creating massive unemployment. The post-war system was created for a society with full employment where marriages were relatively stable, men worked and women stayed at home, and most children stayed at home until they married. Now many women work. Many men do not. Most children leave home and many have families before or out of marriage. So now one in five children are being brought up by lone parents. The present system does not work. It traps people in poverty and destroys honesty, thrift, effort and self-improvement. Fraud is detected in one out of ten claims for income support. One-third of the population lives in households which draw at least one of the major means-tested benefits. Electors refuse to pay more direct taxation, but increasing indirect taxation would hit the poor. Voters increasingly want to make their own choices. The days of the state as universal provider are over.[68]

Fourth, his political sympathies are remarkably broad and unpartisan. He was chosen to give the Keith Joseph Memorial Lecture in 1998 though Joseph is still a hated figure among many on the Left. Field went out of his way to celebrate both his humanity and political acumen. Though he has criticized many aspects of Thatcherism, especially its failure to roll back the state, he writes: 'Bluntly Mrs Thatcher was right to reposition self-interest', and he praises her 'sheer guts and courage' for bringing the unions under the law. For that 'we should be eternally grateful'.[69]

The courage and comprehensive sweep of Field's thinking on welfare have won plaudits from all sides. Yet there are questions to be raised.

First, he argues for the remoralization of society, though he does not use the term. Yet those who would be particularly targeted would be those who come from the social groups which are traditionally suspicious of all official agencies. Working-class men, for example, have been notoriously sceptical about moral exhortations, especially from the governing classes, clergy and politicians. We remember how Mrs Pardiggle was received by the brickmaker's family in *Bleak House*. Victorian Friendly Societies could only help the cooperative and the reliable. How much compulsion or punishment of defaulters would society tolerate? Both Thatcher and Major also tried to remoralize society. Why did they fail? Was it because there was no consensus to which appeal could be made? Or was it because of a gap between the preaching and practice? In 1942 Temple in *Christianity and Social Order* could confidently assume a widespread agreement about the common good. It was there, rather like the monopoly of the BBC, accepted but imposed from above. What about the remoralization of the wealthy? Within the present government there is a variety of financial, sexual and marital styles. Is it in a position to moralize about single parenthood, the permanence of marriage, the demoralizing effects of living on unearned income whether from welfare, the Lottery or a gravy train? A *Tablet* reviewer (12 April 1997) maintained that the moralism of Blair and Field did not resonate with teenagers today:

> I have this picture in my mind of a 16-year old single mum at the Tower Hamlets job centre . . . anxious not to miss

Neighbours, a copy of *Just Seventeen* in her bag . . . Frank Field is sitting on the other side of the desk conducting her evaluation and assessment interview to prepare her personal stakeholder career programme and pension plan, impressing on her the importance of self-improvement. I suspect that she would settle for a ciggie, a satellite dish, and dropping an 'E' with her mates at a rave.

Is there a commonly accepted moral authority today to which Field's programme of remoralization could appeal? Does he over-estimate the diffusion of the Christian ethic in Britain? Or are we too pluralist, too secularized, too post-modern? Would the various faiths, with their schools, be willing to play an active role in attempting to re-create a common ethic?

Second, what happens to those who after much struggle to move into work become the first to be sacked when a recession comes? What kind of welfare will be needed then?

Tony Blair (1953–) is young enough not only to be decisively post-war but almost post-Cold War as well. He came to political maturity when Eastern European socialism was collapsing and Thatcherism was in the ascendent. 'He stands outside many of Labour's traditions . . . He doesn't talk wistfully of bygone days . . . of comrades on winter mornings huddling together amid a brazier outside the factory gates or the historic battles on the picket lines . . .'[70] He has been described as the most overtly religious leader since Gladstone. Though he does not parade his beliefs, or use them for debating purposes, they do give a certain accent to many of his utterances. Surveys show that the Prime Minister's Christian commitment is one of the best-known facts about him.

Blair exemplifies and has powerfully promoted the rediscovery and reinterpretation of the ethical and Christian roots of British socialism. He said in 1995: 'Since the collapse of communism, the ethical basis of socialism is the only one that stood the test of time.' Jack Straw, like Blair, believes that urging people to take responsibility for their actions rather than blaming it on environment is a return to an earlier 'Christian-based' socialism.[71] Blair is an Anglican for whom regular participation in the eucharist (whether Anglican or Roman) is central to his faith. In 1997, for the first time at a Labour Party Conference, it seems at Blair's request, the Conference service was a participation in a Sunday eucharist. It was held at Brighton Parish Church. The Bishop of Chichester presided, the Roman Catholic Bishop of Arundel and Brighton preached and a Methodist conducted the intercessions.

For a number of years Blair, in the tradition of English politics, kept quiet about his faith, though he joined the CSM in 1991. It was the Bulger case in February 1993 which led Blair, then Shadow Home Secretary, to abandon his reticence and to call for the country to be 'unafraid to start talking again about the values and principles we believe in . . . We cannot exist in a moral vacuum.' In March he wrote in *The Sun*: 'There is no excuse for crime. None.'[72] That year he wrote a foreword to a collection of essays on Christian Socialism which included Smith's 1993 Tawney lecture. Christianity, he wrote, promoted change, but was not utopian, believed in equality, justice, compassion and liberty. It was about the union of the individual and the community symbolized by holy communion. The values of democratic socialism were 'closely intertwined with those of Christianity'. When we put our time-bound policies alongside Christianity we discover timeless principles.

> Christianity is a very tough religion . . . It is not utilitarian . . . It is judgemental. There is right and wrong. There is good and bad. We all know this, of course, but it has become fashionable to be uncomfortable about such language.[73]

Those who think of Blair as bland would be surprised to discover that when asked to choose a prayer for a radio programme, he selected one composed by Dietrich Bonhoeffer in 1943 when he was imprisoned by the Nazis.[74] He has returned occasionally to religious themes, directly or obliquely. In his speech to the

Labour Party Conference in 1995 he used biblical language. 'I am my brother's keeper. I will not walk by on the other side . . . Where your child is in distress is my child, your parent ill and in pain, is my parent: your friend unemployed or helpless, my friend; your neighbour, my neigbour'.[75] At the 1996 Conference he claimed the party was in the tradition of the Old Testament prophets and Wilberforce.

At Easter 1996 he took a big risk by writing an article for the *Sunday Telegraph* (reprinted in the *Daily Express*) about his Christian faith. He declared that he could not stand politicians who 'wear God on their sleeves', that he did not believe all Christians should vote Labour and that he did not discuss his beliefs unless asked. Prayer and Bible reading were very important to him. He focussed on Pilate, Peter and Jesus in the Easter story and interestingly, devoted particular attention to Pilate 'the archetypal politician'. Blair said that his Christian values had led him to oppose 'the narrow view of self-interest' of modern Conservatism and also Marxism which suppressed the individual in the interests of the community, whereas in the eucharist the individual is taken into community. 'The Left got into trouble when its basic values became divorced from this ethical socialism, in which Christian socialism is included.' He mentioned the influence of Kierkegaard, Jung, Kant and Macmurray. He rejected 'a purely libertarian ethos . . . unless boundaries are set and agreed, and judgments of good and bad are made, society cannot function well or fairly'. He was, he said, 'an ecumenical Christian', baffled by many inter-church conflicts. 'I have a deep respect for other faiths, and relish the religious pluralism of this country.' Christianity is both 'optimistic' about human nature but knows the human capacity to do evil.[76]

As we saw in chapter 6, socialism has throughout its history been concerned for community, sometimes in utopian, nostalgic or totalitarian forms. After years of Thatcherism, Blair offered a new balance between individual and community. His own security had been shattered at the age of ten, when his father suffered a stroke which deprived him of speech for three years.

Then his mother died suddenly, a fortnight after he had graduated from Oxford. But during that whole period he was sustained by a long experience of different communities – the Durham Choristers' School, Fettes Public School, St John's College Oxford. All of them drew on the Benedictine tradition of worshipping, living, eating and working in community. At Fettes he helped the chaplain with his summer camps for slum children, much as Attlee had done at the beginning of the century. At Oxford he was prepared for confirmation and learned from Peter Thomson, an Australian priest, about the theological understanding of community in the Bible, in the writings of Tawney and Temple (whom Blair calls 'perhaps Britain's greatest Christian Socialist'), in liberation theology and in the philosophy of John Macmurray. 'If you really want to understand what I'm all about,' said Blair in 1994, 'you have to take a look at a guy called Macmurray. It's all there.' In his foreword to a selection of Macmurray's writings, Blair wrote that he taught 'we are what we are, in part, because of the other', but that the personal was not merged in the social. Macmurray, a contemporary of Tawney, was too craggily independent ever to become a source for any kind of oppressive communitarianism. There are obvious similarities between his message that the individual only finds fulfilment in community and what Green, Holland, Gore and Temple had written. One of Macmurray's characteristic phrases is 'All meaningful knowledge is for the sake of action, and all meaningful action for the sake of friendship.'[77]

What Blair seems to have learned at Oxford was not an ideology but a theology and the social ethics derived from it. His concept of the common good probably owes as much to the Bible, Anglican and Roman Catholic moral theology, and Jonathan Sacks (the Chief Rabbi) as to communitarians such as Amitai Etzioni. The title and content of Blair's lecture in 1995, 'The Rights We Enjoy, The Duties We Owe', reflect Etzioni's influence. The libertarian Left (he said) had developed 'a kind of social individualism . . . you "did your own thing". In fact this had very little to do with any forms of left-of-centre philosophy recognizable to the founders of the Labour Party . . . People need rules which we all stand by . . . Duty is the cornerstone of a decent society.' (Blair might have pointed out that if Attlee gave people the welfare state, he also required them to accept National Service.) Lord Plant asks whether the state is like a hotel in which anonymous individuals pursue personal ends, or like a family which shares a common purpose and a common life but allows freedom to its members.

Blair's own family was socially mobile. 'I never felt myself very anchored in a particular setting or class.'[78] One of his favourite quotations from Temple is about mobility: 'Morality demands that you treat people as they have it in themselves to become . . . and raising people from what they are to what they might be is the work of education.'[79] Blair is not a Protestant nationalist and individualist like Margaret Thatcher, but a Catholic European communalist who refers to the eucharist to illustrate his belief that true community individualizes: 'the good of each does depend on the good of all'. '"Community" cannot simply be another word for "state" or "government"', he told a meeting in Southwark Cathedral celebrating ten years of response to *Faith in the City*. He praised the report for exposing the consequences of economic individualism and criticized the individualistic views of the Left represented by John Rawls. He contrasted them with the vision of community in the writings of Chief Rabbi Sacks.[80]

Arthur Marwick in *British Society Since 1945* (1982) coined the term 'secular Anglicanism' to account for the absence of those extremes in English life so common in the United States, Europe and Ireland. Margaret Thatcher despised Anglicanism, both in its religious and secular forms, as a major source of nostalgia, stagnation and fudge, which is one reason why some felt she was 'never one of us'. Blair, like her, is prepared to stand alone. Not very much of the the party was Blairite before he became leader. But he also seeks coalitions and common ground, as he stressed in 1995:

The ultimate objective is a new political consensus of the left-of-centre . . . To reach that consensus we must value the contribution of Lloyd George, Beveridge and Keynes and not just Attlee, Bevan or Crosland. We should start to explore our own history with fresh understanding and an absence of pre-conceptions.[81]

As Blair implies, Labour has often wanted to forget how many of its roots go back to the radical Liberalism of the turn of the century. Like Field, he is not partisan. He has never concealed his admiration for Margaret Thatcher's courage and some of her achievements. So he seeks common ground with Liberals on constitutional issues and with pro–European Conservatives on the European Union. But contrary to popular journalism, he is not afraid to use the word 'socialist'. But he redefines it consciously or unconsciously in line with strands of the Christian Socialist tradition, not in terms of the dominant statist tradition since 1918. 'The solutions of neither the old Left nor the new Right will do.' 'A belief in society, working together, solidarity, cooperation, partnership . . . That is my socialism – and we should stop apologizing for using the word. It is not the socialism of Marx or state control.' 'Socialism to me was never about nationalization or the power of the state; not just economics or politics even. It is a moral purpose to life; a set of values . . . It is how I try to live my life.' Blair's reinterpretations of socialism are reminiscent of those by Westcott in 1890 quoted in chapter 2. Blair believes the political debate has moved on:

> The era of the all-encompassing ideologies in battle to the death – a feature of at least the first part of the twentieth century – has ended . . . There will still be significant differences between political parties in values and priorities . . . But the pot of specific policy prescriptions will be more often held in common. They may be used for different purposes and drawn by different motives, but the right and left hand will sometimes be dipping into the same pot.[82]

Blair wants a 'something for something' community: 'I tell you, a decent society is not based on rights,' he told the Party

Conference in 1997. 'It is based on duty. Our duty to each other.'[83] Devolving power to intermediate groups (he contends) would increase the sense of stakeholding. (Paradoxically he seems to be trying to increase political control over the Church of England, to which uniquely parliament devolved power in 1919. He also appears to be exercising an unprecedented degree of centralized control over his own party and its MPs.) He wants equality of sexuality and gender, but the family is 'the best building block of a good community': we 'cannot be morally neutral about the family'. The government should help to strengthen family life with children ideally raised by two parents. 'The breakup of family and community bonds is intimately linked to the breakdown in law and order.'[84]

Up to now, Blair's references to his Christian faith and practice have been so ethically focussed, so ecumenical towards other Christian traditions and so appreciative of other faiths, that they have won him support not only from Christians but from other faith communities too which also value ethical religion and family life. Many who were attracted to Thatcher and Major because of their moralism and then became disillusioned seem to have been won over to Blair by what he terms his 'compassion with a hard edge'. Conservative Christians, led by Peter Lilley, in 1998 inaugurated a consultation called 'Learning from Britain's churches', a remarkable admission of how alienated from the party many leaders and activists in the churches have become. It is the moral libertarians of the Left who held sway in the 1960s and 1970s who now find Blair's moralism and religion most unacceptable.

It is far too early to make an assessment from a Christian Socialist perspective of Tony Blair after just over only twelve months as Prime Minister. The scale of his achievement so far is clear and impressive. But political success is fragile. So far the government has not had to face any real emergencies, political or economic. The present mutation of Christian Socialism is still very new and depends for its character and visibility upon a comparatively few leading members of the

government. Quite a number of Christian Socialists seem so far
unconvinced by New Labour.

First, we note that there is nothing of the old socialist ruralism
about Blair with his enthusiasm for technology. In one speech he
mused about how he could never have coped with being leader
in 1980 on a three-hour train journey to his constituency without
a mobile phone, fax, personal computer or bleeper. Yet, modernity, like the past, can become a tyranny. His excitement about
modernity and progress tend to drown his occasional references
to human frailty. *The Tablet* (4 October 1997) thought his vision
of society 'unrealistically Utopian, even Pelagian'. Second, as we
have already indicated, the government's welfare proposals seem
to rely upon a moral consensus which may be much more patchy
and incoherent than it imagines. Pope John Paul II, the
Archbishop of Canterbury and the Chief Rabbi themselves all
preside over communities which include great variations in moral
beliefs. Nearly all the government's ethical exhortations seem
directed towards the poor. It appears reluctant to challenge the
wealthy and powerful about *their* responsibilities and duties to
society. A government that morally exhorts ought to cultivate a
greater austerity in its lifestyle than is apparent at the moment.
There is a notable absence of any critique of the acquisitive
society. The market teaches that to be human is to be a consumer,
whatever the consequences. But as the CSU used to insist, consumers also have responsibilities to society, and particularly to the
workers who make or sell the goods they purchase. Third, there
is an unresolved tension between the type of moral liberalism
which Blair condemns (careless conception, feckless parenting,
drug use, callous individualism) and that liberalism which he
espouses (equality for women, gays and religions; uncensorious
treatment of marital problems of Ministers). Sooner or later
this unresolved tension will be exposed and tested in a painful
dilemma. What happens when the twin commitments to
pluralism and to the common good conflict? Which has priority?

A faith in a dynamic God which expresses itself in narratives,
parables and images is more creative and supple than an ideology.

Consciously or unconsciously, Blair has re-expressed socialism in a form which brings him closer to moralists like Tawney, Attlee and Cripps and closer also to the minority strand within Christian Socialism which was more biblical than ideological, advocated devolution rather than statism, co-partnership rather than nationalization, and which saw paternalism as both expressing social obligation and a way of empowering the weak, but asked in return for responsible citizenship. Thus Tony Blair can, if he desires, discover antecedents for his revisionism in features of a lineage which goes back to F. D. Maurice in 1848.

9

Conclusion

Christian Socialism, as we have seen, is (and has always been) a complex and variegated phenomenon, more varied than the Labour Party itself. What positive contributions has it made to church and state? It has retained forms of socialism which the prevailing statism has suppressed. When the Labour Party neglected its Christian and ethical roots, it kept them alive. It has drawn a number of Christians from all classes into politics, social action and work for the poor and for a more just society. Thaxted is inextricably associated with the memory of that flamboyant and romantic socialist priest Conrad Noel. But other priests since have continued something of that tradition. In the churchyard there is an inscription to a lady who died in 1977:

> She gave her life to serving the deprived here, in Africa and in Korea, inspired by the socialist teachings of this Church.

It is very difficult to imagine that the critique of Thatcherism mounted by Anglican bishops and other Christian leaders would have been possible without the Christian Socialist tradition behind them, and in particular without the example and thinking of William Temple, the most influential Christian Socialist bishop in twentieth-century Britain. And in that Christian Socialist tradition, paternalism and *noblesse oblige* was an indispensable element. At the moment the ethics of socialism are being reassessed. Jack Straw and others commend the concept of the responsible citizen and the contribution of the volunteer. The current re-examination of socialist ethics and history should include a more sympathetic understanding of the tradition of paternalism and *noblesse oblige*.

Christian Socialism also opened up lines of communication with, and developed a degree of mutual understanding between, the churches and the Labour movement. This was a major factor in preventing the growth of that anti-clericalism which is so common on the continent. On the continent socialism was almost automatically a sign of atheism, for it was condemned by the pope. Here, by contrast, bishops at the decennial international Anglican episcopal conference at Lambeth in 1888 declared that 'much of what is good and true in Socialism is to be found in the precepts of Christ', and urged the clergy to enter into friendly relations with socialists and to attend their meetings.[1] Christian influence on the British Labour movement saved it from being condemned by the Roman Catholic Church as atheistic and anti-religious. So Roman Catholics did not split the trade union movement here, as they did on the continent in accordance with *Rerum Novarum*, into Catholic and non- (usually anti-) Catholic unions. Another result was that the British Communist Party remained small. The workers did not despair of the democratic process, but worked within it. This is partly because the Labour Party has never been purely a proletarian party, but has drawn some members and support from the middle and upper classes, including bishops and clergy, the kind of people who had access to the levers of power.

But there were also negative features of Christian Socialism. Christian Socialists often encouraged 'new dawnism', and preached that it was possible to establish the kingdom of God in a permanent form and by political means. In reaction against evangelical individualism and the negative views of human nature fostered by Calvinism, Christian Socialists took too rosy a view of human nature and held a too simple belief in progress. They thought it was possible to apply the face-to-face ethics of the Sermon on the Mount in political and international relationships. Their recourse to the Old Testament prophets was a mixed blessing. On the positive side, the prophets were powerful advocates of social righteousness. The pursuit of social justice was a way of knowing God, as Jeremiah reminded the king:

> Did not your father eat and drink and do justice and right-eousness? Then it was well with him. He judged the cause of the poor and needy; then it was well. Is not this to know me? says the Lord (Jer. 22.15–16).

On the other hand, the prophets also encouraged the belief that the verbal denunciation of social evil in emotional, black and white terms was sufficient. But most advances in social welfare have arisen out of the patient, laborious deliberations of com-mittees, investigations and commissions and the painstaking work of legislation. By contrast, Christian Socialist societies often took off into the political stratosphere, largely because they were dominated by clergy who were not in touch with the world of work and commerce and did not experience poverty, job in-security or unemployment.

Christian Socialism has not created a working-class Christianity. Roman Catholicism which once had a strong working-class allegiance has become more middle class, partly through social and demographic changes, but also, as Anthony Archer argued in *The Two Catholic Churches* (1986), through the reforms of Vatican II which created a style of church more attractive to middle-class than to working-class people. Like Nonconformity, British Roman Catholicism has lost much of its desire to dissent from national norms. Christian Socialism has not been a working-class movement, though it has included working-class people. What would a predominantly working-class Christian Socialism (or a predominantly working-class church) led by laypeople, look like?

What about Christian Socialism in the present, and in the future?

Socialism in the past depended upon siege economies where national governments could control the flow of capital, industrial development, interest rates, wages and salaries, and as happened in Eastern Europe, even the movement of people. Membership of the European Union and participation in a global economy and communications network reduces national sovereignty and makes a siege economy impossible. If socialists are committed to internationalism, then a siege economy is also morally undesirable. In a world where a British airline company can shift its whole booking operation through satellite links to India, the imposition of heavy taxation of industry or salaries in one country will simply result in the migration of firms and management to another country with lower taxes.

If the market has made traditional socialism impossible, it has also destroyed traditional Conservatism. So we have the Labour Party trying to recover its traditional values with talk of duties, responsibilities, obligations, interdependence, self-help balancing mutual belonging. But the Conservative Party tries to modernize by greater internal democracy and a more liberal attitude to homosexuals, while being prepared to go to the last ditch against devolution or the abolition of hereditary membership of the House of Lords. As John Gray puts it:

In Britain, the Conservative Party derived its rationale during much of this century from opposition to socialism. When socialism disappeared as a political force – partly as a result of Conservative policies – the Conservative Party lost a large part of its identity and began its drift into disoriented marginality . . . Conservative parties seek to promote free markets, while at the same time defending 'traditional values'. It is hard to think of a more quixotic enterprise. Free markets are the most potent solvents of tradition at work in the world today. As they continuously revolutionize production, they throw all social relationships into flux. Conservatives glorify the incessant change demanded by free markets and at the same time believe that nothing – in family life or the incidence of crime, for example – will be changed by it . . . Free markets undermine some of the central institutions of bourgeois societies. Among these is the institution of the career . . . a lifelong vocation.[2]

Yet it is also time that the churches and the Left more openly reassessed the Thatcher revolution. Both Blair and Field have shown a good deal of political courage in paying tribute to some of its positive features. If Thatcherism was made possible by the breakdown of civic virtues under Wilson and Callaghan, then Blair's revolution was made possible by the positive as well as the negative features of the previous eighteen years. Despite Mrs Thatcher's failure to roll back the state, it was she who made us look again at the voluntary and self-help traditions of the nineteenth century (an important element in Labour's welfare reforms). It was she who challenged statism. Preston contends that Christian Socialists, particularly in the light of what happened in Eastern Europe, should now take a more favourable view of profit, self-interest and competition.[3] Gray maintains that now Communism has collapsed, it is possible to look at Marxism's analysis of capitalism more objectively. He points out how much of Marx's description in the *Communist Manifesto* of a society dominated by the market has been realized in our time:

> Constant revolutionizing of production, uninterrupted disturbance of all social conditions, everlasting uncertainty and agitation . . . All fixed, fast-frozen relations, with their train of ancient and venerable prejudices and opinions, are swept away, all new-formed ones become antiquated before they can ossify. All that is solid melts into air, all that is holy is profaned . . . [4]

If the Marxist picture of society as composed of oppressors and victims is both over-simplified and harmful, the Marxist insistence on taking economic power and motivation seriously remains as important as ever.

Timothy Gorringe writes: 'Tawney's work represents that education of desire which is one of the key functions of prophecy. He opposes, and enables others to oppose, the enemies of hope: silence, submission and fatalism.'[5] Dennis and Halsey claim that ethical socialism gives socialism 'an anti-historicist slant'.[6] (Karl Popper attacked 'historicism', which is the notion that history has a plot which is unfolding by itself. It was this which made him such a formidable opponent of Marxism.) Christian Socialists should also firmly reject historicism. John XXIII, to everyone's astonishment (including his own) in October 1958 became pope at the age of seventy-six. In January 1959 he dumfounded the Vatican and the church by proposing 'without any forethought' (he said) to hold an Ecumenical Council. That Advent he wrote in his diary: 'Above all, one must be ready for the Lord's surprise moves.' Christian Socialists are therefore impelled to challenge those who claim that what Gorringe calls 'the education of desire' is an unwarrantable interference with the rights of citizens to live by the market. Hobbes wrote in chapter XI of *Leviathan*: 'I put for a general inclination of all mankind, a perpetual and restless desire of power after power, that ceaseth only in death.' Yet it is clear that the satisfaction of the perpetual human desire for more and more wants does not necessarily bring a proportionate advance in human welfare, but indeed often the reverse.[7]

The market must be moralized by government and regulatory agencies, through shareholder pressure and customer choice. Even Michael Novak, the leading Roman Catholic protagonist of the New Right, argues:

> Markets are also vulnerable to corruption and defects. Markets have limits; they are not an all-purpose tool; they do not accomplish all necessary social tasks . . . Markets are not a law unto themselves, but operate under both moral and civil law . . . Thus, there are many things that ought never to be bought and sold; the truth, for example, or public office, objects consecrated to divine use, the human body . . . [8]

There ought to be areas of society which are counter-cultural, where, for example, employees are glad to work for less than they could receive in commercial undertakings. Rabbi Jonathan Sacks has written finely in chapter 19 of *Faith in the Future* (1995) about how much a society gains when holy times, holy places, pauses, intervals, enclaves, are carefully created and guarded. Going into a church, a library, a museum, a university, a school ought to feel different from going into a bank or supermarket. Could these be counter-cultural without becoming refugee camps? For clergy, librarians, lecturers, teachers, even nuns and monks, are dependent financially on entrepreneurs and financiers. It always comes as something of a moral shock to the general public to realize that all the churches and even monasteries depend to a lesser or greater extent on investments and on income from property. Peter Selby, Timothy Gorringe and other Christian Socialists are asking for a re-examination of the ethics of usury. They rightly denounce the evil of high rates of interest exacted from the helpless and poor. But they give insufficient attention to the moral value of interest in encouraging thrift and saving or as a method of attracting investment or financing the non-commercial sector of society, including the churches.

Yet there are prophetic signs and acted parables which the churches could perform. For example, the Church of England has since 1972 equalized all stipends for parish priests whatever the size of parish. It could squeeze differentials further between various types of clergy, so that though the expenses paid to a bishop were much greater than those paid to a parish priest, there would be greater similarity between their stipends. Again, the churches need to examine, in the light of the gospel, how they make decisions and exercise power. Again, how salutary it would be if all our very respectable cathedrals had within their precincts either a shelter for the homeless or a home for the mentally disabled. 'He had no form or majesty that we should look at him, nothing in his appearance that we should desire him' (Isa. 53.2).

Why, asked Bishop Gore in 1921, despite all our efforts, have we convinced so few clergy and laypeople about the social implications of Christianity? Is it (we might reply) because the churches attract a high proportion of those who want an individualistic and pietistic religion, but repel those who are mainly convinced by *praxis*? As Frank Field pointed out, *Faith in the City* would have been even more compelling if its publication had been accompanied by a decision to move the church's headquarters into the inner city.

The final question (of many which could be raised about Christian Socialism) is how a specifically *Christian* Socialism can provide an ethical framework for a pluralist society and a pluralist world? As John Atherton said in a sermon commemorating Conrad Noel in 1994 (published by the Jubilee Group): 'There is no longer one grand narrative which can make full sense of our world, whether Christian, socialist, or whatever. There are rather a series of narratives and perspectives in which we search for the gold of Christian insights and values.' Christians need therefore to develop not only middle axioms but moral case studies, narratives which call for a moral and spiritual response, which could be offered as part of an international effort to promote a common moral and political discourse about world issues – for all issues today are global.

Alan Ecclestone in his retirement gathered a 'book of days', quotations of prose and poetry that had nourished him throughout his long life. In his mid-eighties he prepared this collection for publication with the help of Jim Cotter. Two quotations which fitly end this book are found on the same page. The first is from Franz Rosenzweig, a Jewish friend of Martin Buber:

Each of us can only seize by the scruff whoever happens to be closest to him in the mire. This is the 'neighbour' the Bible speaks of. And the miraculous thing is that, although each of us stands in the mire himself, we can each pull out our neighbour, or at least keep him from drowning. None of us has solid ground under his feet; each of us is only held up by the neighbourly hands grasping him by the scruff, with the result that we are each held up by the next man, and often, indeed most of the time . . . hold each other up mutually. All this mutual upholding (a physical impossibility) becomes possible only because the great hand from above supports all these holding hands by their wrists . . . There is no such thing as standing, there is only being held up.

The other quotation is from John Macmurray, who so influenced Tony Blair:

> We need one another to be ourselves.[9]

Bibliography

Place of publication is London, unless otherwise stated

Addison, P. (1977), *The Road to 1945: British Politics and the Second World War*, Quartet Books

Allchin, A.M. (1958), *The Silent Rebellion, Anglican Religious Communities 1845–1900*, SCM Press

Allchin, A.M. (1963), *The Spirit and the Word*, Faith Press

Alison, M. and Edwards, D.E. (1990), (eds) *Christianity and Conservatism*, Hodder

Anson, P. (1956), *The Call of the Cloister: Religious Communities and kindred bodies in the Anglican Communion*, SPCK

Appelbee, E. and Reid, G. (1997), *Powerful Whispers*, Bradford Faith in the City Forum

Arnold, M. (1950), *Culture and Anarchy*, ed J.D. Wilson, CUP

Atherton, J. (1981), 'Trade Unionism: Challenges for Christian Thought', *Theology*, September 1981

— (1992), *Christianity and the Market*, SPCK

— (1994), (ed) *Social Christianity: A Reader*, SPCK

Attlee, C.R. (1949), *The Labour Party in Perspective – and Twelve Years later*, Gollancz

Avis, P. (1988), *Gore: Construction and Conflict*, Churchman Publishing, Worthing

Backstrom, P.N. (1974), *Christian Socialism and Cooperation in Victorian England*, Croom Helm

Barnes, J. (1979), *Ahead of His Age: Bishop Barnes of Birmingham*, Collins

Barnett, C. (1986), *The Audit of War*, Macmillan

Beasley, M. (1997), *Mission on the Margins*, Lutterworth

Bebbington, D.W. (1982), *The Nonconformist Conscience, Chapel and Politics 1870–1914*, Allen & Unwin

Bell, G.K.A. (1940), *Christianity and World Order*, Penguin

— (1952 edn), *Randall Davidson*, OUP

Bettany, F.G. (1926), *Stewart Headlam*, John Murray

Bevir, Mark (1997), 'Labour Churches and Ethical Socialism', *History Today*, April 1997

Binyon G.C. (1931), *The Christian Socialist Movement in England*, SPCK

Birley, R. (1973), 'Maurice and Education', *Theology*, September 1973

Blair, T. (1996), *New Britain*, Fourth Estate

Blatchford, R. (1892), *The Pope's Socialism*, Clarion Press

Bondfield, M. (1948), *A Life's Work*, Hutchinson & Co.

Booth, A. (1990), 'Christian Witness in the New Europe', *Theology*, November 1990

Booth-Clibborn, S. (1991), *Taxes, Burden or Blessing?* Arthur James

Brennan, I. (1990), 'The Gospel and Marxism' in *Fellowship, Freedom and Equality*, David Ormrod (ed), CSM

Briggs, Asa (1954), *Victorian People*, Odhams Press

— (1963), *Victorian Cities*, Odhams Press

— (1979), *The Age of Improvement 1783–1867*, Longmans

Brill, K. (1971), (ed) *John Groser, East End Priest*, Mowbray

Bronowski, J. (1954), *William Blake*, Penguin

Brown, S.J. (1994), '"A Solemn Purification by Fire": Responses to the Great War in the Scottish Presbyterian Churches 1914–19', *Journal of Ecclesiastical History*, January 1994

Bryant, C. (1993), (ed) *Reclaiming the Ground, Christianity and Socialism*, Hodder

— (1994), (ed) *John Smith, An Appreciation*, Hodder

— (1996), *Possible Dreams, A Personal History of the British Christian Socialists*, Hodder

— (1997), *Stafford Cripps*, Hodder

Buchanan, T. (1996), 'Great Britain' in *Political Catholicism in Europe 1918–1965*, Tom Buchanan and Martin Conway (eds), OUP

Burridge, T. (1985), *Clement Attlee*, Cape

Calder, A. (1969), *The People's War: Britain 1939–45*, Cape

Campbell, R.J. (1907), *The New Theology*, Chapman & Hall

Carey, W. (1951), *Good-bye to my Generation*, Mowbray

Carlyle T. (1843; 1909 edn), *Past and Present*, World's Classics, OUP

— (1915), *English and other Critical Essays*, Everyman, J.M. Dent

Carpenter, J. (1960), *Gore, A Study in Liberal Catholic Thought*, Faith Press

Carter, J. (1897), 'The Christian Social Union', *Church Congress Report 1897*, Bemrose & Sons

— (1900), *Preferential Dealing*, CSU

— (1904), *Commercial Morality*, CSU

— (1905), *Christian Socialism*, CSU

Catterall, P. (1989), *The Free Churches and the Labour Party in England and Wales 1918–1939*, unpublished PhD Thesis, University of London

— (1993), 'Morality and Politics: The Free Churches and the Labour Party between the Wars', *The Historical Journal*, 36(3) 1993

— (1994), 'The Party and Religion' in *Conservative Century: The Conservative Party since 1900*, A. Seldon and S. Bell (eds), OUP

— (1996), 'Religion and the rise of Labour' (review), *Journal of Ecclesiastical History*, January 1996

Ceadel, M. (1980), *Pacifism in Britain 1914–1945: The Defining of a Faith*, OUP

Chadwick, O. (1966, 1970), *The Victorian Church*, 2 vols, A. & C. Black (reissued SCM Press 1987)

— (1991), *Victorian Miniature*, CUP

Christian Social Union (1896), *Three Addresses delivered at the Christian Social Union Meeting at the Colston Hall Bristol, December 1st 1896*, W. Crofton Hemmons, Bristol

Clark, H. (1993), *The Church under Thatcher*, SPCK

Clarke, P. (1978), *Liberals and Social Democrats*, CUP

Cockshut, A.O.J. (1966), *Religious Controversies of the Nineteenth Century*, Methuen

Coleman, P. (1980), *Christian Attitudes to Homosexuality*, SPCK

Coleridge, S.T. (1933), *Select Poetry and Prose*, Nonesuch Press

Collingwood, R.G. (1944), *An Autobiography*, Penguin

Coman, P. (1977), *Catholics and the Welfare State*, Longman

Conford, J. (1996), *The Personal World. John Macmurray on self and society*, Floris Books

COPEC (1924), *Commission Report IX: Industry and Property*, Longmans, Green & Co.

COPEC (1924), *The Proceedings*, W. Reason (ed), Longmans, Green & Co.

Cort, J.C. (1988), *Christian Socialism, An Informal History*, Orbis Books, Maryknoll, New York

Creighton, L. (1920) (ed), *Letters of Oswin Creighton*, Longmans, Green & Co.

Cripps, Sir Stafford (1945), *Towards Christian Democracy*, Allen & Unwin

Cunningham, W. (1909), *Christianity and Socialism*, Victoria Institute Transactions

Cupitt, Don (1972), *Crisis of Moral Authority*, Lutterworth Press (reissued SCM Press 1985)

Curtis, G. CR (1947), *William of Glasshampton*, SPCK

Davidson, R.T. (1920), (ed) *The Five Lambeth Conferences* [1867, 1878, 1888, 1897, 1908] SPCK

Davie, P. (1997, *Raising up a Faithful People: High Church Priests and Parochial Education 1850–1910*, Gracewing, Leominster

Davies, D.R. (1961), *In Search of Myself*, Geoffrey Bles

Davies, G. (1983), 'Squires in the East End?', *Theology*, July 1983

Davies, R., George, A.R., Rupp, G. (eds) (1965–88), *A History of the Methodist Church in Great Britain* (4 vols), Epworth Press

Deacon, A. and Mann, K. (1997) 'Moralism and Modernity: The Paradox of New Labour Thinking on Welfare', *Benefits* no. 20

— (1998), 'The Green Paper on Welfare Reform', *Political Quarterly*, vol. 69 no. 3

Dearmer, P. (1907), *The Social Teaching of the Catechism*, CSU

— (1912), 'The Beginnings of the CSU', *Commonwealth*, May 1912

Demant, V.A. (1933), *God, Man and Society*, SCM Press

— (1952), *Religion and the Decline of Capitalism*, Faber

Dennis, N. (1997), *The Invention of Permanent Poverty*, IEA Health and Welfare Unit

— and Halsey, A.H. (1988), *English Ethical Socialism*, OUP

Dictionary of Labour Biography (DLB) (9 vols), J.M. Bellamy and J. Saville (eds), Macmillan 1972–1993

Donaldson, F.L. (*c*1908), *Socialism and the Christian Faith or 'Christian Socialism'*, Mowbray

Duffield, I.K. (1997), *Urban Christ: Responses to John Vincent*, Urban Theology Unit, Sheffield

Eagleton, T. (1966), *The New Left Church*, Sheed & Ward

Eagleton, T. and Wicker, B. (1968), *From Culture to Revolution, The Slant Symposium*, Sheed & Ward

Eagleton, T. (1970), *The Body as Language*, Sheed & Ward

Ecclestone, A. (1967), 'Explosion at Smolny', *New Christian*, 2 November 1967

— (1975), *Yes to God*, Darton, Longman & Todd

— (1976), '*Mystique* and *Politique*', *Theology*, January 1976

— (1993), *Gather the Fragments*, Cairns Publications, Sheffield

Ecclestone, G.S. (1981), *The Church of England and Politics*, CIO Publishing

Eckbert, A.A. (1990), *The Social Thought of the Christian Social Union 1889–1914*, unpublished M.Litt.Thesis, University of Oxford

Evans, S.G. (1965), *The Social Hope of the Christian Church*, Hodder

— (1990), 'Equality' in *Fellowship, Freedom and Equality*, David Ormrod (ed), CSM

Ferguson, R. (1990), *George MacLeod*, HarperCollins

Field, F. (1987), *The Politics of Paradise*, Fount

— (1990), 'Socialism and the Politics of Radical Redistribution' in D. Ormrod (ed) *Fellowship, Freedom and Equality*, CSM

— (1994a), 'William Temple: A Political Evaluation', unpublished lecture

Field, F. (1994b), 'William Temple's Business Ethics: Styming the Left for a Generation', unpublished lecture

— (1996a), 'George Bell: A Uniquely Consistent Life' in *Lambeth*

Palace Library Annual Review (1996)

— (1996b), *Stakeholder Welfare*, IEA Health and Welfare Unit

— (1997), *Reforming Welfare*, Social Market Foundation

Figes, O. (1997), *A People's Tragedy, The Russian Revolution 1891–1924*, Pimlico

Figgis, J.N. CR (1905), 'The Church and the Secular Theory of the State', *Church Congress Report 1905*, Bemrose & Sons

— (1910a), *The Gospel and Human Needs*, Longmans, Green & Co.

— (1910b), *Religion and English Society*, Longmans, Green & Co.

— (1912), *Civilisation at the Cross Roads*, Longmans, Green & Co.

— (1913a), *AntiChrist and other Sermons*, Longmans, Green & Co.

— (1913b), *Churches in the Modern State*, Longmans, Green & Co.

— (1914), *The Fellowship of the Mystery*, Longmans, Green & Co.

— (1919), *Hopes for English Religion*, Longmans, Green & Co.

— (1922 edn), *The Divine Right of Kings*, CUP

Fitzgerald, P. (1977), *The Knox Brothers*, Macmillan

Fletcher, S. (1989), *Maude Royden*, Basil Blackwell

Foot, M. (1981), *Debts of Honour*, Picador

Ford, C.S. (1985), *The Revd John Wilcockson (1872–1969). A Case Study in Relations between Church, Politics and Industrial Society*, unpublished M. Phil. Thesis, University of Leeds

Forrester, D. B. (1981), 'What is distinctive in Social Theology?' in *Christians and the Future of Social Democracy*, M.H. Taylor (ed), G.W. and A. Hesketh, Ormskirk

Forrester, D.B. (1985), *Christianity and the Future of Welfare*, Epworth Press

Fraser, D. (1984), *The Evolution of the British Welfare State*, Macmillan

Freeden, M. (1978), *The New Liberalism: An Ideology of Social Reform*, OUP

Fricker, L. (1958), *New Towns of the Nineteenth and Early Twentieth Centuries*, unpublished Diploma Thesis, University of Reading

Frost, B. (1996), *Goodwill on Fire, Donald Soper's Life and Mission*, Hodder

Girouard, M. (1981), *The Return to Camelot: Chivalry and the English Gentleman*, Yale University Press

Glasier, K.B. (1924), *Memoir of Enid Stacy*, ILP, Manchester

Glass, S.T. (1966), *The Responsible Society, The Ideal of Guild Socialism*, Longmans

Goodfellow, I. (1983), *The Church Socialist League*, unpublished PhD Thesis, University of Durham

Gore, C. (1889; 1892 edn), (ed) *Lux Mundi*, John Murray

— (1891), *The Incarnation of the Son of God*, John Murray

— (1892), *The Social Doctrine of the Sermon on the Mount*, Percival & Co.

— (1896), Sermon in *Report of the Church Congress* (1896), Bemrose & Sons

— (1898), (ed) *Essays in aid of the Reform of the Church*, John Murray

— (1901), *The Body of Christ*, John Murray

— (1902), *St Paul's Epistle to the Ephesians*, John Murray

— (1904), *The Spiritual Efficiency of the Church*, John Murray

— (1905), *Birmingham Bishopric*, Hall & English, Birmingham

— (1907), *The New Theology and the Old Religion*, John Murray

— (1908), *Christianity and Socialism*, CSU/Mowbray

— (1913), (ed) *Property, its Duties and Rights*, Macmillan

— (1918), *Dominant Ideas and Corrective Principles*, Mowbray

— (1921), *The Epistles of St John*, John Murray

— (1922a), *Belief in Christ*, John Murray

— (1922b), introd. *The Return of Christendom*, by A Group of Churchmen, Allen & Unwin

— (1924), 'Richard Meux Benson' in *Spiritual letters of Richard Meux Benson*, W.H. Longridge (ed), Mowbray

— (1926), *Strikes and Locks-Out*, COPEC

— (1928), *Christ and Society*, Allen & Unwin

— (1930), *The Philosophy of the Good Life*, John Murray

Gorringe, T. (1994a), *Alan Ecclestone*, Cairns Publications, Sheffield

— (1994b), *Capital and Kingdom. Theological Ethics and Economic Order*, SPCK

Grasby, D. (1997), 'Henry Scott Holland, Christian Prophet', *Theology*, November 1997

Graves, P.M. (1994), *Labour Women: Women in British Working Class Politics 1918–1939*, CUP

Gray, D. (1986), *Earth and Altar*, Canterbury Press Norwich

Gray, J. (1998), 'Hollow Triumph', *Times Literary Supplement*, 8 May 1998

Groser, St John (1949), *Politics and Persons*, SCM Press

Groves, R. (1967), *Conrad Noel and the Thaxted Movement*, Merlin Press

Habgood, J. (1983), *Church and Nation in a Secular Age*, Darton, Longman & Todd

Hammerton, R.J. (1952), *This Turbulent Priest, The Story of Charles Jenkinson, Parish Priest and Housing Reformer*, Lutterworth Press

Harries, R. (1992), *Is there a Gospel for the Rich?*, Mowbray

Harris, K. (1982), *Attlee*, Weidenfeld & Nicolson

Harvey, J. *et.al.* (1917), *Competition*, Macmillan

Hastings, A. (1991a), *Robert Runcie*, Mowbray

— (1991b), *A History of English Christianity 1920–1990*, SCM Press

— (1994), 'A Prophet in Canterbury', *The Tablet*, 22 October 1994

Hauerwas, S. (1983), *The Peaceable Kingdom*, SCM Press

— (1992), 'In Praise of *Centesimus Annus*', *Theology*, November 1992

Hay, D. (1989), *Economics Today, A Christian Critique*, Apollos

Headlam, S.D. (1907), *The Socialist's Church*, Allen & Unwin

Heidt, J.H. (1975), *The Social Theology of Henry Scott Holland*, unpublished D. Phil. Thesis, University of Oxford

Henderson, P. (1967), *William Morris*, Thames & Hudson

Hennel, M. (1979), *Sons of the Prophets: Evangelical Leaders of the Victorian Church*, SPCK

Hennessy, P. (1993), *Never Again, Britain 1945–1951*, Vintage

Hensman, S. (1996), *Is Tony Blair a Christian Socialist?*, Jubilee Group, Croydon

Higgins, S. (1984), *The Benn Inheritance, The Story of a Radical Family*, Weidenfeld & Nicolson

Hilton, B. (1988), *The Age of Atonement: The Influence of Evangelicalism on Social and Economic Thought, 1795–1865*, OUP

Hinchliffe, P. (1987), *Benjamin Jowett and the Christian Religion*, OUP

Holladay, J.D. (1982), 'Nineteenth Century Evangelical Activism: From Private Charity to State Intervention, 1820–50', *Historical Magazine of the Protestant Episcopal Church*, vol. LI, March 1982

Holland, H.S. and Carter, J. (1905), *Commercial Morality*, CSU
— (1911a), intro. *Lombard Street in Lent*, Robert Scott and Percy Dearmer, (ed)
— (1911b), *Our Neighbours, A Handbook for the CSU*, Mowbray
— (1915), *A Bundle of Memories*, Wells, Gardner, Darton & Co.
— (1916), *So As By Fire*, Wells, Gardner, Darton & Co.
Holman, B. (1987), 'George Lansbury', *Crucible*, October 1987
— (1990), *Good old George: The life of George Lansbury*, Lion
— (1993), 'Reconstructing the Common Good' in *Reclaiming the Ground, Christianity and Socialism*, C. Bryant (ed), Hodder
— (1997), *Towards Equality*, SPCK
Hopkins, A.B. (1952), *Elizabeth Gaskell*, John Lehmann
Howell-Thomas, D. (1993), *William Temple Reviewed*, Jubilee Group, Croydon
Hughes, R. (1987), *The Red Dean*, Churchman Publishing, Worthing

Iremonger, F.A. (1948), *William Temple*, OUP
Jasper, R.C.D. (1967), *George Bell*, OUP
Jenkins, D.E. (1976), *The Contradiction of Christianity*, SCM Press
— (1988), *God, Politics and the Future*, SCM Press
— and Jenkins, R. (1991) *Free to Believe*, BBC Books
Jeremy, D.J. (1990), *Capitalists and Christians, Business Leaders and the Churches in Britain 1900–1960*, OUP
Johnson, H. (1939), *The Socialist Sixth of the World*, Gollancz
— (1956), *Christians and Communism*, Putnam
Jones, P.d'A. (1968), *The Christian Socialist Revival 1877–1914*, Princeton University Press

Kendall, G. (1947), *Charles Kingsley and his Ideas*, Hutchinson
Kenyon, R. (1928), *A Syllabus for Study Circles on Catholicism and Industry*, (no publisher)
Kent, J. (1980), 'From Temple to *Slant*' in *Agenda for Prophets*, R.Ambler and D. Haslam (eds), Bowerdean Press
Kitson Clark, G. (1973), *Churchmen and the Condition of England 1832–1885*, Methuen
Knight, F. (1995) *The Nineteenth-Century Church and English Society*, CUP

Koss, S. (1975), *Nonconformity in Modern British Politics*, Batsford

Kumar, K. (1987), *Utopia and Anti-Utopia in Modern Times*, Blackwell, Oxford

Lambeth Conference Report (1920), SPCK

Lansbury, E. (1934), *George Lansbury, My Father*, Sampson Low, Marston & Co.

Lansbury, G. (1928), *My Life*, Constable

— (1935), *Looking Backwards and Forwards*, Blackie & Son

Lash, N. (1981), *A Matter of Hope*, Darton, Longman & Todd

Lawson, J. (1949), *Peter Lee*, Epworth Press

Leech, K. (1965), 'What Has Happened to Christian Social Theology?', *Theology*, March 1965

— (1968), 'Stewart Headlam' in *For Christ and the People*, M.B. Reckitt (ed), SPCK

— (1974), 'The Resurrection of the Catholic Social Voice', *Theology*, December 1974

— (1976), 'Believing in the Incarnation', *Theology*, March 1976

— (1977), *Soul Friend*, Sheldon Press

— (1980), 'The Christian Left in Britain' in R. Ambler and D. Haslam (eds), *Agenda for Prophets*, Bowerdean

— (1981a), 'The Thought of Juan Luis Segundo', *Theology*, July 1981

— (1981b), *The Social God*, Sheldon Press

— (1986), *Spirituality and Pastoral Care*, Sheldon Press

— (1988), *Struggle in Babylon* Sheldon Press

— (1990), 'Religion and the rise of racism' in *Fellowship, Freedom and Equality*, David Ormrod (ed), CSM

— (1993), (ed) *Conrad Noel and the Catholic Crusade*, Jubilee Group, Croydon

— (1994), (ed) *Who will sound the Trumpet? The Jubilee Group and the Future of the Left*, Jubilee Group, Croydon

— (1995), *Stanley Evans 1912–1965*, Jubilee Paper

— (1997), *The Sky is Red*, Darton, Longman & Todd

Le Quesne, A.L. *et al* (1993), *Victorian Thinkers: Carlyle, Ruskin, Arnold, Morris*, OUP

Liddon, H.P. (1893–7), *Life of Edward Bouverie Pusey* (4 vols), Longmans, Green & Co.

Lloyd, R. (1966), *The Church of England 1900–1965*, SCM Press

Lockhart, J.G. (1949), *Cosmo Gordon Lang*, Hodder

McCabe, M. (1994), 'On Jordan's Stormy Banks: Evangelicalism and the Socialist Revival in Scotland c1890–1914' in *After Socialism? The Future of Radical Christianity*, A.R. Morton (ed), University of Edinburgh Press

MacCarthy, F. (1989), *Eric Gill*, Faber

— (1994), *William Morris*, Faber

McLeod, H. (1996), *Religion and Society in England 1850–1914*, Macmillan

McSmith, A. (1993), *John Smith*, Verso

Marchant, J. (1924), *Dr John Clifford C.H.*, Cassell

Markham, I.S. (1994), *Plurality and Christian Ethics*, CUP

Marquand, D. (1996), 'Moralists and Hedonists' in *The Ideas that Shaped Post-War Britain*, D. Marquand and A. Seldon (eds), Fontana

Marx, K. (1904), *A Contribution to the Critique of Political Economy*, N.I. Stone (trs) Charles Kerr, Chicago

Mason, A. (1993), *SSM: History of the Society of the Sacred Mission*, Canterbury Press Norwich

— (1994), 'Jenkinson and Southcott' in *Religion in Leeds*, A. Mason (ed), Alan Sutton, Stroud

Matthews, W.R. (*et.al.*) (1946), *William Temple: An Estimate and An Appreciation*, James Clarke

Maurice, F. (1884), *The Life of Frederick Denison Maurice* (2 vols), Macmillan

Maurice, F.D. (1838; Everyman edn n.d.), *The Kingdom of Christ* (2 vols), J.M. Dent

Mayhew, P. (1987), *All Saints: Birth and Growth of a Community*, All Saints, Oxford

Mayor, S. (1967), *The Churches and the Labour Movement*, Independent Press

Meacham, S. (1987), *Toynbee Hall and Social Reform 1880–1914*, Yale University Press

Messinger, G.S. (1985), *Manchester in the Victorian Age*, Manchester University Press

Mews, S. (1976), 'The Churches' in *The General Strike*, M. Morris (ed), Penguin

Milbank, J. (1986), 'The Body by Love Possessed: Christianity and late Capitalism in Britain', *Modern Theology*, 3, 1, 1986

— (1990), *Theology and Social Theory*, Blackwell, Oxford

— (1993), 'Against the Resignations of the Age' in *Things Old and New: Catholic Social Teaching Revisited*, F.P. McHugh and S.M. Natale (eds), University Press of America

— (1996), 'Socialism of the Gift, Socialism by Grace', *New Blackfriars*, December 1996

— (1997), *The Word Made Strange*, Blackwell, Oxford

Mingay, G.E. (1981), (ed) *The Victorian Countryside* (2 vols), Routledge

Morris, W. (1891; 1993 edn), *News from Nowhere, and Other Writings* Penguin

Morisy, A. (1997), *Beyond the Good Samaritan*, Mowbray

Morton, A.R. (1994a), (ed) *After Socialism? The Future of Radical Christianity*, University of Edinburgh Press

— (1994b), (ed) *God's Will in a Time of Crisis: A Colloquium Celebrating the 50th Anniversary of the Baillie Commission*, University of Edinburgh Press

Munby, D.L. (1956), *Christianity and Economic Problems*, Macmillan

— (1958), 'The Importance of Technical Competence' in *Essays in Anglican Self-Criticism*, D.M. Paton (ed), SCM Press

— (1961), *God and the Rich Society*, OUP

Munson, J. (1991), *The Nonconformists*, SPCK

Neave, D. (1991), *Mutual Aid in the Victorian Countryside*, Hull University Press

Nettleship, L.E. (1982), 'William Fremantle, Samuel Barnett and the Broad Church Origins of Toynbee Hall', *Journal of Ecclesiastical History*, October 1982

Newell, J. Philip (1981), *A.J. Scott and his Circle*, unpublished PhD Thesis, University of Edinburgh

Newsome, D. (1966), 'The Assault on Mammon: Charles Gore and John Neville Figgis', *Journal of Ecclesiastical History*, October 1966

Nicholls, D. (1962), *Authority in Church and State*, unpublished PhD Thesis, University of Cambridge

— (1967), *Church and State in Britain since 1820*, Routledge

— (1975; 1994 edn), *The Pluralist State*, St Martin's Press

— (1982), 'Fractions', *Crucible*, January 1982

— (1984), 'William Temple and the Welfare State', *Crucible*, October 1984

— (1986), 'Two Tendencies in Political Theology' in *Tradition Renewed*, G. Rowell (ed), Darton, Longman & Todd

— (1989a), 'Christianity in Politics' in *The Religion of the Incarnation*, R. Morgan (ed), Bristol Classical Press

— (1989b), *Deity and Domination*, Routledge

— (1991), *God and Government*, Jubilee Group, Croydon

— (1993), 'Trinity and Conflict', *Theology*, January 1993

Niebuhr, R. (1932; 1960 edn), *Moral Man and Immoral Society*, Charles Scribner's Sons, New York and SCM Press

Noel, C. (1910), *Socialism in Church History*, Frank Palmer

— (1945), *An Autobiography*, J.M. Dent

Norman, E.R. (1976), *Church and Society in England 1770–1970*, OUP

— (1984), *The English Catholic Church in the Nineteenth Century*, OUP

— (1985), *Roman Catholicism in England*, OUP

— (1987), *The Victorian Christian Socialists*, CUP

Novak, M. and Preston, R.H. (1994), *Christian Capitalism or Christian Socialism?*, IEA Health and Welfare Unit

Oliver, J. (1968), *The Church and Social Order: Social Thought in the Church of England 1918–1939*, Mowbray

Orwell, G. (1961), *Collected Essays*, Mercury Books

Osborne, C.E. (1905), *The Life of Father Dolling*, George Newnes Ltd

Paget, S. (1921), *Henry Scott Holland*, John Murray

Palmer, B. (1993), *Reverend Rebels*, Darton, Longman & Todd

Papal Encyclicals,

    Rerum Novarum (1891)

Quadragesimo Anno (1931)
Populorum Progressio (1967)
Laborem Exercens (1981)
Sollicitudo Rei Socialis (1987)
Centesimus Annus (1991)

Parsons, G. and Moore, J.R. (1988), (eds) *Religion in Victorian Britain* (4 vols), Manchester University Press

Pawson, G.P.H.C.R. (1954), *Edward Keble Talbot*, SPCK

Peart-Binns, J.S. (1988), *Maurice B. Reckitt*, Bowerdean Press and Marshall Pickering

Pierson, S. (1979), *British Socialists, The Journey from Fantasy to Politics*, Harvard University Press

Pinnington, J. (1997), *Kingdom and Commonwealth: The Christian Social Union and its legacy to radical social thought in the Church of England 1889–1941*, Jubilee Group, Croydon

Plant, R. (1985), 'The Anglican Church and the Secular State' in *Church and Politics Today*, G. Moyser (ed), T. & T. Clark

— (1995), 'Markets, Theology and the Common Good', (unpublished) 1995 Gore Lecture

Prestige, G.L. (1935), *The Life of Charles Gore*, Heinemann

Preston, R.H. (1942), 'The Malvern Conference' in *Modern Churchman*, April 1942

— (1966), 'R.H. Tawney as a Christian Moralist', *Theology*, April, May, June 1966

— (1979), *Religion and the Persistence of Capitalism*, SCM Press

— (1981), *Explorations in Theology 9*, SCM Press

— (1983a), *Church and Society in the Late Twentieth Century: The Economic and Political Task*, SCM Press

— (1983b), 'Pope John Paul II on Work', *Theology*, January 1983

— (1985), 'William Temple', *Crucible*, July 1985

— (1987), 'Theology and the Economy', *Crucible*, July 1987

— (1989), 'Twenty Years after *Populorum Progressio*', *Theology*, November 1989

— (1992), '*Centesimus Annus*: An Appraisal', *Theology*, November 1992

Preston, R.H. *et. al.* (1994), *Archbishop William Temple: Issues in*

Church and Society Fifty Years on, William Temple Foundation, Manchester

— (1997), 'The Common Good', *Epworth Review*, January 1997

Price Hughes, D.P. (1904), *The Life of Hugh Price Hughes*, Hodder

Purcell, W. (1983), *Odd Man Out. A Biography of Lord Soper of Kingsway*, Mowbray

Ramsey, A.M. (1951), *F.D. Maurice and the Conflicts of Modern Theology*, CUP

Raven, C.E. (1920), *Christian Socialism 1848–1854*, Macmillan

Read, D. (1979), *England 1868–1914*, Longman

— (1982) (ed), *Edwardian England*, Croom Helm

Reckitt, M. (1932), *Faith and Society*, Longmans, Green & Co.

— (1945) (ed), *Prospect for Christendom*, Faber

— (1947), *Maurice to Temple*, Faber

Rentoul, J. (1995), *Tony Blair*, Little, Brown & Co.

Report of the Pan-Anglican Congress (1908), SPCK

Richter, M. (1964), *The Politics of Conscience: T.H. Green and his Age*, Weidenfeld & Nicolson

Roberts, D. (1979), *Paternalism in Early Victorian England*, Croom Helm

Rowlands, J.H.L. (1989), *Church, State and Society: The Attitudes of John Keble, Richard Hurrell Froude and John Henry Newman 1827–1845*, Churchman Publishing, Worthing

Royle, E. (1983), *The Victorian Church in York*, University of York

Ruskin, J. (1862; 1985 edn), *Unto This Last and Other Writings*, Penguin

Sandford, E.G. (1906), *Memoirs of Archbishop Temple* (2 vols), Macmillan

Sedgwick, P. (1997), 'Theology and Society' in *The Modern Theologians*, D.F. Ford (ed), Blackwell, Oxford

Selby, P. (1997), *Grace and Mortgage*, Darton, Longmann Todd

Seymour-Jones, C. (1992), *Beatrice Webb, Woman of Conflict*, Allison & Busby

Simon, U. (1978), *Sitting in Judgement*, SPCK

Smith, L. (1992), 'Religion and the ILP' in *The Centennial History of the Independent Labour Party*, D. James, T. Jowitt, K. Laybourn (eds), Ryburn Publishing, Keele

— (1993), *Religion and the Rise of Labour: Nonconformity and the Independent Labour Movement in Lancashire and the West Riding 1880–1914*, Ryburn Publishing, Keele

Snowden, P. (1903), *The Christ that is to be*, ILP

Soloway, R.A. (1969), *Prelates and People: Ecclesiastical Social Thought in England 1783–1852*, Routledge

Sopel, J. (1995), *Tony Blair*, Bantam Books

Soper, D. (1935), *Christ and Tower Hill*, Hodder

— (1984), *Calling for Action*, Robson Books

— (1990), 'Socialism, an enduring Creed' in *Fellowship, Freedom and Equality*, David Ormrod (ed), CSM

Speaight, R. (1966), *The Life of Eric Gill*, Methuen

Stacy, Paul (1907), *The Socialist Meaning of the Church's Facts*, Elland

Stanford, P. (1994), *Lord Longford*, Heinemann

Stedman Jones, G. (1983), *Languages of Class*, CUP

Stephenson, G. (1936), *Edward Stuart Talbot 1844–1934*, SPCK

Stranks, C.J. (1954), *Dean Hook*, Mowbray

Studdert-Kennedy, G.A. (1982), *Dog-Collar Democracy, The Industrial Christian Fellowship 1919–1929*, Macmillan

Suggate, A. (1981), 'William Temple's Christian Social Ethics', *Crucible*, October 1981

— (1987), *William Temple and Social Ethics Today*, T. & T. Clark

Tawney, R.H. (1921), *The Acquisitive Society*, G. Bell & Sons Ltd

— (1931; 1964 edn), *Equality*, Unwin Books

— (1926; 1948 edn), *Religion and the Rise of Capitalism*, Penguin

— (1953), *The Attack and other Papers*, Allen & Unwin

— (1964), *The Radical Tradition*, Allen & Unwin

— (1972), *Commonplace Book*, J.M. Winter and D.M. Joslin (eds), CUP

Taylor, A.J.P. (1975), *English History 1914–1945*, Penguin

Taylor, M.H. (1981), (ed) *Christians and the Future of Social Democracy*, G.W. & A. Hesketh, Ormskirk

Temple, F.S. (1963), (ed) *William Temple: Some Lambeth Letters*, OUP

Temple, W. (1940a), *Thoughts in War-Time*, Macmillan
— (1940b), *The Hope of a New World*, SCM Press
— (1941a), *Citizen and Churchman*, Eyre & Spottiswoode
— (1941b), intro. *Malvern, 1941: The Life of the Church and the Order of Society*, Longmans, Green & Co.
— (1941c), intro. *The Archbishop of York's Conference, Malvern. The Life of the Church and the Order of Society*, ICF
— (1944), *The Church Looks Forward*, Macmillan
— (1942; 1956 edn), *Christianity and Social Order*, Penguin
— (1958), *Religious Experience and Other Essays and Addresses*, A.E. Baker (ed), James Clarke
Terrill, R. (1974), *R.H. Tawney and His Times: Socialism as Fellowship*, André Deutsch
Thompson, D.M. (1986), 'John Clifford's Social Gospel', *Baptist Quarterly*, January 1986
— (1990), 'The Emergence of the Nonconformist Social Gospel in England' in *Protestant Evangelicalism, Studies in Church History, Subsidia 7*, K. Robbins (ed), Blackwell, Oxford
— (1993), 'F.D. Maurice, Rebel Conservative' in *Modern Religious Rebels*, Stuart Mews (ed), Epworth Press
Thorpe, A. (1997), *A History of the British Labour Party*, Macmillan
Tillotson, K. (1954), *Novels of the Eighteen-Forties*, OUP
Trevelyan, G.M. (1946), *English Social History*, Longmans, Green & Co.
Tucker, M.G. (1950), *John Neville Figgis*, SPCK
Tuckwell, G.M. (1931), *Constance Smith*, Duckworth

Uglow, J. (1993), *Elizabeth Gaskell*, Faber

Vidler, A.R. (1976), 'The Limitations of William Temple', *Theology*, January 1976
Villa-Vicencio, C. (1992), *A Theology of Reconstruction*, CUP
Vincent, J. (1962), *Christ in a Nuclear World*, Crux Press, Manchester
— (1976), *Alternative Church*, Christian Journals Ltd, Belfast
Vincent, J. (1992), (ed) *A Community Called Ashram*, Ashram Community Trust, Sheffield

— (1993), 'Jesus as Politician' in *Reclaiming the Ground, Christianity and Socialism*, C. Bryant (ed), Hodder

— (1996), Interview in *Reviews in Religion and Theology*, August 1996

Wagner, D.O. (1930), *The Church of England and Social Reform since 1854*, Columbia, New York

Wainwright, H. (1991), 'New Forms of Democracy for Socialist Renewal' in D.McLellan (ed), *Socialism and Democracy*, Macmillan

Walvin, J. (1987), *Victorian Values*, André Deutsch

Ward, M. (1945), *Gilbert Keith Chesterton*, Sheed & Ward

Ward, W.R. (1993), 'The Way of the World. The Rise and Decline of Protestant Social Christianity in Britain' in his *Faith and Faction*, Epworth Press

Waterman, A.M.C. (1990), 'Denys Munby on Economics and Christianity', *Theology*, March 1990

— (1991), *Revolution, Economics and Religion: Christian Political Economy 1798–1833*, CUP

Webb, B. (1938), *My Apprenticeship* (2 vols), Penguin

Webb, S. (1890; 1987 edn), *Socialism in England*, Gower, Aldershot

Welsby, P.A. (1970), (ed) *Sermons and Society: An Anglican Anthology*, Penguin

Westcott, B.F. (1890), *Socialism*, The Guild of St Matthew

— (1895), *The Christian Social Union*, Rivington, Percival & Co.

— (1896), *The Christian Law*, CSU

Whitbourn, J. (1997), (ed) *The Best of my Belief*, SPCK Triangle

Wicker, B. (1966), *Culture and Theology*, Sheed & Ward

Wiener, M.J. (1981), *English Culture and the Decline of the Industrial Spirit 1850–1980*, CUP

Wiles, M. (1976), 'Believing in the Incarnation', *Theology*, July 1976

Wilkinson, A. (1986), *Dissent or Conform? War, Peace and the English Churches 1900–1945*, SCM Press

— (1988a), 'Three Sexual Issues', *Theology*, March 1988

— (1988b), 'Victorian Priest's faith in the city', *Church Times* 27 May 1988

— (1990), 'The Politics of the Anglican Modernists' in *Chesterton and the Modernist Crisis*, A. Nichols (ed), Augustine Publishing Co., Chulmleigh

— (1992), *The Community of the Resurrection. A Centenary History*, SCM Press

— (1978; 1996, edn), *The Church of England and the First World War*, SCM Press

Wilkinson J.T. (1971), *Arthur Samuel Peake*, Epworth Press

Williams, B. (1982), *The Franciscan Revival in the Anglican Communion*, Darton, Longman & Todd

Williams, R. (1961), *Culture and Society 1780–1850*, Penguin

Wilson, A.N. (1986), *Hilaire Belloc*, Penguin

Wolffe, J. (1995), (ed) *Evangelical Faith and Public Zeal: Evangelicals and Society in Britain 1780–1980*, SPCK

Wood, I.S. (1990), *John Wheatley*, Manchester University Press

— (1994), 'John Wheatley and Catholic Socialism' in *After Socialism? The Future of Radical Christianity*, A.R. Morton (ed), University of Edinburgh Press

Worrall, B.G. (1978), 'R.J. Campbell and his New Theology', *Theology*, September 1978

Wright, A. (1987), *R.H. Tawney*, Manchester University Press

Wrigley, C. (1990), *Arthur Henderson*, University of Wales Press

Yeo, S. (1968), 'Thomas Hancock' in *For Christ and the People*, M. Reckitt (ed), SPCK

Young, G.M. (1936), *Victorian England: Portrait of an Age*, OUP

Notes

The details of all books referred to in the Notes are to be found in the Bibliography.

Preface

1. Blair (1996) 7, 15
2. Morris xxxiii

1 Nineteenth-Century Background

1. Norman (1976) 15–18
2. Kitson Clark 55, 61; Norman (1976) 187–90
3. Hilton 209–10; Hennel 10, 67; Wolffe 11–20
4. Kitson Clark 37; Norman (1976) 37; Waterman (1991) 74–5, 162–5
5. cit. Kitson Clark 9
6. Welsby 231–8; Chadwick (1991) 70–1
7. Hilton 297, 300; Norman (1976) 40–3; Soloway 93
8. cit. Soloway 96
9. Atherton (1994) 351; Soloway 96–101, 108–9; Waterman (1991) 162–9
10. Soloway 118–25
11. Davie *passim*; Kitson Clark 122; Norman 163; Stranks 64–6
12. cit. Royle 32
13. Hilton 98–9; Soloway 163
14. Chadwick (1991) 53, 55, 81; Knight 69–70, 105
15. Kitson Clark 168–73, 182–90, 206–16; Wilkinson (1986) 77–8
16. Roberts 74, 258; Soloway chs IV and V; Waterman (1991) 179
17. cit. Norman (1976) 63

18. Briggs (1979) 280; Soloway 161, 174–5; Hilton 245
19. Norman (1976) 62; Soloway 180–2; Mingay II:599
20. Hilton 84, 242–3; Parsons and Moore II:122–3, 136–7, II:115–6
21. Hilton 109, 273–4, 255–6 *et passim*; Holladay *passim*; Wolffe 38, 45
22. Cupitt 98–104
23. *Quarterly Review* XCVII (1855) 144
24. Rowlands 52–8; Liddon II:37, 82, III:171
25. Rowlands 116–7, 225; Dennis and Halsey 44; Chadwick (1966) I:336; Sandford II:477
26. Briggs (1979) 288–9; Williams (1961) 43–7
27. Waterman (1991) 196–203; Soloway 421–2
28. Kitson Clark xvii–xviii
29. Hilton 314; Bronowski 120, 91
30. Norman (1987) 10
31. Coleridge 476–7
32. cit. Cockshut 41, 43
33. cit. Bryant (1996) 24
34. Carlyle (1909) 1–2; Carlyle (1915) 208
35. cit. Kitson Clark 75; Nicholls (1967) 36
36. cit. Norman (1976) 138
37. Soloway 209
38. cit. Norman (1976) 139; see also Walvin *passim*
39. Young 63; Kitson Clark 32; Trevelyan 471
40. Briggs (1954) 220–1; Roberts 190; Kitson Clark 223
41. Recent studies of Maurice's socialism include Bryant (1996), Norman (1987) and Thompson (1993)
42. cit. Kendall 46; Norman 49
43. Raven 108
44. Norman (1987) 1; contrast Thompson (1990) 258
45. Maurice (1884) II:35, 36; cf. II:550
46. cit. Birley 455; Maurice (1884) II:32, 83
47. see Preston (1983a) 16–20; Atherton (1992) 141–6; Reckitt (1947) 85; Welsby 243
48. Maurice (n.d.) II:222
49. Ramsey 47, 55
50. Maurice (n.d.) II:320–1, 323

51. Bettany 20
52. This section is indebted to Newell
53. Uglow 86–9, 192–3, 214; Messinger; Hopkins
54. Roberts 171–83; Mingay II:458–9
55. *Birkenhead News* 24 November 1900 cit. Fricker 51–2; Jeremy 3
56. Mayor 99–115. For the role of Nonconformity in preparing working-class people for leadership, see Parsons and Moore I:95–6, IV:102–3. For working-class attitudes to religion, see Parsons and Moore II chap 3; McLeod; Wilkinson (1996). For the role of Friendly Societies in working-class life, see Neave. On Samuel Smiles see Briggs (1954) ch. V.
57. Briggs (1963) 197–205; Parsons and Moore II:47–8, III:298–9, 206; Chadwick (1970) II:272; Thompson (1990) 263–4
58. Norman (1987) 131–2
59. Ruskin 164, 167, 209, 172, 176
60. See Milbank (1986) 51 on Ruskin's critique of industrialism and its attraction for socialists; Wilkinson (1986) 11–12; Wiener
61. MacCarthy (1994) 487
62. Henderson 277, 279, 303–4
63. MacCarthy (1994) xvii–xviii, 548
64. Read (1979) 140, 324–9; Smith (1992) 264–5; Bevir; McLeod 120, 208–11; Parsons and Moore II:56–7
65. Read (1979) 294–5, 443; Walvin *passim*
66. Davidson 136–41, 265–9
67. Bebbington 42–3; Parsons and Moore III:284–6, 305–12
68. Backstrom 93; this paragraph is indebted to this book
69. Davidson 270
70. Holland (1915) 89
71. Webb (1938) I:208–9. On *noblesse oblige* and 'Christian Chivalry' see Girouard chs 9, 16
72. cit. Nettleship 577
73. Oliver 14–15; Seymour-Jones 77–9; Fraser 130–2, 270–1
74. Webb (1938) I:221–43; Kitson Clark 271–89; Oliver 15–17
75. Meacham *passim*; Mayor 58–9; Holland (1915) 91; G. Davies (1983); Stedman Jones 247
76. Fletcher 14, 31, 217; Davies, George and Rupp III:211–2; Koss 211

77. Wilkinson (1988b); Palmer
78. Davies, George and Rupp III:136–47
79. Norman (1984) 196–9, 274–82; Parsons and Moore I:300–5
80. Blatchford; Norman (1985) 117–8
81. On Headlam, see Leech (1968); Norman (1987); Bettany; Jones ch. V
82. Coleman 149–50
83. On Hancock, see Yeo; Allchin (1963) 51–87
84. Norman (1987) 98; Leech (1968) 78
85. cit. Jones 146
86. cit. Parsons and Moore IV:85; cit. Osborne 179
87. Smith (1993) 75–6. For Clifford see Jones 340–6, Thompson (1986), Marchant. For Hughes see Bebbington; Price Hughes; Norman (1987) ch. 8
88. cit. Jones 345; Wilkinson (1986) 23; Norman (1987) 153, 154
89. cit. Koss 173
90. Catterall (1993) 679
91. Habgood 105–6; Wilkinson (1986) chs 1–3
92. Wilkinson, J. T. (1971) 147–9

2 Henry Scott Holland and the Christian Social Union

1. For the origins of the CSU, see Dearmer (1912); for its outlook and history see Eckbert; Jones.
2. On Green, see Nicholls (1989b) 32–3, 74–81; Freeden 16f., 55f.; Meacham; Richter. Freeden (17–18) believes that even if Green had not existed, Liberalism would have still become collectivist.
3. Holland (1911a) x; Collingwood 17
4. Wilkinson (1992) 4–5
5. Davidson 109, 136–41
6. Paget 170–1
7. Paget 242
8. Reckitt (1947) 139
9. Bebbington 14–15, 97, 115–17, 152–7; Davies, George and Rupp III: 146–7
10. Eckbert 33; Jones 185
11. Pinnington 25

12. see Wilkinson (1990)
13. Eckbert 131–3
14. Dennis and Halsey ch. 4
15. Graves 25
16. Peart-Binns 13, 74–5, 132; *DLB* VI; Jones 184–5, 290; Tuckwell
17. Carter (1897) 325
18. Stephenson 69, 333
19. Freeden 14f., 27–8; Clarke 9
20. Freeden 27, 47; Webb (1890) 98–101
21. Wilkinson (1992) 1–3, 71–8
22. Westcott (1890) 1–8; on Westcott's socialism, see Norman (1987) ch. 9
23. Westcott (1895) 4, 8, 11, 12, 14
24. Westcott (1896) 6, 11, 12, 13
25. cit. Reckitt (1932) 89n
26. *The Guardian* 11 March 1896
27. M. Ward (1945) 71–3; Hastings (1991b) 175
28. Bell (1952) 488–92; Jones 75n, 186–8; Paget 226–7; *Anecdota Westmonasteriensia* (Westminster Abbey Library)
29. See also Cunningham
30. *Report, Pan Anglican Congress*
31. Donaldson *passim*; Leech (1993) 48–9
32. Bettany 120–1
33. D. Gray (1986) 159
34. Wilkinson (1992) 39, 118–25, 165
35. For Hancock's sermon see Parsons and Moore III:98–101
36. Thompson (1990) 259, 266, 269; Dearmer (1907)
37. Stacy; Headlam 77; Noel (1910)
38. Smith (1993) 90–2
39. Campbell 173
40. Eckbert 96–107, 131–9; Heidt 364–8
41. Prestige 274, 281–2; Wilkinson (1992) 117–22; for the CSL see Goodfellow
42. Oliver 49. On the National Mission and the subsequent reports on church and society, see Wilkinson (1996) 70–90
43. Lambeth Conference *Report* 1920, 62f, 133; for the ICF, see Studdert-Kennedy; for COPEC see Oliver 65–78

44. Noel (1910) 257; Reckitt (1932) 91n; Jones 217
45. Webb (1890) xiii, 20, 63–73; Eckbert 34; Jones 166–7
46. Jones 217–8
47. Pinnington 12, 17, 19, 28
48. Paget 250; Wilkinson (1992) 137
49. On Holland, see Heidt; Paget; Nicholls (1989b) 56–60
50. Paget 130, 135; cf. Holland (1915) 63–4
51. Paget 26–8, 94–6, 150–1, 166–7, 224; Pawson 106
52. Lockhart 147–8, 260; Prestige 4, 18; Carey 37
53. Paget 29–32, 67; Holland (1915) 145
54. Heidt 139–40, 159–60, 198
55. Worrall 344
56. Paget 33, 81, 100; Heidt 17–21, 308–10
57. Paget 172
58. Welsby 322, 323, 328–9; Paget 320
59. Heidt 336–8, 343–4
60. Holland (1911b) 62
61. Ibid. 75
62. Ibid. 81
63. Ibid. 86
64. Ibid. 100–2
65. Preston (1983a) 76; Holland (1911b) 126, 128; Holland in: Guild of the Epiphany: *Lecture Series No 51* (January 1915)
66. Heidt 217–18, 228–9
67. Paget 286
68. Heidt 242–50
69. D. Gray (1986) 122, 127
70. Grasby 419
71. Paget 61
72. Ibid. 88
73. Pinnington 34; Jones 218; Holland (1916) 115
74. Paget 235
75. Holland (1911b) 173
76. Christian Social Union (1896) 18–24; Holland (1915) 193; Paget 211–2, 313; Grasby 420
77. Heidt 60

3 Charles Gore

1. On Gore, see Avis; Carpenter; Prestige; Wilkinson (1992)
2. *Church Times* 30 September 1921
3. Gore (1891) 110, 211
4. Gore (1928) 31; Gore (1930) 155
5. Gore (1930) 182–3; Gore (1928) 50, 51–2, 55; Gore (1902) 19, 123, 273; Gore (1921) 97, 106; Gore (1892) 15
6. Gore (1928) 84; Stephenson 157; Gore (1901) 325; Wilkinson (1992) 19
7. Gore (1907) 278–91
8. *Guardian* 8 May 1907; Gore (1891) 36, 38
9. Gore (1898) 16, 25; Wilkinson (1988a); Gore (1930) 181, 192; Christian Social Union (1896) 34; Gore (1889, 1892) xxx, 233; Gore (1922a) 317
10. Wilkinson (1992) 142; Wilkinson (1996) *passim.*; Gore (1926) 13–14; Gore (1928) 148, 169–70; *Church Times* 21 May 1920
11. Prestige 180, 275–8, 335
12. Gore (1904) 30
13. *Church Times* 5 September 1919
14. See e.g. Gore (1908)
15. *Church Times* 10 May 1907
16. Gore (1928) 125, 162; Gore (1918) 4–8; *Challenge* 3 December 1920
17. Gore (1924) xv; Gore (1896) 563; Gore (1908) 6
18. Gore (1908) 7–9; Gore (1922b) 10
19. *Birmingham Daily Post* 13 November 1907; *Church Times* 9 February 1906; Gore (1928) 15, 162, 175
20. Gore (1928) 142; *Manchester Guardian Weekly* 3 September 1926; Gore (1926) 5–9; *Times* 7 January 1927; Christian Social Union (1896) 32–3; Gore (1896) 563; Wilkinson (1992) 42, 68, 70; Lambeth Conference (1920) resolution 74.
21. *Church Times* 25 April 1913, 21 May 1920
22. Studdert-Kennedy 96; Gore (1926) 1, 5–6
23. Oliver 90–1; Mews 318, 330–3, 336–7; Bell (1952) 1308
24. Oliver 95–7; Catterall (1989) 134–44; Catterall (1993) 672, 677–8; Catterall (1994) 645–52

25. *Edinburgh Review* October 1926; cf. Bell (1952) 1316–7; on Stamp, see Jeremy 178–83
26. *Times Weekly Edition* 10 April 1912
27. Gore (1907) 299, 305; Gore (1926) 8; Lambeth Conference (1920) 70–1; Oliver 54–5
28. *Guardian* 19 November 1900; Gore (1905) 20–1
29. Gore (1898) 15–16; Gore (1926) 4, 12

4 R. H. Tawney

1. Dennis and Halsey 153
2. Meacham 157–61; Terrill 28–35
3. Wright 11, 16, 140–2; Tawney (1921) 171
4. Tawney (1964) 82; Dennis and Halsey 171; Terrill 100, 135, 185
5. Wright 29, 34–5, 52; Tawney (1953) 84–5; Preston (1983a) 28
6. Wright 134
7. Tawney (1972) 15, 54; Terrill 82; Tawney (1921) 222; Tawney (1953) 16
8. Tawney (1972) 63–8
9. Tawney (1953) 191; Tawney (1948) 153, 280; Tawney (1921) 30, 48, 221
10. Tawney (1948) 188; Norman (1976) 317
11. Terrill 59
12. Dennis and Halsey 180; Terrill 75, 276; Groser 9, 10
13. Tawney (1953) 163; Preston (1966) 158
14. Tawney (1953) 164–5; Terrill 268
15. Tawney (1953) 163, 179, 181, 185, 188, 190; Tawney (1964) 143–4
16. Tawney (1931; 1964 edn) 56; Tawney (1953) 14; Tawney (1921) 7, 106, 186
17. Tawney (1964); Terrill 12, 175; Williams (1961) 220
18. Tawney (1964) 168
19. Atherton (1981) 351
20. Tawney (1972) 14, 79
21. Tawney (1953) 67, 68; Terrill 6, 262–3
22. Tawney (1972) 70; Tawney (1921) 43–4; Tawney (1953) 184–5
23. Tawney (1964) 168, 194, 197; Tawney (1921) 227

24. Terrill 122, 187; Tawney (1953) 183; Tawney (1931; 1964 edn) 56, 57, 14, 150, 164; Tawney (1921) 119
25. Tawney (1964) 167
26. Hastings (1991b) 185; Tawney (1964) 214; Preston (1966) 160; Dennis and Halsey 151
27. Atherton (1992) 137
28. Tawney (1931; 1964 edn) 85
29. Waterman (1991) 1–4; Wiener 115, 194; Wolffe 38–9, 75; Terrill 59–60; Dennis and Halsey 254
30. Preston (1966) 209, 211–12, 264, 267, 268
31. Leech (1990) 59–60; Terrill 15, 232–3; Norman (1976) 270–2, 355–6
32. Dennis and Halsey 256, 259
33. Wright 131, 144–6

5 *William Temple*

1. Hinchliffe ch. 9; Hastings (1991b) 184; Iremonger 488
2. Creighton 218; on Oswin Creighton, see Wilkinson (1996)
3. Oliver 106; on the National Mission, see Wilkinson (1996) 70–90; also 285–7 on post-war bishops
4. On COPEC see: Kent 116–34; Suggate (1987) 33–8; Oliver 65–78; Norman (1976) ch. 7
5. Hastings (1991b) 252–3
6. Iremonger 341–2; Norman (1976) 280–1
7. Field (1987) 104–6
8. For Temple's changing theological attitudes 1938–9, see Wilkinson (1986) 216–8
9. Niebuhr 22; on Niebuhr, see Wilkinson (1986) 206–14
10. Wilkinson (1986) 223–7
11. Simon 58
12. Iremonger 537; Temple (1940a) 106; Temple (1956) 76; Temple (1958) 244
13. Temple (1940b) 51–4, 60, 104
14. Temple (1941a) 83
15. Howell-Thomas 7
16. See Temple (1941b); also Iremonger ch. XXV, Kent 148–68 and Suggate (1987) 66–8

17. Temple (1941b) 10–14; Kent 154
18. Temple (1941b) 105, xv, 169, 173, 3
19. *Guardian* 23 August 1940
20. Temple (1941b) 125, 142, 147, 192
21. Iremonger 431; Gorringe (1994a) 68
22. Temple (1941b) 215–25; Calder 483
23. Preston (1942) 16–19; Suggate (1987) 147; Howell-Thomas 7
24. Temple (1944) 105, 107, 110, 111, 113
25. Ibid. 118, 119, 127, 148, 15, 155–6
26. Ibid. 72
27. Temple (1956) 32
28. Ibid. 59
29. Ibid. 77–8
30. Ibid. 99–100
31. Ibid. 101, 102, 121
32. See Wilkinson (1986) 262–72
33. See Temple F. S. 89–95
34. Temple (1956) 17; Welsby 343; Oliver 121
35. Nicholls (1984) 163–4; Suggate (1981) 156
36. Kent 20; Hastings (1994)
37. Suggate (1987) 40, 65, 106–25; Kent 164; Matthews 72
38. Wilkinson (1986) 253
39. Bell (1940) 140; Temple (1956) 93; Kent ix, 1–2; Sedgwick 292–3
40. Temple (1941b) vii; Preston (1981) 76–7; Preston (1983a) 145, 147, 153; Suggate (1987) 149; Villa-Vicencio 9–10, 280–3
41. Hauerwas (1983) 25; Bryant (1996) 306–7; Taylor (1981) 33–43
42. Preston (1994) 2, 10, 24, 40, 43
43. Iremonger 547; cf. 500, 504; Vidler 37–8
44. Atherton (1992) 135, 179; Field (1994a), (1994b); Barnett ch. 1; Wiener 116–8; Nicholls (1989b) 44–52
45. Iremonger 475; Kent 4–5; Preston (1994) 4
46. Wolffe 12

6 *The Search for Community*

1. Kitson Clark 168–78
2. Munson 35–6, 40, 228, 232–3

3. Knight 202
4. Mason (1993) 84, 217, 297 (n111); Wilkinson (1992) 287–8, 304
5. Orwell 224; Norman (1987) 88–92; Kumar 2–65, 420–4
6. On Figgis see, Newsome; Nicholls (1994); Tucker; Wilkinson (1992)
7. Unpublished letter, St Catharine's College Cambridge Archives
8. Figgis (1910a) 15
9. Figgis (1919) 17, 22, 24, 106
10. Figgis (1912) 86–8
11. Figgis (1910b) 30
12. Figgis (1919) 53
13. Figgis (1912) 70–1, 125–6
14. Figgis (1919) 38, 284
15. Figgis (1905) 189, 191; Figgis (1914) 100
16. Figgis (1913a) 284
17. Figgis (1910a) 87
18. Figgis (1912) 171
19. Figgis (1922) 292; Jones 22, 45, 278–80; Glass 1–8, 22, 23, 44, 54–5, 58–9
20. Glass 21–2, Wilson 185, 293; M. Ward (1945) ch. XXVI; Buchanan 259–60
21. Jones 263, 275–300; Goodfellow ch. 7
22. Oliver ch. 6; Reckitt (1932) 167–8, 227–8 (italics original)
23. See Denys Munby's savage review of Mairet's book in *Theology*, March 1957 and Mairet's lame reply, May 1957
24. Reckitt (1947) 197; Peart-Binns 67; Gore (1922b) 20, 129, 143
25. Kenyon 5, 21; for Slesser, see *DLB* vol. IX
26. Reckitt (1945) 76, 105, 125, 253
27. Peart-Binns *passim*
28. Munby (1956) 243–50, (1958) 45–58, (1961) 3n, 158; Waterman (1990); Reckitt (1947) 198–9; Peart-Binns 166–7; Markham 23, 29–62
29. Milbank (1997) 276, (1996) 544, (1990) 1, 9
30. Preston (1983a) 87
31. Temple (1956) 66–7
32. Milbank (1993) 23
33. Preston (1989) 519

34. Preston (1992) 406; Hauerwas (1992) 417
35. George Carey 'Self-interest is not the way to serve others', *The Independent*, 16 November 1996
36. Plant 7, 23
37. Atherton (1992) 199, 220, 256, 265, 274; Preston (1997) 14–19
38. See Harries (1992) 52–3
39. Preston (1983b) 18–23
40. Ibid. 21–3
41. Preston (1989) 524, (1987) 101
42. William Rees-Mogg, 'Bishops, or Party Pawns', *The Times*, 23 October 1996; Paul Brett, *Theology*, March 1989 136–7
43. Brown 97–104
44. Morton (1994b) *passim*; Forrester (1985) 38–41
45. Speaight xvii. This section is indebted to biographies by Speaight and MacCarthy (1989)
46. MacCarthy (1989) vii
47. Speaight 265
48. This section is indebted to Ferguson.
49. *What is the Iona Community?*, Wild Goose Publications, Glasgow (1996)
50. Gore (1892) 15, 16
51. Wilkinson (1992)
52. Williams (1982) 32–59; Allchin (1958) 245; Curtis 20, 27–8
53. Williams (1982) 63–6; Mayhew 203–4
54. Anson 106–22
55. This section is indebted to Groves; Leech (1993); Noel (1945)
56. Milbank (1996) 544
57. Noel (1945) 91
58. Leech (1993) 33–4
59. This section draws on Brill and personal knowledge
60. This section draws on Gorringe (1994a) and personal knowledge.

7 Dissenters

1. Wilkinson (1986) xiii
2. Higgins 109, 116, 129; Foot 13
3. Niebuhr 19, 21, 62, 199

4. Groves 180–1
5. Norman (1976) 351; Terrill 237–8
6. Marx 11
7. Lash 268, 270, 277, 286
8. The following section is indebted to Hughes
9. Barnes 305, 378–9
10. Johnson (1939) 15, 16
11. Ibid. 21
12. Johnson (1956) 17, 44–5, 147
13. Norman (1976) 355
14. Brill 83; Hughes 203; Hastings (1991b) 320
15. This section is largely derived from Gorringe (1994a) and personal knowledge.
16. Gorringe (1994a) 14
17. Ecclestone (1976) 30; Ecclestone (1975) 121; Ecclestone (1967)
18. *Church Times*, 19 June 1992
19. See particularly Leech (1995)
20. Evans (1965) 224; Leech (1986) 99
21. Leech (1980) 71; Evans (1990)
22. Eagleton and Wicker (1968) 3
23. Coman 84
24. Eagleton (1966) 26, 142, 6, 179
25. Hastings (1991b) 571–3; Eagleton (1970) 76
26. Kent (1980) 81; Brennan 73, 76
27. Booth (1990) 444–5
28. Gray (1998)
29. Freeden 112
30. In *The Independent*, 26 August 1991
31. T. Tastard discussing D. McLellan, *Theology*, November 1988, 547–8
32. Preston (1983a) 91, 92
33. Morton (1994a) 15
34. This section is based on Frost; Purcell; Soper (1935); Soper (1984); Soper (1990) and personal knowledge.
35. Frost 74; Purcell 99, 136; Ulrich Simon private communication; Frost 56
36. Frost 215

37. Purcell 111–2
38. *Methodist Recorder* 8 February 1996; Purcell 118, 123
39. Soper (1990) 46
40. Soper (1984) 134; Frost 117, 193
41. On CSM see Bryant (1996) ch. 10
42. Frost 229
43. Ibid. 254
44. This section is based on Duffield; Vincent (1962); Vincent (1976); Vincent (1992); Vincent (1993); Vincent (1996) and personal knowledge.
45. Duffield 14, 17, 54–5, 26, 36, 31
46. Ibid. 67–76; *Theology*, May 1990, 249
47. Duffield 81; Vincent (1993) 71–3, 77–8, 81, 89
48. Vincent (1996) 83–4
49. Ibid. 84
50. This section draws upon Sedgwick, Leech's works listed in the bibliography, Jubilee Group material and personal knowledge.
51. Leech (1997) 3
52. Leech (1965) 135, 138, 139; Leech (1974) 63–6
53. Leech (1976) 72, 74; Wiles (1976) 230–1; Leech (1981a) 263
54. Leech (1977) 191, 192; Leech (1981b) 6
55. See Leech (1994) for the origins and history of the Jubilee Group
56. Leech (1994) 9
57. Jones 149–56
58. Leech (1988) 134–50
59. Leech (1997) 15, 153–6
60. Leech (1994) 26
61. Leech (1997) 147. For a critique of Leech see Sedgwick 298–300
62. This section is derived from obituaries (e.g. *The Independent*, 18 June 1996), the works listed in bibliography and personal knowledge
63. Nicholls (1994) ix–xiv; Nicholls (1989a) 179; Nicholls (1994) 108
64. Nicholls (1989b) 57–70
65. Ibid. 44–50; Nicholls (1984); Preston (1985) criticized Nicholls' view of Temple

66. Nicholls (1989a) 180; Nicholls (1993) 20, 21
67. Nicholls (1986) 147, 150; Nicholls (1989a) 174–8
68. Nicholls (1982); Nicholls (1989a) 183–4
69. Leech (1994) 5
70. Holman (1990) 194–6; Holman (1993) 29–52; Holman (1997) 68–9
71. Beasley 60, 77, 100
72. Morisy 7, 8
73. Appelbee and Reid. See Wainwright on informal intermediate groups as a way to socialist renewal

8 *Politicians*

1. I am indebted to Ford's thesis for this section on Wilcockson.
2. On the National Mission, see Wilkinson (1996) 70–90.
3. Ibid. 86–8
4. For Jenkinson, see Hammerton; Groves; Mason (1994); Lloyd ch. 15.
5. Hammerton 107; Lloyd 328
6. For Lee, see Lawson and *DLB* II:230–4
7. *DLB* II:231–2
8. For Lansbury, see Holman (1987); Holman (1990); Lansbury (1928); Lansbury (1934); Lansbury (1935); *DLB*:II 214–21
9. Groser 23–4; Williams (1982) 103, 111, 173
10. Taylor (1975) 191n
11. Lansbury (1928) 265; Groser 22–3; *DLB* II:221
12. Ceadel 278, Wilkinson (1986) 212, 288. For an analysis of twentieth-century Christian pacifism, see Wilkinson (1986) chs 4–6; Lansbury (1928) 205
13. Lansbury (1934) 117; Lockhart 160–1; Groser 25; Holman (1990) 73
14. cit. Fitzgerald 101–2
15. Lansbury (1928) 285, 130–1
16. For Henderson, see *DLB* I:161–6; Wrigley
17. cit. Wrigley xii
18. Wrigley 41–4
19. cit. Catterall (1993) 667–8; Smith (1993) 166–7

20. McCabe 26
21. Catterall (1996); Davies (1961) ch. VI; Koss 184–6, 199–200; Mews 323–4
22. For Bondfield, see Bondfield; *DLB* II:39–45
23. Bondfield 358; *DLB* II:44
24. For Wheatley, see Wood (1990), Wood (1994), *DLB* VII:250–5
25. Wood (1990) 18
26. *DLB* VII:254; Bryant (1996) 168
27. The following section draws on Buchanan and Coman
28. Bryant (1996) 171
29. For Attlee, see Burridge; Harris
30. Attlee 37
31. Harris 563–4
32. Burridge 22
33. Ibid. 317; *The Listener*, 20 January, 22 September 1983
34. Burridge 315
35. Hennessy 194. Much of this section is indebted to Bryant (1997)
36. Bryant (1997) 11
37. Ibid. 350–1
38. Hennessy 195; Bryant (1997) 447, 464
39. Stanford 136. This section is indebted to Stanford and Coman.
40. Coman 45
41. Stanford 210; Jasper 285–6, 302, 344, ch. 15
42. Stanford 459
43. McSmith 6–12; see also Bryant (1994)
44. Bryant (1993) chap 6.
45. Bryant (1996) 291–3
46. See Clark; Hastings (1991a); Marquand 28
47. Jenkins (1988) 8; Jenkins (1976) 33–4; Jenkins (1991) 11, 118, 113–4, 118
48. See Atherton (1994) ch. 14
49. Hastings (1991a) 74–7
50. Text from TUC
51. Bryant (1996) 285–97, 312–3
52. Field (1987) 114–8
53. Field (1990) 57
54. cit. Field (1997) 15

55. Ibid. 27; Field (1996b) 39; Neave 76–81, 86–99; Dennis and Halsey 150

56. Field (1997) George Orwell lecture (unpublished); (1998) Keith Joseph Memorial Lecture (unpublished)

57. Field (1996b) 31–2

58. Dennis, iv, 2, 46, 153–4

59. cit. Field (1996b) 69

60. Ibid. 97, 98 cf. Deacon (1997) and (1998)

61. Ibid. 24; Field (1997) 29, 44–9

62. Field (1997) 28, 46; cf. 75, 112

63. Field (1996b) 111

64. Ibid. 60–5, 111; cf. Marquand 21–3. On COS and poverty see Read (1982) 77–8

65. Field: 'William Temple; A Political Evaluation' (unpublished lecture); Field (1997) 13

66. Field (1997) 30–1

67. Field (1997) 18, 54, 76; Field (1996b) 19–20, 37, 107–8

68. Field (1996b) 8–15, 27, 32

69. Field (1997) 77; *The Tablet*, 10 February 1996

70. Sopel 2–3

71. Blair 16; Bryant (1996) 296–7

72. Sopel 154–5; Rentoul 290

73. Bryant (1993) 9–12

74. Whitbourn 16–17

75. Blair 62, 71

76. Ibid. 57–61

77. Rentoul 41; Conford 9–10, 17; on the influence on Blair of Peter Thomson, see *New Statesman* 31 May 1996

78. Blair 236–7, 45. Plant (1995)

79. Blair 159

80. Ibid. 16, 236, 297–9

81. Ibid. 32, 60, 7, 14–15

82. Ibid. 38, 62; *The Independent*, 22 April 1996

83. Blair 298; *The Independent*, 1 October 1997; cf. Marquand 21–3, 28

84. Blair 153, 189, 68, 247, 249; *The Independent*, 27 April 1996

9 Conclusion

1. Davidson 140
2. Gray (1998) 4
3. Novak and Preston 30–2
4. Gray (1998) 4
5. Gorringe (1994b) 53
6. Dennis and Halsey 4
7. Atherton (1992) 211
8. Novak and Preston 15–6
9. 'Letter to Ilse Hahn, March 1920' in N. N. Glatzer, *Franz Rosenzweig: His Life and Thought*, Schocken Books 1953; John Macmurray, *Persons in Relation*, Faber 1957: cit. Ecclestone (1993) 52–3

Index